2nd edition

masterMind

Student's Book

Mickey Rogers

Joanne Taylore-Knowles

Steve Taylore-Knowles

with Ingrid Wisniewska

Concept development:
Mariela Gil Vierma

Level 1

MACMILLAN

Contents

⚙ Grammar review   pages 6–7

PRONUNCIATION	GRAMMAR	VOCABULARY	LIFESKILLS
WORDS: emphatic *do/did* for contrast	**REVIEW OF PAST TENSES** **FUNCTION** talking about a past experience **WOULD, USED TO, BE + ALWAYS + –ING** **FUNCTION** talking about family identity	**PERSONAL IDENTITY** **FUNCTION** talking about your family background **SENSE** **FUNCTION** talking about learning a new language	**SELF & SOCIETY:** Understanding stereotypes **FUNCTION** discussing the consequences of negative stereotypes
		LANGUAGE WRAP-UP	
SOUNDS: voiced and voiceless consonant sounds	**VERBS WITH STATIVE AND DYNAMIC USES** **FUNCTION** talking about the spread of multinationals **REPEATED AND DOUBLE COMPARATIVES** **FUNCTION** talking about the growth of social media	**GLOBALIZATION** **FUNCTION** talking about the positive and negative aspects of a global market **VERBS FOR TAKING SOCIAL ACTION** **FUNCTION** talking about ways of supporting your local economy	**STUDY & LEARNING:** Understanding internet search terms **FUNCTION** studying the effect of globalization on your local economy
		LANGUAGE WRAP-UP	
SOUNDS: silent letters—consonant sounds	**REPORTED SPEECH—MODAL VERBS AND PAST PERFECT** **FUNCTION** talking about 15 minutes of fame **REPORTED SPEECH—OPTIONAL BACK-SHIFTING** **FUNCTION** talking about lookalikes	**WAYS TO BECOME FAMOUS** **FUNCTION** talking about famous people in your country **GUESSING MEANING FROM CONTEXT** **FUNCTION** talking about the effects of celebrity	**WORK & CAREER:** Evaluating arguments **FUNCTION** discussing a proposal
		LANGUAGE WRAP-UP	
WORDS: reduced forms of *would you* and *did you*	**NOUN CLAUSES AS OBJECTS** **FUNCTION** talking about laughter therapy **REVIEW OF CONDITIONAL FORMS** **FUNCTION** talking about taking a year off before college	**LIFE SATISFACTION** **FUNCTION** talking about wealth and happiness **MOOD** **FUNCTION** talking about your state of well-being	**WORK & CAREER:** Being a positive team member **FUNCTION** focusing on solutions to problems
		LANGUAGE WRAP-UP	
SOUNDS: word stress in adjective + compound noun phrases	**THE PASSIVE** **FUNCTION** talking about problems caused by the monsoon season **EXPRESSIONS OF PURPOSE** **FUNCTION** understanding FAQs about water	**MARKETING** **FUNCTION** talking about how packaging can affect your buying decisions **ENVIRONMENTAL ISSUES** **FUNCTION** discussing responsibility for solving environmental problems	**SELF & SOCIETY:** Developing empathy **FUNCTION** discussing your water usage
		LANGUAGE WRAP-UP	
SOUNDS: stress in words with *–tion/ –sion*	**BE USED TO / GET USED TO** **FUNCTION** describing habits and customs **VERB + OBJECT + INFINITIVE** **FUNCTION** comparing traditional and nontraditional jobs	**INSTITUTIONAL TRADITIONS** **FUNCTION** discussing customs and rituals **PHRASAL VERBS FOR PERSONAL RITUALS** **FUNCTION** discussing why you have rituals	**STUDY & LEARNING:** Managing distractions **FUNCTION** making a plan to change your habits
		LANGUAGE WRAP-UP	

	READING	LISTENING	SPEAKING	WRITING	
UNIT 7 DESIGNED TO PLEASE *page 80*	⚙ **INFERRING FACTUAL INFORMATION:** an article	Listening to a radio call-in **FUNCTION** discussing fashion styles	**DISTANCING LANGUAGE:** a polite conversation	Writing a biography **FUNCTION** writing about a designer **WRITING WORKSHOP** **FUNCTION** writing a hotel review	
UNIT 8 A FAIR DEAL? *page 92*	Reading biographical profiles **FUNCTION** understanding a summary of someone's life	⚙ **LISTENING FOR MAIN IDEAS:** a lecture about Fair Trade	Talking about social justice **SPEAKING WORKSHOP** **FUNCTION** proposing a solution	**SENTENCE VARIETY:** expressing your opinion of international aid	
UNIT 9 COMPETITIVE EDGE *page 104*	**UNDERSTANDING TEXT ORGANIZATION:** a scientific article	Listening to experts' opinions **FUNCTION** understanding the main arguments	**PARAPHRASING:** a scientific study	Writing a description **FUNCTION** giving an opinion about reality TV **WRITING WORKSHOP** **FUNCTION** writing a business letter	
UNIT 10 RISKY BUSINESS *page 116*	Reading an opinion article **FUNCTION** talking about taking risks	**RAPID SPEECH:** a conversation about a TV stunt	Speculating about events **SPEAKING WORKSHOP** **FUNCTION** responding to a question asking for a choice	**REQUESTING ACTION:** writing clear and concise points	
UNIT 11 THROUGH THE LENS *page 128*	⚙ **UNDERSTANDING TEXT ORGANIZATION:** an online article	Listening to a podcast **FUNCTION** understanding the description of a picture	**MAKING COMPARISONS:** an informal conversation	Writing a memo **FUNCTION** summarizing key points from a phone message **WRITING WORKSHOP** **FUNCTION** writing a report about tourism in your area	
UNIT 12 BRIGHT LIGHTS, BIG CITY *page 140*	Reading a guidebook **FUNCTION** talking about a description of a place	⚙ **RAPID SPEECH:** a guided tour	Talking about cities of the future **SPEAKING WORKSHOP** **FUNCTION** giving a short presentation	**WRITING A LETTER OF COMPLAINT:** expressing specific details clearly	

⚙ Communicative wrap-ups   pages 152–163   ⚙ Grammar reference   pages 164–175

PRONUNCIATION	GRAMMAR	VOCABULARY	LIFESKILLS
WORDS: 's after names that end in /s/, /ʃ/, or /z/	**POSSESSIVE APOSTROPHE** **FUNCTION** talking about celebrities' clothing sale **PAST PERFECT VS. PAST PERFECT PROGRESSIVE** **FUNCTION** understanding a biography	**DESIGN** **FUNCTION** talking about revolutionizing the design process **PHRASAL VERBS** **FUNCTION** talking about fashion design and trends	**WORK & CAREER:** Showing initiative **FUNCTION** identifying opportunities to show initiative
		LANGUAGE WRAP-UP	
WORDS: the contracted form of *would*	***WOULD RATHER* AND *WOULD PREFER*** **FUNCTION** talking about donating to charities **NOUN CLAUSES AS SUBJECTS** **FUNCTION** talking about unemployment	**SOCIAL ISSUES** **FUNCTION** talking about humanitarian causes **SOCIAL JUSTICE** **FUNCTION** talking about a fair society	**SELF & SOCIETY:** Understanding rights and responsibilities **FUNCTION** sharing your ideas on the rights and responsibilities in your country
		LANGUAGE WRAP-UP	
WORDS: nouns and verbs with different pronunciation	**GERUNDS AFTER PREPOSITIONS** **FUNCTION** talking about personality types **VERB + GERUND** **FUNCTION** talking about reality shows	**SCIENTIFIC NOUNS AND VERBS** **FUNCTION** talking about psychology and the effects of competition **EXPRESSIONS OF EMOTION** **FUNCTION** talking about feelings and desires	**STUDY & LEARNING:** Synthesizing information **FUNCTION** preparing and presenting a report
		LANGUAGE WRAP-UP	
WORDS: reduction of *have*	**EXPRESSING ABILITY** **FUNCTION** talking about entrepreneurs **PAST MODALS OF DEDUCTION** **FUNCTION** working out how something happened	**SAFETY AND RISK** **FUNCTION** discussing freedom and security **EXPRESSIONS WITH *RISK*** **FUNCTION** talking about high-risk situations	**SELF & SOCIETY:** Managing stress **FUNCTION** creating strategies to help you relax
SOUNDS: stress timing	**VERB + GERUND/INFINITIVE WITH A CHANGE IN MEANING** **FUNCTION** talking about a past memory **CONNECTORS OF ADDITION / CAUSE AND EFFECT** **FUNCTION** talking about image manipulation	**DESCRIBING PICTURES** **FUNCTION** explaining what you like and dislike about pictures **MAKING COMPARISONS** **FUNCTION** finding similarities and differences between pictures	**WORK & CAREER:** Giving and receiving feedback **FUNCTION** discussing a campaign to boost local tourism
		LANGUAGE WRAP-UP	
SOUNDS: connected speech	**CONNECTORS OF CONTRAST** **FUNCTION** talking about a visit to a city **WAYS OF TALKING ABOUT THE FUTURE** **FUNCTION** talking about cities of the future	**FORMAL LETTERS** **FUNCTION** writing a letter of complaint **DESCRIBING PLACES** **FUNCTION** talking about a city that you know	**STUDY & LEARNING:** Recognizing and avoiding plagiarism **FUNCTION** discussing strategies to make your work original
		LANGUAGE WRAP-UP	

Grammar review

1 Correct the mistakes in each sentence.

1 I've taken all my vacation days yet.
2 He didn't used to be a troublemaker at school.
3 Did you use give presentations in your old job?
4 You should help your mother, should not you?
5 The happiness is important in life.
6 By the time I arrived, he left the office already.

2 Complete the sentences with one word.

1 How long has it _____ raining?
2 Why haven't you gone home _____? It's 5 p.m.
3 I _____ to have long hair when I was a child, but now it's short.
4 You're going to develop the marketing strategy, _____ you?
5 Only a few colleagues _____ signed up for the seminar when I spoke to them.
6 You registered online, _____ you?

3 Complete the sentences with the verb in parentheses in the present perfect or present perfect progressive. In one case, both are possible.

1 Emily _____ (retrain) as a teacher. She's almost finished her training program.
2 She _____ (study) part-time for her master's degree for six months.
3 I feel a little nervous. I think it's because I _____ (step out) of my comfort zone.
4 My brother _____ (apply) to lots of graduate schools recently.
5 Is Tom OK? He _____ (push) himself really hard lately in his new job.

4 Complete each sentence so that it has the same meaning as the first one.

1 Do you give refunds without a receipt?
Could you tell me _____?
2 What other models do you have?
Do you know _____?
3 I would like someone to create a website for me.
I would like to have _____.
4 My hair is too long.
I need to get _____.
5 Mark doesn't like that his friend always talks through movies.
Mark wishes _____.

5 Choose the correct options to complete the sentences.

1 The interview was *too long / long enough*. It was over an hour and a half!
2 Sophia felt *dissatisfied / dissatisfying* with the poor-quality service.
3 It's a great book, but kind of *frustrated / frustrating* at times.
4 I really enjoyed the movie. It was *such / so* entertaining.
5 James was always *such / so* a troublemaker at school.

6 Complete the statements and questions to report the direct speech.

1 "I've worked on this project for a long time."
Mark said _____.
2 "We'll give you a loan when the business plan is accepted."
The bank's business advisor told Harry _____.
3 "This song reminds me of my high school days."
My aunt told me _____.
4 "Did you have time to chat with the students yesterday?"
Mr. Todd asked _____.
5 "Where are you going to take us for lunch tomorrow?"
Mike and Naomi asked me _____.

7 Complete the sentences with a modal verb: *must*, *might*, *could*, or *can't*.

Amy: Have you seen Joe? He was supposed to be here an hour ago.

James: I can see his car outside. This **(1)** _____ be him now.

Amy: No, Joe left his car here last night.

James: He **(2)** _____ be at soccer club. He sometimes has practice on Sundays.

Amy: I already called Tom and he told me he didn't go today. I guess he **(3)** _____ be sick.

James: No, Joe's never sick. Wait! Do you think he **(4)** _____ be at Sara's place?

Amy: He **(5)** _____ be at Sara's—she's on vacation. I'm really worried!

8 Complete the sentences with the correct form of the verb in parentheses.

1 If only I _____ (*buy*) that dress when I saw it. Now it's sold out.

2 If I _____ (*not feel*) so tired, I would have remembered everyone's names.

3 I think more people would have found out about the product if the company _____ (*advertise*) it better.

4 I _____ (*not show up*) late if you had given me better directions.

5 I wish I _____ (*study*) Portuguese, so I could understand my colleagues in São Paolo.

9 Choose the correct options to complete the sentences.

1 I usually try to avoid *using / use* the internet late at night before I go to bed.

2 My colleague had to admit *send / sending* an embarrassing text to the wrong person.

3 I refuse *to read / reading* articles that have pointless arguments.

4 We finally persuaded Dad to go to the doctor when he admitted *feel / feeling* dizzy.

5 The magazine has denied *start / starting* the rumor and spreading gossip about the singer.

6 When you finish *register / registering* online, log in and check out the pictures I uploaded.

10 Complete the sentences with a defining or non-defining relative clause. Remember to use correct punctuation.

1 *The Grapes of Wrath* is a famous American novel. It is set during the Great Depression.
The Grapes of Wrath ,*which is a famous American novel, is set during the Great Depression* _____.

2 There is a great restaurant in Brooklyn. You can eat the best matzo ball soup there.
There is a great restaurant in Brooklyn _____.

3 The Burj Khalifa is the world's tallest building. It is over 2,716 feet high.
The Burj Khalifa _____.

4 Jennifer Lawrence won Best Actress at the 2013 Oscar Award Ceremony. She had wanted to be a doctor.
Jennifer Lawrence _____.

11 What advice or criticism would you give in these situations? Complete the sentences with the words from the box and the correct form of the verb in parentheses. There may be more than one possible answer.

advisable   good   should have   shouldn't have   understandable

Your friend is coughing and sneezing after walking all day in the country without warm clothes.

1 It's _____ _____ _____ the weather before you go out. (*check*)

2 You _____ _____ _____ a coat and scarf. (*wear*)

She hit the "reply to all" button when sending a friend a personal email at work.

3 It's _____ _____ embarrassed about things like that. (*feel*)

4 You _____ _____ _____ a personal email at work. (*send*)

I feel really lonely and depressed lately.

5 It's _____ _____ _____ friends. (*see*)

6 You _____ _____ _____ me sooner. (*tell*)

12 Find the four incorrect sentences and correct the mistakes.

1 Dan called. Did you call back him? _____

2 I promise to copy everyone in this time. _____

3 What about your essay? Did you hand in it? _____

4 Did you run Jonas into at the café this afternoon? _____

5 My parents like Susie. She gets along with them. _____

6 That music is too loud. Can you turn down it? _____

IN THIS UNIT YOU

- learn language to talk about identity
- read about identity when speaking a second language
- talk about personal identity
- listen to an immigrant talking about how his identity has changed
- write a comment about peer pressure
- learn about stereotypes
- ► watch a video about personal identity

READING
for different purposes

Do you read different types of texts in different ways? How? Think about a novel, a dictionary, a magazine, etc.

SPEAKING
agreeing and disagreeing

In what situations might you need to disagree with someone politely?

LIFE SKILLS

SELF & SOCIETY

understanding stereotypes A stereotype is an idea we have about what someone, or a group of people, is like when we don't know them. What common stereotypes do people have about teenagers? Or about elderly people?

A 🗣 Work in pairs. Identify each type of group in the pictures and say which similar groups you belong to.

B 🗣 Think about each group you belong to and how important that group is to your identity. Choose the two groups you think have the biggest influence on your identity. Then compare with your partner and explain your choice.

1 LISTENING: to a podcast interview

A The following factors can all influence our personal identity. Number them 1–8 in order of importance to your identity. Number 1 is the most important.

clothes ☐   friends ☐   values ☐   language ☐
studies ☐   interests ☐   family ☐   job ☐

B 🎧 **1.01** Listen to the first part of a podcast interview with a Mexican man who has moved to the U.S.A. Choose the things in the list in Exercise A that he says were important for his sense of identity in the past. Does he mention anything not on the list?

C 🎧 **1.02** Listen to the second part of the interview and answer the questions.

1 In general, how does Armando say he has changed since moving to Miami?
2 Which specific factors in his sense of identity have changed? Why?

D **VOCABULARY: PERSONAL IDENTITY** Match the phrases (1–6) with the definitions (a–f).

1 family values   a) the kind of family you come from
2 sense of identity   b) the things you hope to achieve in the future
3 social status   c) beliefs that you learn from your family
4 family background   d) position in society; class
5 life goals   e) your friends
6 social group   f) the feeling of who you are

E 🗣 **VOCABULARY: PERSONAL IDENTITY** Work in groups. Ask and answer the questions.

1 Is your family background an important part of your sense of identity? Which family values are important to you?
2 What's the difference between family background and social status? How might they be related to each other?
3 Do you and the people in your social group share the same life goals? Is that important?

2 SPEAKING: agreeing and disagreeing

⚙ There is a variety of words and phrases that you can use to express agreement, partial agreement, or disagreement. In more formal situations, we often apologize as we disagree.

A 🗣 Work in pairs. What phrases do you know already for agreeing, partially agreeing, and disagreeing? Make a list.

B 🎧 **1.03** Listen to part of a seminar on identity. What does Sean think about expressing personal identity?

C 🗣 Work in pairs. Listen again and complete the phrases from the conversation. Compare your answers with another pair. Which phrases are used to agree, partially agree, or disagree?

1 Well, yes, to a _____ extent …
2 _____ and no.
3 I'm _____, but I just don't think that's true.
4 I'm _____ I can't agree.
5 In a _____, you're right, but …
6 I _____ agree more.

D 🗣 Work in small groups. Discuss the question.

Do you think it is important to "be yourself" at all times, even if sometimes it may upset people?

3 GRAMMAR: review of past tenses

A LANGUAGE IN CONTEXT Read the blog extract. What was difficult for Akna when she moved to the city?

IDENTITY CRISIS

the blog of a woman living in two worlds   HOME   ABOUT ME   ARCHIVE   LINKS

ABOUT ME
Hi, I'm Akna! I grew up in remote northern Canada, as a member of an indigenous community. My people are Inuit, and up to the age of 18 I spent my days in a very traditional way: fishing and cooking, as well as attending a local school. And then my life changed completely when I met Jordan. Jordan had arrived in my area as an anthropologist a year before I met him, and he was studying our language and traditions. We fell in love and eventually we got married and moved to Montreal. I did try to fit in, but I really suffered from culture shock and felt out of place. I was scared of losing my identity and didn't know who I was anymore. After a long struggle I finally realized that my family background and community had made me who I was, but that my choices have made me who I am today.

NOTICE!
Underline all the verbs in the text in a past tense. Which past tenses appear in the text? What auxiliary verb is sometimes used for emphasis?

B ANALYZE Read the extract in Exercise A again.

Form Complete the table with examples from the text.

Tense	Form	Example
simple past simple past with *did* for emphasis	–*ed*, irregular forms (*was, had,* etc.) *did* + base form	*I* **(1)** _____ *up in remote northern Canada …* *… my life* **(2)** _____ *completely …* *I* **(3)** _____ *to fit in …*
past progressive	*was/were* + –*ing* form	*… he* **(4)** _____ *our language …*
past perfect	*had* + past participle	*… my family background and community* **(5)** _____ *me who I was …*

WATCH OUT!
✓ When I was young, I went fishing almost every day.
✗ When I was young, I was going fishing almost every day.

Function Write the names of the correct tenses to match the explanations.

1   _____: This tense describes a completed event, action, or state that took place before another past event, action, or state. It is used to talk about things that happened before the main action.

2   _____: This tense describes a completed event, action, or state in the past. It is usually the main tense used to talk about the past.

3   _____: This tense describes actions or states in progress at a particular time in the past. It is often used to describe background action (e.g., the weather).

C PRACTICE Complete the entry from Akna's blog with the correct form of the verbs in parentheses.

This **(1)** _____ (*happen*) soon after Jordan and I **(2)** _____ (*move*) here. That day, it **(3)** _____ (*snow*) and the wind **(4)** _____ (*blow*) really hard. I **(5)** _____ (*be*) in Montreal for just two months, and I **(6)** _____ (*miss*) my family really badly. The St. Lawrence River **(7)** _____ (*freeze*) over a month before, and I **(8)** _____ (*decide*) to go ice fishing. Some of the local men **(9)** _____ (*fish*) out on the ice, and they **(10)** _____ (*look*) a bit strangely at this young Inuit woman with her traditional equipment. Anyway, I **(11)** _____ (*start*) catching fish, and pretty soon people **(12)** _____ (*notice*) that I **(13)** _____ (*catch*) more than the men with their high-tech equipment! People **(14)** _____ (*applaud*) every time I caught a fish and soon everyone **(15)** _____ (*laugh*) and congratulating me! It really **(16)** _____ (*help*) me feel just a little more at home!

D 🎨 **NOW YOU DO IT** Work in groups. Think of a time when you felt out of place or like you didn't fit in. Describe what happened. Did you all have similar experiences?

We read different texts for different purposes and in different ways. Before you read a text, think about why you are going to read it.

A Work in pairs. Look at the purposes for reading. For each one, think of types of texts you might read for that purpose. Write as many as you can. Remember to include electronic texts as well as print texts.

1 for pleasure *a novel, a story, a poem* _____
2 to find out about a product you are interested in _____
3 to find out news or opinions _____
4 to learn information for school or work _____
5 to find information you need in order to do something _____

B Look at the text below. Decide what kind of text it is. Then choose the reasons why someone might read a text like this. More than one answer is possible.

1 Text type: _____
2 Possible reasons for reading the text:
   a) to keep up to date with current developments
   b) to prepare for a meeting at work
   c) to decide whether to watch something
   d) to compare your opinion with someone else's
   e) to decide whether to travel to a place
   f) to research becoming an English teacher

New **country,** new **language,** ... new **identity?**

[1]Take four recent immigrants in an English-speaking country and place them with host families for a month. Ask the families to teach them English and film the results. That's the idea behind *Lost in Translation*, the new show from ABTV, which you sense is going to be a hit. In the first episode broadcast last night, we met a young woman, Amaal, 22, from Somalia, who was staying with the Wilson family. Mr. Wilson, a businessman, decided to take Amaal with him to work. The resulting clash of cultures, though predictable, made for fascinating viewing. Back in Somalia, Amaal lived a nomadic life where she tended goats, sheep, and cattle, and where she knew everyone around her. Though Mr. Wilson did try, in his clumsy way, to teach her, and though Amaal is clearly a very intelligent, sensible young woman, she struggled to make sense of much of what goes on in the anonymous business world. Fortunately, her common sense and ready sense of humor got her through.

[2]The most interesting, and unexpected, aspect of the show, though, was the insight we gain into learning a foreign language. In a mix of English and Somali, Amaal explained that she feels like a different person when she speaks in English. It seems that using another language makes it easier for her to talk about certain things. For example, dating and relationships can be sensitive subjects in her country, parts of which are very conservative. As a result, she finds it easier to talk about relationships between men and women in English. Also, her country has been affected by war. Amaal, who is clearly a very sensitive person, can talk about that more easily in English. It appears to give her some distance from a difficult topic.

[3]However, Amaal also talked about some aspects of speaking English that make her uncomfortable. She worries that as she learns more and more about the world beyond Somalia, she may lose contact with her background. She finds herself being defensive about her identity as a Somali and Somali traditions as she encounters the English-speaking world of business, travel, and culture.

[4]The show is available on demand, so if you missed it, make sure you watch this fascinating insight into language and identity.

C Read the text on page 12 and choose the correct answers.

1 Why was there a "clash of cultures"?
   a) Amaal wasn't interested in Mr. Wilson's business.
   b) The Western workplace was new to Amaal.
   c) Mr. Wilson didn't understand anything about farming.
2 How did Amaal's sense of humor help her?
   a) It helped her learn English more quickly.
   b) It helped her deal with a difficult situation.
   c) People liked her because she made them laugh.
3 Why does Amaal find it easier to talk about relationships in English?
   a) The subject is more sensitive in her own country and language.
   b) English-speaking people know more about that kind of thing.
   c) Mr. Wilson teaches her the right vocabulary to use.
4 Why does Amaal find it easier to talk about her country's past in English?
   a) In a foreign language, the topic is less emotional.
   b) English has more ways of talking about war than Somali.
   c) She doesn't like speaking Somali when she is so far from home.

D VOCABULARY: SENSE Find and underline words and phrases in the text that include or are derived from the word *sense* and complete the sentences (1–7). Use the definitions in parentheses to help.

1 I couldn't _____ what she was saying to me. (*understand*)
2 We can usually _____ when a family member has a problem. (*feel*)
3 You have to have a _____ to work in this crazy place! (*ability to see the funny side*)
4 My sister is very _____ and cares about other people's feelings. (*understanding of others' emotions*)
5 Try to think before you act and be a little more _____ next time. (*reasonable, practical*)
6 Religion can be a very _____ topic of conversation in my country. (*needing to be dealt with carefully*)
7 He's very intelligent, but he doesn't have much _____! (*ability to use good judgment*)

E 🗣 **VOCABULARY: SENSE** Work in groups. Discuss the questions.

1 Is your sense of identity connected to your language? Is your identity in your first language the same as your identity when you speak English?
2 What topics do you think are sensitive in the classroom? Should there be classroom discussions of sensitive issues, or is it more sensible for schools to avoid those topics?
3 Which do you think is most important in life—a sense of humor, a sense of responsibility, common sense, or a sense of loyalty?

5 PRONUNCIATION: emphatic *do/did* for contrast

A 🎧 **1.04** Listen to the conversations. For each "B" response, notice that the words in italics are stressed.

A: Do you think it's important for friends to share the same values and life goals?
B: No, but I *do* think it's important to share the same sense of humor.
A: You went to Somalia last year, didn't you?
B: No. I *did* go to Africa, but I didn't go to Somalia.

B 🎧 **1.05** 🗣 Work in pairs. Listen and practice the conversation below. Make sure you stress the words in italics.

A: I don't have a big social group, but I *do* have a few close friends.
B: Did you meet your friends at school?
A: No. I *did* make some friends there, but we've lost touch now.

6 GRAMMAR: *would, used to, be + always + –ing*

A LANGUAGE IN CONTEXT Read the magazine excerpt. Which person remembers an annoying habit that a family member had? What was it?

FAMILY IDENTITY

Family memories are one of the things that help a family bond as a unit and create a sense of family identity. Even things that used to annoy us sometimes become favorite memories!

Kyle:

My dad always used to throw a softball for me so I could practice my batting. He would never say he was too tired, even after working all day. He was sensitive and really understood how I felt. I try to remember that now when my little boy wants me to play with him!

Sandy:

My little sister was always sneaking into my room and trying on my clothes. I used to get mad at her because she would leave my nice clothes all over the floor! Now we're the same size, and we're always borrowing each other's clothes!

> **NOTICE!**
> Find and underline all the examples of *always* and *never* in the text. Which structures are they used with?

B ANALYZE Read the excerpt in Exercise A again.

Form Complete the table with examples from the text.

Form		Example
a	*would (always/never)* + base form	(1) _____
b	*(always/never) used to* + base form	(2) _____
c	*be + always + –ing* form (present or past progressive)	(3) _____ (4) _____

Function Match the structure (a–c) to the rule (1–2).

1 We use these two structures to talk about habits or customs which are only in the past. ☐ ☐
2 We use this structure to talk about present or past habits and customs. ☐

> **WATCH OUT!**
> ✓ You are always interrupting me.
> ✗ You always are interrupting me.

C PRACTICE Complete the family story with one of the structures used to talk about habits. In some cases, more than one answer is possible.

My brother is six years younger than me, and when he was little, he **(1)** _____ (*ask*) me to read him stories. He **(2)** _____ always _____ (*make*) me read the same story about four times, and he **(3)** _____ never _____ (*get*) bored! He **(4)** _____ (*carry*) his favorite book around with him. I **(5)** _____ (*hide*) it so he couldn't find me and make me read it to him! And then he **(6)** _____ (*cry*) and I **(7)** _____ (*feel*) bad. Now I'm always **(8)** _____ (*ask*) him if he wants me to read him a story! It's a family joke.

D 🎦 NOW YOU DO IT Work in groups. Think of a past habit of yours or of someone in your family. Tell your group. Ask each other questions about the effects of the habit and report back to the whole class on what you discussed.

I remember that my cousin Laura always used to …
I used to think it was … but now I think …

7 WRITING: contributing to a question-and-answer page

A Read the contributions to the question-and-answer page. What do you think "peer pressure" means?

Gina: I live in a small town, and I feel like there's so much pressure on everyone to fit in and have the same identity. Everyone seems to do the same things and go to the same places. People are always criticizing what other people do. It's hard because I feel like an outsider, both at work and socially. I feel like my interests are different from everyone else's, and it's only my online life that keeps me sane! Have other people experienced something similar or is it just me?

Maura: I feel sorry for you, Gina, but remember that it's not true of all small towns. I live in a small town where people are very happy to let you be yourself. Maybe it's more to do with your country or culture, rather than the size of the town. Here, the only place where peer pressure is a problem is in high school.

 **Len:** Peer pressure can certainly be a problem at work. I work in finance, and there's so much pressure to wear the right clothes, drive the right car, you know, keep up the high-flyer image. People are always going on about all that stuff. It doesn't make any sense to me.

GaryG: It's important to remember that peer pressure can have positive effects, too. When all my friends were doing well at school, the pressure forced me to work hard. The same thing is true at work. I know everyone else is working hard and I don't want to let them down. Being yourself doesn't mean you shouldn't think about other people!

 **Aran:** I'm from Thailand, and I'm interested in hearing from people in other countries. Does peer pressure exist in every culture? There is definitely peer pressure in my country, but sometimes it can be positive, like when there's pressure to work hard or get good grades in school.

B Work in groups. Read Aran's comment. Make a list of positive and negative examples of peer pressure that you know about in your social or professional group. Decide whether each item on your list usually has more positive or negative effects.

C With your group, use your list to write an answer to Aran. Include the following information.

- information about your social or professional group—country, city, age, occupation(s)
- examples of peer pressure
- whether you think peer pressure is positive or negative

D "Post" your answer in your classroom. Read the other answers to see if other groups have similar ideas to yours.

HOW TO SAY IT

In my social group, there's a lot of pressure to …, and I think that's …

People in my town/college/ office are always saying that …

In my last school/job, people were always … They would …

UNDERSTANDING STEREOTYPES

- Be aware of different kinds of stereotypes.
- Consider the stereotypes you hold and what they are based on.
- Think about the negative impact of certain stereotypes.

A Read the joke in the first paragraph of the article below. What positive and negative stereotypes does the joke imply about each of the nationalities?

B In your opinion, are national stereotypes based on real characteristics? Read the article to find out if the study supports your opinion or not.

SCIENCE GETS THE LAST LAUGH ON ETHNIC JOKES

"HEAVEN IS WHERE THE POLICE ARE ENGLISH, the cooks are French, the mechanics are German, the romantic poets are Italian, and everything is organized by the Swiss. Hell is where the police are German, the cooks are English, the mechanics are French, the romantic poets are Swiss, and everything is organized by the Italians."

Obviously, the national stereotypes in this old joke are generalizations, but such stereotypes are often said "to exist for a reason." Is there actually a sliver of truth in them? Not likely, an international research team now says.

The study, which compares "typical" personalities in many cultures with the personalities of real individuals from those cultures, appears in Friday's issue of the journal *Science*, published by AAAS, the nonprofit science society.

Generalizations about cultures or nationalities can be a source of identity, pride, … and bad jokes. But they can also cause a great deal of harm. Both history and current events are full of examples in which unfavorable stereotypes contribute to prejudice, discrimination, persecution, or even genocide.

"National and cultural stereotypes do play an important role in how people perceive themselves and others, and being aware that these are not trustworthy is a useful thing," said study author Robert McCrae of the National Institute on Aging.

The new findings also call into question other stereotypes, such as age stereotypes, according to McCrae.

The researchers tested the possibility that cultural stereotypes might be based, at least partly, on real experiences that people have interacting with each other. If this were true, then such stereotypes would reflect the average personality of real members of that culture.

But McCrae and his colleagues studied real and perceived personalities in roughly 50 countries, and found this wasn't the case.

"These are, in fact, unfounded stereotypes. They don't come from looking around you and doing your own averaging of people's personality traits," McCrae said.

C 🔊 **Work in groups. Make a list of stereotypes you've heard about your region, country, or culture. Then look at your list and discuss the questions.**

1 Are most of the things on your list positive or negative? Are they true? How do they make you feel?
2 Which of the following do you think cause stereotypes about your culture?
   • people from your country living in other countries
   • impressions tourists get when they visit your country
   • the media
   • jokes and other forms of oral stereotyping
3 How can people avoid believing stereotypes about other countries?

D 🔊 **Work in pairs. Look at the groups of people in the diagram. For each group of people, write as many stereotypes as you can. Then compare your list with another pair.**

People say that teenagers are lazy and sleep too much.

> ### HOW TO SAY IT 🔊
> *People are always saying …*
> *The media is always showing …*
> *People assume that …*
> *Teenagers are seen as …*
> *People tend to think that teenagers …*

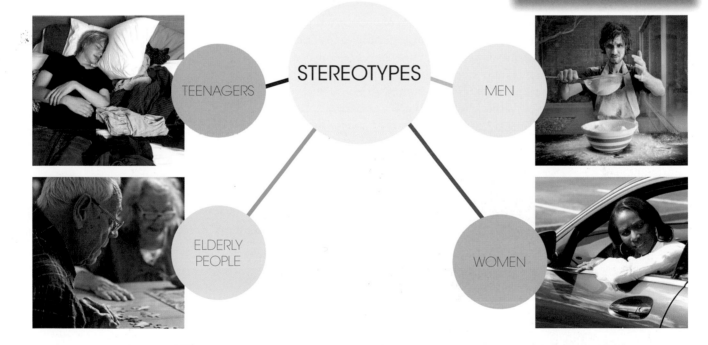

E 🔊 **Work in pairs. For each set of people in Exercise D, decide what the consequences of the negative stereotypes you have identified might be.**

Someone might not give a hard-working teenager a job because of the stereotype that teenagers are lazy.

F 🔊 **Work in groups. Discuss the questions.**

1 Do you feel you now have a better understanding of stereotypes? In what ways?
2 Will you be more able to recognize stereotypes in the future when they refer to you?

 REFLECT … How can the skill of understanding stereotypes be useful to you in **Work & Career** and **Study & Learning**?

 RESEARCH …

Find out about a person who has been stereotyped and the negative impact this has had on them. In your next class, tell the class about the person you read about.

Language wrap-up

1 VOCABULARY

A Complete the conversation with the words from the box. One of the words can be used more than once. (6 points)

family   identity   life   sense   social

Alicia: Do you think your **(1)** _____ background has made you who you are?

Byron: Well, yes, I guess it's given me a strong sense of **(2)** _____. And we all learn values from our parents, don't we?

Alicia: Hmm, it's not always easy to make **(3)** _____ of your own past. I'm not sure how much my family made me who I am today. I have very different **(4)** _____ goals from my parents. I think my sense of identity is really connected to my **(5)** _____ group.

Byron: Maybe, but I'm sure your parents influenced you, too. They taught you common **(6)** _____, didn't they?

B Choose the correct options to complete the rest of the conversation. (6 points)

Alicia: Yes, of course! But things like social **(1)** *level / status* are very important to my parents and not so important to me. The people in my social **(2)** *crowd / group* come from all kinds of backgrounds.

Byron: But your parents have influenced you in different ways. You and your dad have exactly the same sense of **(3)** *funny / humor*. And you and your mom are both very **(4)** *sensitive / sensible* when people are unhappy or upset.

Alicia: That's true. My mom and I can both **(5)** *know / sense* what the other person is feeling.

Byron: On the other hand, she's very **(6)** *sensible / thinking*, but you're …

Alicia: Hey!

10–12 correct: I can talk about personal identity and use words and phrases with *sense*.

0–9 correct: Look again at Sections 1 and 4 on pages 10 and 13.   **SCORE:**   /12

2 GRAMMAR

Choose the correct options to complete the text. (12 points)

When I was a kid, my dad **(1)** *had done / was always doing* silly things. Like sometimes, we **(2)** *had waited / would be waiting* in a movie line or whatever, and he **(3)** *was used to / used to* stand on his head. Stuff like that. He did it even after I **(4)** *had asked / would ask* him to just be a normal, sensible dad. He never **(5)** *used to / would* listen and I **(6)** *found / was finding* it very embarrassing. My uncle (my dad's brother) **(7)** *used to tell / had told* my dad to act his age. I remember he **(8)** *would say / was saying*, "Act your age, not your kid's age." My dad **(9)** *had tried / did try*, but soon, he **(10)** *was forgetting / would forget* and do something silly. Well, now I'm all grown up, and so is my dad. Now I **(11)** *would always ask / am always asking* him to do some of the things that **(12)** *used to embarrass / were embarrassing* me. But my dad is 90 years old, and he doesn't have as much energy. Funny how we don't appreciate things until we don't have them anymore!

10–12 correct: I can use past tenses and expressions describing habits in the past.

0–9 correct: Look again at Sections 3 and 6 on pages 11 and 14.   **SCORE:**   /12

WRITING WORKSHOP

A Read the article. In your own words, explain what advice the writer gives.

How to survive
CULTURE SHOCK

Are you thinking of moving to another country, either to work or to study? If you are, there's a chance you'll face a number of challenges. You might find it hard to make sense of your new country or you may feel that people are always stereotyping you and not seeing the real you. What can you do about it?

Well, first of all, lighten up and don't be so sensitive! You may encounter stereotypes, but now's your chance to prove them wrong! And no one expects you to understand your new environment right away. People are generally happy to give you time to figure things out. Ask questions and don't be afraid to make mistakes. Usually, people enjoy explaining their culture to people from other countries.

Second, if you find that people expect certain things from you because of their stereotypes, don't see it as a problem. See it as your chance to show them that you're an individual. Try to explain, in a sensitive way, why their view of people from your country is wrong or incomplete.

Above all, you have to be open to new experiences and not worry about losing your identity. Instead, you need to be ready to accept your new identity. Welcome to your new life!

B Look back at the article and choose *T* (true) or *F* (false). The writer …

1 uses a question to engage the reader.   *T / F*
2 uses a conversational, chatty style.   *T / F*
3 mentions a few potential problems and then solutions to those problems. *T / F*

C You are going to write an article giving advice to people who are going abroad to study or work. First, make notes below.

1 Make a note of two or three problems someone who has recently arrived in a new country might face.

_____

2 For each problem you have identified, make notes on what advice you could give.

_____

_____

_____

D Now use your notes to write your article. Write about 200 words.

HOW ARE YOU DOING?
○ I have tried to engage the reader in the article.
○ I have used a conversational, chatty style.
○ I have given clear advice on the problems.

UNIT 2 GLOBAL VIEWS

IN THIS UNIT YOU

- learn language to talk about globalization and taking social action
- listen to a discussion about globalization
- write a formal email to organize a meeting
- read about shopping locally
- talk about the advantages and disadvantages of social media
- learn about effective internet search terms
- ▶ watch a video about the advantages of eating locally-produced food

LISTENING
understanding discourse markers

Do you sometimes hear words or phrases that don't seem to have much meaning? Why do you think people use them?

WRITING
a formal email

When do you need to write a formal email? How is a formal email different from an informal email?

LIFE SKILLS

STUDY & LEARNING

understanding internet search terms
The internet provides huge amounts of information on almost every topic. What are some effective ways you have found to search for information on the internet?

A 🗣 **Work in pairs. Look at the pictures and discuss the questions.**

1 Which, if any, of these aspects of globalization affect your country? In what ways?

2 What do you think are the positive and negative features of each of these three aspects of globalization, both in general and specifically for your country?

1 trade

2 human migration

3 communication

B 🗣 **Work in groups. What other aspects of globalization can you think of? Do you think they have mostly positive or mostly negative consequences? Why?**

1 LISTENING: understanding discourse markers

Discourse markers or "fillers" such as *like, you know,* or *well* are often used in informal speech. Such words and phrases can have several meanings, but when used as fillers, they don't mean very much at all. Fillers are often used to give the speaker time to think about what they want to say.

A »? **1.06** Listen and write the missing discourse markers.

Speaker 1 _____, it's easier for countries to export goods.

Speaker 2 … companies increase their profits by, _____, setting up factories in poorer countries.

Speaker 3 _____, you see the same fast-food restaurants … wherever you go.

Speaker 4 I _____ think it's sad that regional cultures are disappearing.

Speaker 5 And … _____ … that helps everyone.

B Listen again to the five people discussing globalization. Match the speakers (1–5) with their opinions (a–e).

Speaker 1   **a)**   benefits economies

Speaker 2   **b)**   destroys local cultures

Speaker 3   **c)**   harms local businesses

Speaker 4   **d)**   improves communication

Speaker 5   **e)**   creates inequality

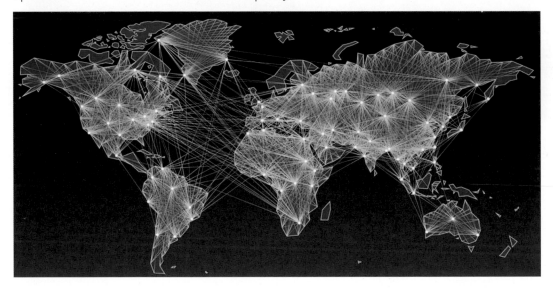

C VOCABULARY: GLOBALIZATION Choose the definitions that match the words or phrases in bold.

1   "There's been huge **economic growth** in recent decades."
    a)   increase in size of the economy   **b)**   decrease in size of the economy

2   "Companies increase their **profits** by setting up factories in poorer countries."
    a)   financial gain   **b)**   financial loss

3   "**Multinational** companies are completely taking over."
    a)   in one country   **b)**   in many countries

4   "**Regional** cultures are disappearing."
    a)   local   **b)**   international

5   "The same music and movies **dominate** popular culture everywhere."
    a)   destroy   **b)**   control

6   "The internet **facilitates** information sharing."
    a)   makes easier   **b)**   demands

D 🗣 **VOCABULARY: GLOBALIZATION** Work in pairs. Decide how much you agree with each of the statements in Exercise C. Explain why.

2 GRAMMAR: verbs with stative and dynamic uses

A LANGUAGE IN CONTEXT Read the text. What positive aspects of multinational corporations are mentioned?

MULTINATIONAL SPREAD

Walk around almost any city in the world and you see signs advertising multinational corporations. They are having a major effect on emerging economies around the world. These companies often have branches in many countries and can offer varied job opportunities, especially for young people. A recent study showed that more young people than ever are thinking of applying for jobs with such companies. However, some people think that large companies take money out of the country. They would prefer local companies to do well. Whatever the pros and cons are, it looks as if multinational corporations are here to stay.

NOTICE!
Underline the verbs in the text that are in the simple form. Then circle the same verbs that are used in the progressive form. How does the form of the verb change the meaning?

B ANALYZE Read the text in Exercise A again.

Form & Function Read the information and complete the table with examples from the text.

Some verbs are rarely used in progressive forms. They are called stative verbs because they usually refer to states or conditions that continue over a period of time, for example, *know*, *prefer*, or *agree*. However, some stative verbs commonly have both stative and dynamic uses, with different meanings.

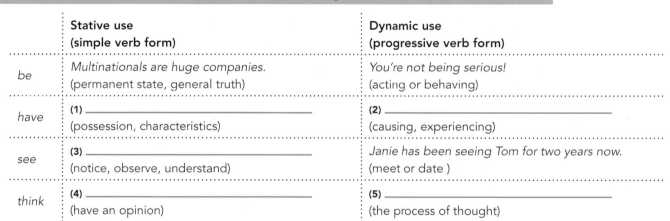

	Stative use (simple verb form)	Dynamic use (progressive verb form)
be	*Multinationals are huge companies.* (permanent state, general truth)	*You're not being serious!* (acting or behaving)
have	**(1)** _____ (possession, characteristics)	**(2)** _____ (causing, experiencing)
see	**(3)** _____ (notice, observe, understand)	*Janie has been seeing Tom for two years now.* (meet or date)
think	**(4)** _____ (have an opinion)	**(5)** _____ (the process of thought)

C PRACTICE Choose the correct options to complete the sentences. Explain your choice.

1 I *think / am thinking* of applying for a job with a large company.
2 We *don't have / are not having* an office in Australia.
3 Stop behaving like that! You *are / are being* ridiculous!
4 Yes, I *see / am seeing* your point of view.
5 What *do you think / are you thinking* of multinational corporations?
6 There *are / are being* fewer jobs for young people these days.
7 I saw Jim and Davina having dinner together. *Do they see / Are they seeing* each other?

WATCH OUT!
✘ She is being an intern at a multinational company.
✓ She's an intern at a multinational company.

D NOW YOU DO IT Work in pairs and do the role-play. Write three sentences to convince your partner about your opinion. Use some of these verbs: *be, have, see, think*. Then tell your partner.

Student A
You agree with the spread of multinational corporations.

Student B
You disagree with the spread of multinational corporations.

3 SPEAKING: talking about social media

A Read the definition of social media. What social media do you use?

Web terms: Your questions answered

Q: What is social media?

A: The term *social media* refers to websites and networks that help us communicate with each other. It includes websites where we post comments, share pictures or videos, or interact with friends and large groups of people. Social media is contributing to globalization by connecting everyone around the world.

B 🎧 **1.07** Listen to three people giving their opinions about social media. Complete the table with the information.

Speaker	Social media used	Advantage / Disadvantage
1		
2		
3		

C Think about one form of social media you use. Make brief notes to complete the table.

Social media	
How often you use it	
Advantages	
Disadvantages	
Effect on communication	

D 👥 **Independent Speaking** Work in pairs. Student A, tell your partner about the type of social media you have chosen. Student B, as you listen, take notes in your notebook. Change roles. When you have finished, tell the class what you learned about your partner.

4 PRONUNCIATION: voiced and voiceless consonant sounds

A 🎧 **1.08** Listen to each pair of words. Put your hand on your throat and say the first word of each pair. You should feel a vibration. Put the palm of your hand a few inches in front of your mouth and say the second word in each pair. You should feel a puff of air after the first letter.

1	vast	fast	4	drain	train
2	do	too	5	goal	coal
3	base	pace			

B 🎧 **1.09** Listen to five sentences. Choose the word you hear in Exercise A.

C 🗣 Work in pairs. Take turns saying one word from each pair. Your partner will identify the word.

5 GRAMMAR: repeated and double comparatives

A   LANGUAGE IN CONTEXT Read the opinions.
Which person do you agree with more?

"Communication <u>has gotten faster and faster,</u> and all forms of social media are becoming more and more popular. People around the world feel closer to each other and understand each other better. The more we understand each other, the more peaceful the world will be."
Monica, San Luis Obispo, California

"We live in a global village, and we have friends all over the world. But the faster communication becomes, the less interesting our messages become. We send more and more messages about unimportant things. Sometimes slower is better."
Luca, Modena, Italy

NOTICE!

Look at the underlined phrase. Why do you think *faster* is repeated?

B   ANALYZE Read the opinions in Exercise A again.

Form & Function Complete the table with examples from the text.

Form	Function	Examples
comparative + *and* + comparative *more and more* + multisyllable adjective *less and less* + multisyllable adjective	**Repeated comparatives** used to describe something that is changing	**(1)** Communication has gotten _____ and _____, and … **(2)** … social media are becoming _____ and _____.
the + *more* (+ noun) + verb phrase, *the* + comparative + verb phrase ··· *the* + comparative + *the* + noun + verb phrase, *the* + comparative + verb phrase	**Double comparatives** used to describe how two things are changing at the same time, or how one thing changes as a result of a change in something else	**(3)** … better. _____ we understand …, _____ the world will be. **(4)** But _____ communication becomes, _____ our messages become.

More and *less* can be used with nouns: *The more work I get, the less time I have. We send more and more instant messages these days.*

More and *less* can also be used on their own: *The more I see, the less I understand.*

If we use a comparative adjective with a noun, we add *the* before the noun: *The better the teacher, the quicker you learn.*

Some expressions can leave out the verb: *The sooner the better.* (NOT: *The sooner it is, the better it is.*)

WATCH OUT!

✓ Social media is getting more and more powerful.

✗ Social media is getting more powerful and more powerful.

C   PRACTICE Complete the sentences with the words in parentheses.
Use either a repeated or a double comparative.

1   People are becoming _____ toward people in other countries. (*sympathetic*)
2   The world is becoming _____ with each new form of media that appears. (*small*)
3   _____ I use Twitter, the _____ I am in its possibilities. (*more, interested*)
4   _____ I read his blog, _____ I find it. (*more, funny*)
5   _____ you use social media, _____ it becomes. (*more, confusing*)
6   _____ broadband becomes, _____ it is to transmit information. (*fast, easy*)

D   NOW YOU DO IT Complete the sentences with your own ideas. Work in pairs.
Compare your ideas with a partner.

1   The more I _____, _____.
2   The less we _____, _____.
3   I believe the world is becoming _____ and _____.

A Work in pairs. Where do you prefer to shop: in a small local store, in a large department store, or online? Tell your partner and explain why. Then read the magazine article and find out if any your ideas are mentioned.

GOING LOCAL

¹ It's Saturday morning and the farmer's market in Seattle, Washington, is already busy with shoppers looking for locally-grown fresh fruit and vegetables as well as locally-produced eggs, cheese, and bread. "I'm here because I want to **support** local farmers, and I feel that I'm buying real food that has a connection to the place I live in," says Liz Minty. "It's also just nice to meet the farmers and producers—you get a real sense of community."

² Markets like this are becoming increasingly popular in towns and cities across America as consumers move away from food produced and packaged by large multinational companies. "Fresh food in supermarkets is rarely fresh," says Luisa Gonzalez, who **campaigns** for local farmers and growers. "It's usually been packed and refrigerated several days or weeks before it reaches the store. It often uses additives to extend shelf life and also consumes more energy as it is transported over long distances."

³ "Shop Small" is an initiative that helps to **promote** local businesses. "Small Business Saturday" now follows the Thanksgiving holiday and is intended to encourage shoppers to avoid large stores, and instead do their shopping at small independent stores. "It helps to **boost** our business at the start of the holiday season," says Anne Marshall of Newport, Rhode Island. "The Shop Small campaign definitely **generates** more interest in shopping locally."

⁴ Large supermarkets and department store chains often have better discounts and are able to provide a greater choice, especially of larger consumer items such as furniture or household appliances, but most of the money spent there goes to owners and suppliers in other parts of the country or abroad. Small businesses can't compete with their prices and still make a profit, which is why the campaign to go local is so important. "We **value** the experience of going into these small stores, speaking with the owners, and finding a range of items that are unique to this local community," says Hal Carter of Portland, Maine. "That's something you won't find in big department stores or online." And for lots of people, it's this experience that makes it worth paying a little more for certain items.

⁵ **Participating** in the "go local" movement doesn't mean completely ignoring the advantages of large stores or of online shopping, but it does mean thinking about ways to spend your money that can help **sustain** the local economy in the face of increasing globalization of the manufacturing and food industries.

B Work in pairs and answer the questions.

1 Find at least six reasons for shopping locally that are mentioned in the article.
2 Find two reasons for shopping in a large department store or supermarket.
3 Is the writer of this article for or against "going local"? How do you know?

C VOCABULARY: VERBS FOR TAKING SOCIAL ACTION Match the words with synonyms from the article in bold. Use the infinitive form.

1 encourage _____
2 create _____
3 keep alive _____
4 help _____
5 appreciate _____
6 take part _____
7 increase _____
8 fight _____

D 🔊 **VOCABULARY: VERBS FOR TAKING SOCIAL ACTION** Work in pairs. Choose the correct options to complete the sentences. Then discuss the questions with your partner.

1 How do your shopping habits *sustain / promote* local businesses?
2 How do store owners in your town or city try to *value / generate* business?
3 What could shoppers do to *generate / support* small stores in your neighborhood?
4 What do you *campaign / value* about the experience of shopping in small stores?

7 WRITING: a formal email

⚙ We can use different levels of formality in English to suggest particular meanings. More formal language can be used to be respectful to people we don't know very well, or who are more senior to us, or if we want to appear more serious. We can use less formal language if we want to seem friendlier, or if we know the person we are talking to well.

A 🔊 Work in pairs. In which situations would you need to send a formal email? Brainstorm ideas and tell the class.

B Read the emails about arranging a global citizenship meeting. Which email is more formal? Which language helps you identify it?

Hi, Kathy,

Thanks so much for volunteering to help organize the meeting about global citizenship.
Can you contact our guest speaker, Andrew Scott, with more information? He's been to lots of places and seen global citizenship projects in action. Tell him:
– date: March 28 or 31—which does he prefer?
– venue: Beckett Auditorium
His email address is: andrew01@netglobe.com
Oh, and see if he has any pictures of places he's visited recently. It would be great if he could base the talk on real examples. The more examples we can give people, the better.

Thanks a lot!

Jerry

Dear Mr. Scott,

My name is Kathy Allen, and Jerry Knibloe has asked me to write to you about the global citizenship meeting. Thank you for agreeing to be our guest speaker. We're all looking forward to meeting you and hearing about your experiences.

The meeting will take place on campus at the Beckett Auditorium. There are two possible dates for the meeting: March 28 or 31. Could you please let us know which one you prefer? The sooner you can do that, the sooner we can finalize the other details. We would also appreciate it if you could bring any pictures you might have from recent trips. Examples will really help people understand what it means to be a global citizen.

Please contact me if you have any questions.

Regards,

Kathy Allen

C 🔊 Work in pairs. Are the expressions formal or informal? Check the correct column and discuss your answers.

		Formal	Informal
1	Dear Mr. Scott,	☐	☐
2	Hi, Andy!	☐	☐
3	Thanks very much.	☐	☐
4	Thanks a lot!	☐	☐
5	With love,	☐	☐
6	Sincerely,	☐	☐

D You have agreed to help organize a meeting. Write an email based on the note on the right.

To do

Email guest speaker (Carol Sinclair) for global citizenship meeting.
Details: Victory Hotel, either September 5 @ 6 p.m. or September 19 @ 8 p.m.
Ask if she needs any equipment for the talk.

lifeSkills

UNDERSTANDING INTERNET SEARCH TERMS

- Determine what information you need to find.
- Choose effective search terms.
- Evaluate search results and refine your search if necessary.

A Read the essay topic. Make notes on what kind of information you will need to include in the essay.

> Choose two international fast-food chains that have branches in India. Describe how they have impacted the local economy and discuss whether these effects have been mainly positive or negative.

B Work in pairs. Discuss the internet search terms. How effective are they? What results do you think you would get?

← → fast food   >

top fast-food companies India

non-Indian fast-food companies

fast-food effects in India

effects on Indian economy of fast-food chains

HOW TO SAY IT

The problem with this search term is that it's too specific / not specific enough / too general.

This search term would probably return results that …

C Work in pairs. Many search engines allow you to refine your search in various ways using specific terms. Discuss what each of these five searches means.

- fast-food restaurants in India
- India AND food AND industry
- McDonald's OR KFC India
- India culture −celebrity
- India * industry

D Work in pairs. Think of the last time you used a search engine. Did you find the information you wanted? Is there anything that you would do differently now?

E Work in pairs. A search engine can give a wide variety of results in response to a keyword search. Discuss which ones you think might be useful for the essay in Exercise A, and why.

← →   india globalization   >

India globalization
Influence of globalization on developing countries
www.globalmonitor.com/globalization/developing-countries.html
India has benefited from globalization, but … There have been a number of negative effects on local culture …

American fast food—no thanks!
www.blogmasterglobal.com/vijay
It's time we got foreign influences out of India … We need to protect our culture. In my experience, we've been affected by foreign investment …

IBC NEWS Fire strikes fast-food outlet, Delhi, India
indiabc.com/headlines/delhi-fire.html
A fire broke out in a BestBurger restaurant in the early hours of yesterday morning … The police have described the damage as "devastating" …

India fast-food industry—statistics
www.india-food.in/statistics/
This page contains various statistics related to the fast-food industry in India … Local companies … International companies … Public opinion …

F Work in groups. Complete the Internet Research Plan for the task below.

You are going to study the effect of globalization on your local economy. Your professor has asked your group to prepare a short presentation for the next class. You have been asked to include some specific statistics, as well as broad concepts.

Internet Research Plan

Topic to be researched: _____

Information we want to find: _____

Key phrases we might use in searches: _____

Search terms to try: _____ _____ _____

G Tell the class about your Internet Research Plan. Listen to the other plans and take notes about good ideas you would like to add to your plan.

 REFLECT … How can the skill of understanding internet search terms be useful to you in **Work & Career** and **Self & Society**?

H Work in groups. Discuss the questions.

1 Do you feel you now have a better understanding of internet search terms? Give examples of things you have learned.
2 Will you apply what you have learned when you are using the internet for research? Why or why not?

RESEARCH …

Make notes for an internet research plan on the essay topic below.

What effect has globalization had on work and employment in your country? Give examples from two different industries and explain how jobs and working conditions have been affected.

Language wrap-up

1 VOCABULARY

Complete the paragraph with the words from the box. (12 points)

> boost   campaign   dominated   economic growth   facilitate   generating
> multinational   profits   promote   regional   support   value

Globalization has had a great impact on the **(1)** _____ of emerging economies.
Many **(2)** _____ companies have set up factories and offices around the world
that create employment and **(3)** _____ cheaper production while at the same
time **(4)** _____ huge **(5)** _____ for themselves. Many countries have
benefited dramatically from this process. Some experts, however, are worried that the
global economy will become **(6)** _____ by a few powerful companies and that
(7) _____ cultures and traditional skills will disappear.
In contrast to the trend toward increasing globalization, some communities are seeing
more people who **(8)** _____ the experience of shopping locally. People are going
to local farmers' markets to **(9)** _____ local growers and producers. Shop Small
Saturday every November is also part of a growing **(10)** _____ to **(11)** _____
local businesses and **(12)** _____ profits for local stores.

> **10–12 correct:** I can talk about globalization and social action.
> **0–9 correct:** Look again at Sections 1 and 6 on pages 22, 26, and 27.   SCORE: /12

2 GRAMMAR

Choose the correct options to complete the conversation. (12 points)

Vicky: I've been reading a lot recently about the effects of globalization on the world
economy.

Alex: Really? **(1)** *Do you think / Are you thinking* it's a good thing, or not?

Vicky: That's difficult to say. There are many advantages. For example, companies now
(2) *have / are having* factories all over the world, so economies are more closely
connected. **(3)** *More connected / The more connected* economies become, the
more we depend on each other. On the other hand, there are disadvantages,
too. These days, many countries **(4)** *have / are having* financial problems caused
by economic issues in other countries around the world. It's becoming **(5)** *more
and more / the more and more* difficult to avoid a global economic crisis in a
globalized world.

Alex: I **(6)** *see / am seeing* what you mean. But the internet makes it
(7) *easier and easier / more and more easy* to share information. **(8)** *More /
The more* we communicate, **(9)** *better / the better* we will understand each other.

Vicky: That's true. Now, it **(10)** *is / is being* **(11)** *more common and more common /
more and more common* to have friends and co-workers all over the world.

Alex: I **(12)** *think / am thinking* of going to the café. Why don't we go together and talk
about it some more?

Vicky: Good idea!

> **10–12 correct:** I can use verbs with stative and dynamic uses and repeated and double
> comparatives.
> **0–9 correct:** Look again at Sections 2 and 5 on pages 23 and 25.   SCORE: /12

SPEAKING WORKSHOP
Describing a picture

A 🎧 **1.10** 🗣 Listen to someone describing the picture and take notes on the main points the speaker makes under the following headings. Work in pairs and compare your notes.

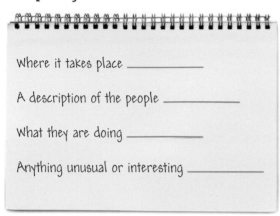

Where it takes place _____

A description of the people _____

What they are doing _____

Anything unusual or interesting _____

B Listen again and check the points the speaker mentions.

The speaker …
- ☐ describes the background
- ☐ describes the foreground
- ☐ describes the person who took the picture
- ☐ describes the people and what they are doing
- ☐ describes the general setting and context
- ☐ makes an inference about where the people come from
- ☐ makes an inference about the relationship between the people

C 🗣 Look at the picture below. You are going to describe it. Make notes with your own ideas under the following headings. Work in pairs and compare your ideas.

- Where was it taken?
- Who are they?
- What are they doing?
- Are they doing anything interesting or unusual?

D 🗣 Work in groups.
Present your description.

HOW ARE YOU DOING?
- ◯ I described all the details in the picture
- ◯ I spoke clearly.
- ◯ I varied the tone of my voice.

UNIT 3 FAME AND FORTUNE

IN THIS UNIT YOU

⚙ learn language to talk about fame

⚙ read about the drawbacks of wanting to be famous

⚙ talk about the advantages and disadvantages of being famous

⚙ listen to a gossip columnist's opinions about different levels of fame

⚙ write a blog post about someone you admire

⚙ learn about evaluating arguments

▶ watch a video about an actor working in Los Angeles

READING
for different purposes
Why do you think we read different types of texts in different ways?

SPEAKING
clarifying misunderstandings
What phrases can you use to explain or clarify what you are saying when someone misunderstands you?

LIFE SKILLS

WORK & CAREER

evaluating arguments The word *argument* has two meanings. It can be a disagreement, or it can be ideas and evidence that someone presents to convince other people to agree. Think of a time when you argued for or against something. Were you able to convince other people to agree with you?

A Work in pairs. Who do you think are five of the most famous people in the world? Try to think of a variety of famous people, not just entertainers. Use the pictures to help you. Share your ideas with the class.

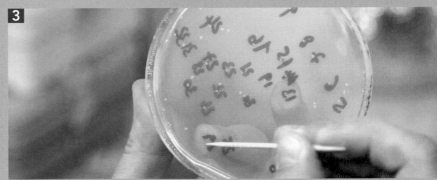

B Work in groups. Do you think the famous people you chose in Exercise A are different or special compared to ordinary people? If so, how?

A LANGUAGE IN CONTEXT Read the magazine article. Was each person's experience of fame positive or negative? Why?

The artist **Andy Warhol** once said that everyone would be famous for 15 minutes. Here we look at two people who have had their 15 minutes of fame and what the experience meant to them.

STEVE JENNINGS was just 17 when he appeared as Des in the popular TV series *Angels* back in the 90s. He became famous overnight, but Steve said no one had told him what to expect and how to deal with it. Although he enjoyed aspects of his celebrity, he admitted that he would do things differently if he became famous now, and confessed that he had had to get help to deal with the pressures of fame.

And then there's **TOM REYNOLDS** from San Diego, who unexpectedly inherited a fortune from an uncle he never knew and became famous when the news was widely publicized by reporters. Within a short time, Tom had spent his entire inheritance and ended up living on the streets. He commented that people in a similar situation should get advice on handling and investing their money. But he also suggested that lots of people might not admit that they need help.

B ANALYZE Read the article in Exercise A again.

NOTICE!
Find and underline five reporting verbs. Can you think of any more examples?

Form Answer the questions. Then complete the table with the correct verb or modal forms.

1 In reported speech, what usually happens to the verb after the reporting verb? Does the tense change?

2 Now look at the reporting verbs you underlined in the article. Does the verb that follows the reporting verb always change form in reported speech?

No tense change	Examples
past perfect → past perfect	Direct: *"I hadn't thought about what fame would really be like."* Reported: *He admitted that he* **(3)** _____ *about what fame would really be like.*
Modal change	**Examples**
can → could *may → might* *must → had to* *will → would*	Direct: *"I may never work in television again."* Reported: *He suggested (that) he* **(4)** _____ *never work in television again.*
No modal change	**Examples**
could—could *should—should* *might—might* *would—would*	Direct: *"Would you do things differently?"* Reported: *She asked if he* **(5)** _____ *do things differently.*

C PRACTICE Rewrite the direct quotes in reported speech with the reporting verbs in parentheses.

1 Andrew: "I would like to see Katy Perry in concert." (*said*)

_____

2 *Entertainment Weekly*: "Jay Z may perform at the new stadium." (*reported*)

_____

3 Clare: "Will I see some celebrities during my vacation in Los Angeles?" (*asked*)

_____

4 Security Officer: "You have to leave your cameras at the door." (*told us*)

_____

5 Dylan: "I had never used Twitter before I started college." (*said*)

_____

WATCH OUT!
✓ He said he had to give an interview yesterday.
✗ He said he must give an interview yesterday.

D 🗣 **NOW YOU DO IT** Work in pairs. Complete the statements about the disadvantages of fame and tell a partner what you think. Then report your partner's opinions to another pair.

Celebrities have to / don't have to …　　*If I were famous, I would/wouldn't …*
Famous people can/can't …　　*It would/wouldn't be difficult to …*

2 LISTENING: to a gossip columnist

A 🗣 Work in pairs and discuss the questions.
1　Does being a *celebrity* mean the same as being *famous*?
2　Do you think all famous people are celebrities?

B 🗣 Work in pairs. Look at these pictures of famous people. Say if you know of them and what you know about them. Which ones are celebrities?

C 👂 **1.11** 🗣 Listen and then discuss the questions as a class.
1　According to the gossip columnist, what is the difference between A-, B-, and C-list celebrities?
2　Look at the people in Exercise B that you considered to be celebrities. In your opinion, what categories do they belong to?
3　Think of some famous people in your country. According to the definitions of A-, B-, and C-list celebrities, which category would each person be in?

D **VOCABULARY: WAYS TO BECOME FAMOUS** Listen again and complete the phrases with the words from the box. Then add any other ways to become famous you can think of.

| break | cause | come up with | discover | inherit | run | write |

1　_____ a world record
2　_____ a global company
3　_____ a fortune
4　_____ a best-selling novel
5　_____ a cure for a disease
6　_____ a scandal
7　_____ a new invention/idea

E 🗣 **VOCABULARY: WAYS TO BECOME FAMOUS** Work in pairs. Think of three people who became famous for one of the reasons in Exercise D and write sentences about them as in the example. Do you think they are celebrities? If so, say whether you think they are A-, B-, or C-list celebrities and why.

The American swimmer Missy Franklin became famous for breaking a world record at the 2012 Olympic Games in London, at the age of 17. I think she's a B-list celebrity because she's probably only known in the U.S.

F 🗣 Work with another pair. Talk about your ideas.

We said Missy Franklin had become famous because she broke a world record at the Olympics.

When you've identified why you're reading something, the next step is to identify how to read it. Different texts require different ways of reading.

A Match each text type (a–j) with the way you normally read it (1–4).

a) newspaper articles ☐   f) textbooks ☐
b) novels/stories ☐   g) internet articles ☐
c) reference books ☐   h) phone directories ☐
d) magazine articles ☐   i) poetry or lyrics ☐
e) advertisements ☐   j) text messages ☐

1 Skimming: Looking quickly at an article or a book to get a general idea of what it is about. This includes looking at visuals, headings, and subheadings.

2 Scanning: Looking for specific information in a text, such as headings and key words.

3 Reading in detail: Reading a text carefully in order to learn concepts and details. This often involves marking important information or taking notes.

4 General reading: Reading a text completely, but without concentrating on learning specific information.

B Read the first question below and write the best strategy (1–4) from Exercise A to answer it. Then read the text in that way to find the answer. Do questions 2–5 in the same way.

1 What is the text about? ☐ _____
2 What careers did children want to have 25 years ago? What careers do they want to have now? ☐ _____
3 What has caused the changes in children's career ambitions, and how does the author feel about these changes? ☐ _____
4 According to the author, what has made people believe that it's easy to become famous and wealthy? ☐ _____
5 According to the author, why do fame and fortune sometimes have negative effects on people? ☐ _____

---

www.family.values.com

WHEN I GROW UP . . . TEACHER OR ROCK STAR?

[1] "What do you want to be when you grow up?" For generations, children have been asked this question, but it seems their answers are changing. A recent study has revealed a dramatic and rather worrying shift in children's **ambitions**.

[2] Twenty-five years ago, the most common **aspiration** of the average American child was to be a teacher, followed by a career in finance, and then medicine. Today's younger generation, on the other hand, say they want to be a sports star, a singer, or an actor: all careers associated with great wealth and, perhaps more significantly, fame.

[3] We now live in a culture that worships celebrities, so perhaps it is not surprising that so many children grow up with a desire to be famous. Some would argue that this is a positive thing; that it is good to aim high and that there is no harm in dreaming. However, others feel that this trend will ultimately lead to dissatisfaction.

[4] This cult of celebrity has been intensified by an increasing number of TV talent competitions through which winners can acquire wealth and fame in a very short time. This quick route to fame and fortune creates unrealistic expectations and the belief that a celebrity lifestyle is easy to achieve. For the majority who inevitably will not reach their goal, failure can lead to intense feelings of disappointment and even low **self-esteem**. In addition, individuals can waste years of their lives pursuing their dream, missing out on opportunities for education and training that would make them employable in the real world.

[5] Even for the lucky few who do **make it big**, fame and fortune do not always have a positive impact on their lives. Many careers **in the spotlight** are brief—an athlete's physical peak lasts only a few years, and a lot of musicians have only one successful album. The careers of reality-show celebrities are likely to be even shorter. When the sole focus of their lives suddenly disappears and their earnings **dwindle**, these former stars can suffer feelings of **worthlessness** and a complete lack of control. It can also be difficult for them to adapt to normal life again. Many **washed-up** celebrities end up competing in "celebrity" reality shows, desperate to be famous again.

[6] It is worrying that so many young people these days value fame above more realistic aspirations, not only because so few of them will achieve it, but because fame can be a **traumatic** experience for those who actually succeed and become celebrities. Unfortunately, these changing aspirations could have a very negative impact on the happiness of a generation.

C VOCABULARY: GUESSING MEANING FROM CONTEXT Read the text again and choose the correct options.

1   **Aspiration** and **ambition** have *similar / different* meanings.
2   **Self-esteem** refers to the state of a person's *mind / body*.
3   If you **make it big** you are very *successful / unsuccessful*.
4   **In the spotlight** relates to *fame / happiness*.
5   **Dwindle** refers to *an increase / a decrease*.
6   **Worthlessness** has a *positive / negative* meaning.
7   **Washed-up** has a *positive / negative* meaning.
8   **Traumatic** has a *positive / negative* meaning.

D VOCABULARY: GUESSING MEANING FROM CONTEXT Complete the questions with the correct form of a word or phrase from Exercise C. Then work in pairs and discuss the questions.

1   Do you agree with the author that many children's _____ to become rich and famous is a bad thing? Why or why not?
2   Do you think personal problems are more or less _____ for people who are _____?
3   If you were a celebrity, what would you do when your fame started to _____?

4 WRITING: a website post

A Look at the picture. What do you know, or what can you guess, about Ellen Ochoa? Read the website post and check your ideas. Why is she the writer's hero?

● ● ●　　　　　　www.family.values.com

My personal HERO

Written by Laney from New Orleans Updated on May 16 11:32:09 p.m.

Why do we look up to "celebrities" who have achieved nothing more than appearing on some mindless reality TV show? Why are these people our heroes? I want to talk about a real hero.

Ellen Ochoa was born in 1958, in Los Angeles, and is half Mexican. When she was a college student and couldn't decide what career she wanted, she asked her engineering teacher for advice. He told her that engineering was too hard for a girl, but thanks to her enthusiasm and courage, she followed her engineering dreams and achieved great things. In fact, she became the first Hispanic woman astronaut!

She showed enormous courage in doing something that so few women have done at a time when many people still believed that being an astronaut was "a man's job." That's why I admire her.

B Think of someone you admire and write a website post about him or her.

C Work in pairs. Tell your partner why you admire the person.

5 PRONUNCIATION: silent letters — consonant sounds

A 🎧 1.12 Listen to the words. Notice that the underlined consonant sound in each word is silent.

b: num<u>b</u>, de<u>b</u>t, dou<u>b</u>t　　k: <u>k</u>nown, <u>k</u>not　　g: forei<u>g</u>n, si<u>g</u>n
p: <u>p</u>sychology　　h: <u>rh</u>yme, <u>h</u>ours, w<u>h</u>en　　l: cou<u>l</u>d, shou<u>l</u>d

B 🎧 1.13 Now listen to the words and underline the silent consonant sound in each one. Work in pairs and practice saying the words in Exercises A and B.

comb   designer   ghost   honest   knee   knife   knock   resign

6 GRAMMAR: reported speech — optional back-shifting

A LANGUAGE IN CONTEXT Read the article. How does Ilham Anas feel about looking like a famous person?

NOTICE!
Underline the five examples of reported speech in the text. Which tense is used after the reporting verb?

U.S.A. News Bulletin

January • Volume 4

Take a look at the two pictures. Can you tell which one is Barack Obama and which is a lookalike? No, we couldn't either, but the guy in the left-hand picture isn't President Obama! His name is Ilham Anas, an Indonesian photographer who suddenly became a celebrity in Jakarta when Mr. Obama was first elected in 2008.

At first, when Mr. Anas's relatives pointed out his similarity to the president, he said he couldn't see a strong likeness. Then colleagues asked him to pose for photographs with an American flag, wearing a suit and tie, and suddenly everything changed. Before long, the pictures were all over the internet, and Mr. Anas was receiving calls from TV stations and an advertising agency. His life hasn't been the same since. He has appeared on a national talk show and in a television advertisement, among other things.

Surprisingly, Mr. Anas revealed that he is a shy person who doesn't like being in the spotlight. However, he explained that he sees looking like Mr. Obama as a blessing. He said that he'll keep taking all the opportunities that come along as long as they do not conflict with his personal values. Of course, the excitement of the president's election has worn off now, and Mr. Anas told reporters that he isn't getting much "Obama work" anymore and is returning to a more normal life. There may be less demand for Barack Obama lookalikes, but while Mr. Obama is President of the United States, we're certain that Mr. Anas's life won't be completely normal.

B ANALYZE Read the article in Exercise A again.

Form Read the information and complete the table with examples from the text. Then answer the question.

> When we report speech, we generally shift the verb tense back into the past. This is called back-shifting. Sometimes this is optional.

WATCH OUT!

✗ He said he will never get used to being famous, but he seems to like it now.

✓ He said he would never get used to being famous, but he seems to like it now.

Back-shifting is *optional* when reporting …	Direct speech	Reported speech— back-shifting	Reported speech— no back-shifting
… a general truth.	"I am a shy person."	He revealed that he was a shy person.	He revealed that he is a shy person.
… something that is true at the moment of reporting.	"I'm not getting much 'Obama work' anymore."	He told reporters (1) _____.	He told reporters (2) _____.
… future possibilities or plans.	"I'll keep taking all the opportunities that come along."	He said (3) _____.	He said (4) _____.
Back-shifting is *necessary* when reporting something that is no longer true.	"I can't see a strong likeness."	At first, he said (5) _____.	

6 Look at the pairs of sentences below. For each pair, which is correct—a, b, or both?

i **a)** He said he doesn't like being in the spotlight.

   b) He said he didn't like being in the spotlight.

ii **a)** At first, he claimed he can't see a strong likeness.

   b) At first, he claimed he couldn't see a strong likeness.

C PRACTICE Rewrite the direct speech as reported speech with and without back-shifting. In one example, only back-shifting is possible.

1 **John:** "They are holding an Oscars party downtown."
John announced _____. John announced _____.

2 **Nadia (yesterday):** "I'm really excited about the concert this evening."
Nadia told us _____. Nadia told us _____.

3 **Professor:** "Technological advances will change the way we watch movies."
The professor declared _____. The professor declared _____.

4 **Jimena:** "You don't have to be 18 to get a backstage pass."
Jimena stated _____. Jimena stated _____.

D  **NOW YOU DO IT** Work in pairs. Imagine you are suddenly famous. Tell your partner about your experiences of celebrity. Swap roles and listen to your partner. Then work with a different person and report on what your previous partner told you.

7 SPEAKING: clarifying misunderstandings

When you feel you haven't explained something clearly enough, there are phrases you can use to clarify what you mean.

A Work in pairs. Look at the picture and the quote. Discuss what you think are the disadvantages of being famous.

"The image is one thing and the human being is another. It's very hard to live up to an image, put it that way."—Elvis Presley

B))) 1.14 Listen to six short conversations about the disadvantages of fame. Complete the phrases the speakers use to clarify what they mean.

1 Well, what I _____ was …
2 What I'm trying to _____ is …
3 Maybe I'm not _____ myself clear.
4 Maybe I should _____ that.
5 _____, that's not what I meant.
6 _____ it that way.

C Complete the sentences with an appropriate phrase from Exercise B. There is more than one correct answer for some of the sentences.

1 "I didn't mean that fame had brought Elvis Presley a huge amount of unhappiness. _____ that it didn't bring him the happiness he thought it would."

2 "_____. I didn't mean all celebrities have problems. I just meant that a lot of them seem to."

3 "I'm not saying the media was responsible for Michael Jackson's difficulties, but I don't think they made his life easy, _____."

4 "_____. It's not that actors who cause scandals are less talented. It's just that they become more well known for their scandals than for good acting."

D Work in pairs. Discuss your opinions about fame. Rephrase to clarify what you mean where appropriate.

A: *I think it would be really difficult being famous.*
B: *Really? I think it would be really fun!*
A: *Maybe I should rephrase that. I'm not saying that it wouldn't be fun sometimes. What I meant was that certain things, like going out in public, would be difficult.*

lifeSkills

EVALUATING ARGUMENTS

- Identify claims made and evidence for those claims.
- Understand strong and weak points.
- Evaluate the argument based on the strength of the points.

A Read the definition of *argument*. Then read the proposal to change the content of a large city newspaper and look at the sentences in bold. Underline the sentences which are claims and circle the sentences which provide evidence to support the claims.

- a claim (a statement that may or may not be true)
- evidence (provable factual information to support the claim)

> **argument (*n.*)** /ˈɑrɡjəmənt/ **[COUNT./NON-COUNT.]:**
> a reason or reasons used to persuade other people to support an idea. An argument usually includes an introduction to the situation or problem, one or more claims, and evidence. It also often includes personal opinion.

To:	Editorial Board
From:	Tanya Stevens
RE:	Proposal to reduce extent of print edition
Date:	February 12, 2015

As you are aware, newspaper sales started to drop in the 1960s when TV became widely available, and more recently, sales have dropped further due to the availability of news and other information on the internet. **(1) According to a Pew Research Center survey, the number of people who read a newspaper daily dropped from 41% in 2002 to 23% in 2012.** Consequently, the newspaper industry has to make adjustments if it is to survive.

One approach is to cut costs, and **(2) the best way to do this is to decrease the size of the newspaper.** Therefore, I propose that we cut one of the less important sections of the paper. **(3) Newspaper readers in the 21ˢᵗ century are a smaller and more specific group than a decade ago.** They tend to be older, college educated, and interested in international and national affairs. **(4) A recent survey by the Newspaper Association of America revealed that 87% of readers read the front page and main news, 85% read the local news, and 54% read the international and national news. In contrast, only 45% read the lifestyle and entertainment section.**

It makes sense to offer only the most popular sections of our newspaper. We could consider cutting sections like travel, or science and technology, but I think that those sections are too small to have an impact on our costs. Based on the data, I propose that we cut our Lifestyle and Entertainment section. I appreciate that this change will not be easy. However, as in any type of evolution, those who do not adapt cannot survive. **(5) If we start targeting our newspaper at the 21ˢᵗ century reader, it will not only survive, but it will also grow.**

B 🎧 **1.15** Listen to an excerpt from the Editorial Board meeting. What action do they decide to take?

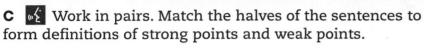

C **Work in pairs. Match the halves of the sentences to form definitions of strong points and weak points.**

1 A strong point …   **a)** states a personal opinion or makes a claim not based on evidence.

2 A weak point …   **b)** makes a claim based on evidence from a reliable source.

D **Work in pairs. Decide if each claim in the table is a strong or a weak point, and label it S (strong) or W (weak).**

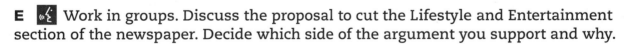

Against cutting the L&E section	For cutting the L&E section
1 ☐ We get dozens of letters to the editor each week with comments about articles in the L&E section. In fact, last week we got 50 letters related to that section.	1 ☐ Newspaper readers in the 21ˢᵗ century are a smaller and more specific group than a decade ago.
2 ☐ If L&E disappears, we're going to get lots of complaints.	2 ☐ What these 21ˢᵗ century readers want is news; the news sections are read by many more people than sections such as lifestyle and entertainment.
3 ☐ People in our community want a newspaper that offers a variety of content.	3 ☐ A recent survey by the Newspaper Association of America[ii] revealed that 87% of readers read the front page and main news, and an average of 69.5% read international or local news. In contrast, an average of only 45% read the lifestyle section.
4 ☐ Also, several national surveys have shown that when young people *do* read the newspaper, they tend to read the L&E sections.	4 ☐ I believe that if we start targeting our newspaper at the 21ˢᵗ century reader, it will not only survive, but it will also grow.
5 ☐ If we cut that section, we'll lose any young readers that we have!	5 ☐ Yes, but we get hundreds of letters about the news stories and editorials, far more than we get for L&E.
	6 ☐ People want to read real news.

E **Work in groups. Discuss the proposal to cut the Lifestyle and Entertainment section of the newspaper. Decide which side of the argument you support and why.**

F **Work in groups. Discuss the questions.**

1 Do you feel that you are now able to recognize strong and weak arguments? Why or why not?

2 Do you think the side with the most points is usually the strongest? Explain your answer.

RESEARCH …

Compare a print newspaper to its online version. Consider these questions and make notes in order to report back to the class.

1 If you do not have a subscription to an online paper, are you able to access all sections?

2 How does the price of an online subscription compare with the print version?

3 Do both versions of the newspaper have the same content and layout?

HOW TO SAY IT

Tanya Stevens claimed that … / said she thought that …

I think this is a good/bad argument because …

This point is weak/strong because …

I agree / don't agree with Tanya Stevens's claim that …

I think it would be a better idea to …

REFLECT … How can the skill of evaluating arguments be useful to you in the areas of **Study & Learning** and **Self & Society**?

Language wrap-up

1 VOCABULARY

A Complete the sentences with a verb in the correct form from the box. (7 points)

> break cause come up with discover inherit run write

1 Madonna **(1)** _____ a scandal in 2009 when she adopted a child from Malawi.
   She is a singer, but she has also **(2)** _____ a best-selling children's book.
2 Allegra Versace **(3)** _____ her fortune after her uncle was killed in 1997. She now
   (4) _____ a fashion company.
3 Scientists in this country **(5)** _____ the gene that causes certain types of cancer.
4 Usain Bolt **(6)** _____ the world record for the 100-meter sprint in the 2012 Olympics.
5 This man is famous for **(7)** _____ a new machine that made cartoon characters look more realistic.

B Complete the sentences with a word or phrase from the box. Change the form if necessary. (5 points)

> ambition dwindle in the spotlight make it big washed-up

1 For every person who **(1)** _____, there are thousands of others who don't
   succeed in becoming famous.
2 If your **(2)** _____ is to become a famous singer, actor, or sports star, you have to be
   prepared to work very hard.
3 Celebrities should be prepared for the time when their fame **(3)** _____ and they
   are no longer **(4)** _____.
4 Many **(5)** _____ celebrities will do anything to become famous again.

10–12 correct: I can talk about fame and ways to become famous.
0–9 correct: Look again at Sections 2 and 3 on pages 35, 36 and 37.   **SCORE:**   /12

2 GRAMMAR

Rewrite the direct speech as reported speech in two different ways with the verbs in parentheses. (10 points)

1 The manager: "You have to wear a tie if you want to get into the club." (*said*)
   _____
   _____

2 Rachel: "You have to be very self-confident to be an actor." (*commented*)
   _____
   _____

3 Vicki: "Will the movie industry change a lot in the near future?" (*asked*)
   _____
   _____

4 Anton: "I've seen lots of celebrities around here." (*revealed*)
   _____
   _____

5 Sonia: "I can help you find an agent." (*told me*)
   _____
   _____

8–10 correct: I can use reported speech with modals and optional back-shifting.
0–7 correct: Look again at Sections 1 and 6 on pages 34 and 38.   **SCORE:**   /10

WRITING WORKSHOP
Writing a short essay

A Read the essay and choose T (true) or F (false).

In general, are celebrities a positive or negative influence on others?

It is true that some celebrities are not a positive influence on young people. They constantly cause scandals or get into trouble. However, many celebrities use their position in the spotlight to do good things, and they have a very positive influence on society.

One important thing celebrities do is donate money, time, and their names to good causes. When there is a disaster such as a hurricane or an earthquake, many celebrities help raise money. For example, when model Grisele Bündchen said that she would donate $1.5 million to the Red Cross after a hurricane in Haiti, that inspired the public to donate, too. Another generous celebrity is the singer Bono, who gives benefit concerts and meets with world leaders to raise money and promote programs to help poor children around the world.

Apart from supporting good causes, celebrities can also be good role models for young people. When celebrities have qualities such as compassion, honesty, and tolerance, they can influence teenagers and younger children to develop those same qualities. There are definitely many celebrities who use their fame in positive ways.

1 The writer thinks that many celebrities have a positive influence on society.   *T / F*
2 People tend to give money to charity if a celebrity donates money.   *T / F*
3 Bono gives many benefit concerts in support of environmental charities.   *T / F*

B Look back at the essay and choose the correct options to complete the statements.
1 The purpose of the first paragraph is to …
  a) present the writer's general opinion.   **b)** give reasons for the opinion.   **c)** explain who the writer is.
2 In paragraph 2, the author gives … examples of charitable celebrities to support his point.
  a) two   **b)** three   **c)** four
3 In paragraph 3, the author gives … examples of positive qualities to support his point.
  a) two   **b)** three   **c)** four
4 The last sentence of the essay …
  a) gives an example.
  b) gives a reason for the writer's opinion.
  c) restates the writer's general opinion.

C You are going to write a short essay giving your opinion about the question in Exercise A. If you agree with the writer of the sample essay, give different reasons in your essay. Write notes for your essay.

Introductory topic sentence: _____
Reasons for your opinion (at least two): _____
Supporting details or examples (at least one or two): _____
_____
Concluding sentence: _____

D Use your notes to write your essay. Write about 200 words.

HOW ARE YOU DOING?

○ My opening paragraph states my general opinion.
○ I have given enough reasons to support my opinion.
○ My paragraphs include a topic sentence summarizing the main point of the paragraph.

UNIT 4 UPS AND DOWNS

IN THIS UNIT YOU

- learn language to talk about mood and life satisfaction
- listen to a lecture about wealth and happiness
- write a thank-you note
- read about research on happiness
- talk about having a positive attitude
- learn about being a positive team member
- ▶ watch a video about the concept of Gross National Happiness

LISTENING
understanding discourse markers

What are some phrases you might hear that signal a change of topic or the conclusion of a topic?

WRITING
a thank-you note

In what situations do you need to write a thank-you note? Would different situations require a different style? Why?

LIFE SKILLS

WORK & CAREER

being a positive team member When you are working on a team, it is important to be positive. What are some characteristics of a positive team member?

A 🗣 Work in pairs. Do you agree with these definitions of happiness? Explain why or why not.

1 Happiness is having good friends you can talk to.

2 Happiness is feeling you've done your best.

3 Happiness is helping other people.

4 Happiness is feeling peaceful and safe.

5 Happiness is having enough money to buy whatever you want.

6 Happiness is being independent.

B 🗣 Work in pairs. First, complete the definition in your own words. Then explain your definition to your partner.

Happiness is …

Discourse markers often act as signposts, giving a listener clues about what they might hear next. They might introduce additional points, contrasting ideas, or a conclusion.

A 🎧 **1.16** Listen to the introduction to a lecture. What is the lecture going to be about?

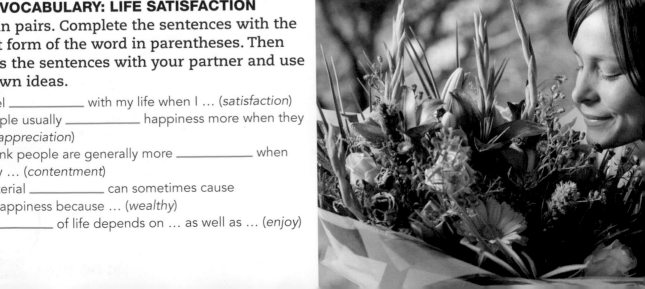

B 🎧 **1.17** Listen to the full lecture. As you listen, write one word to complete the phrases. Then write each phrase in the correct place in the table.

_____ general   _____ the other hand
_____ a result   _____ addition

Phrases used to talk generally	Phrases used to introduce a contrasting point	Phrases used to introduce a result	Phrases used to introduce an additional point
(1) _____ On the whole To a great extent	(2) _____ That said Nevertheless	(3) _____ As a consequence Consequently	(4) _____ What's more Furthermore

C 🗣 Listen to the lecture again and answer the questions. Work in pairs and discuss your answers.

1 What did the first study find out?
2 How did the second study contradict the first study?
3 What is the difference between satisfaction and happiness?
4 Why do you think wealthier people enjoy everyday pleasures less?

D VOCABULARY: LIFE SATISFACTION Complete the tables with the correct form of each word.

Adjective	Noun
happy	_____
wealthy	_____
_____	pleasure
_____	contentment

Verb	Noun
_____	appreciation
enjoy	_____
_____	satisfaction

E 🗣 **VOCABULARY: LIFE SATISFACTION**
Work in pairs. Complete the sentences with the correct form of the word in parentheses. Then discuss the sentences with your partner and use your own ideas.

1 I feel _____ with my life when I … (*satisfaction*)
2 People usually _____ happiness more when they … (*appreciation*)
3 I think people are generally more _____ when they … (*contentment*)
4 Material _____ can sometimes cause unhappiness because … (*wealthy*)
5 _____ of life depends on … as well as … (*enjoy*)

2 GRAMMAR: noun clauses as objects

A 🎧 **1.18 LANGUAGE IN CONTEXT** Read the notice. Then listen to the conversation below. According to Michelle, how does laughter therapy work?

Rita: Look at this! Laughter therapy!

Michelle: Yeah, I've read about that. Apparently, laughing can help people feel happier and less stressed, so now they're using it as a therapy!

Rita: That sounds really interesting. Do you know what it involves?

Michelle: I'm not sure exactly, but I think they explain how laughter could help you deal with a problem. I think you learn techniques to see the positive side of a situation.

Rita: That sounds useful! I wonder when they're holding the workshop. Does it say where we can get more information?

Michelle: I'm sure there's more information on the website. I think we need to register online, and we might need to explain why we want to attend the course.

Rita: So, do you want to try it?

JOIN OUR ONE-DAY
LAUGHTER THERAPY WORKSHOP

LAUGHTER CAN CHANGE YOUR LIFE!
Venue: Main Hall
Time: 9–5
Limited to 40 participants.
http://laughtertherapy.campusworkshops.net

REGISTER TODAY!

B ANALYZE Read the conversation in Exercise A again.

NOTICE!
Underline all the examples of **what**, **where**, **when**, **why**, and **how** in the conversation. What do you notice about the word order in the clauses that follow each one?

Form Complete the table with examples from the text.

	Noun clause	
Do you know	(= the thing(s)) **(1)** _____	it involves?
They explain	(= the way) **(2)** _____	laughter could help you deal with a situation.
I wonder	(= the time) **(3)** _____	they're holding the workshop.
Does it say	(= the place) **(4)** _____	we can get more information?
We might need to explain	(= the reason) **(5)** _____	we want to attend the course.

C PRACTICE Complete the sentences with *what*, *where*, *when*, *why*, or *how*. More than one answer may be possible.

1 I think you'll be interested in _____ they have to say about happiness.
2 I don't understand _____ laughter therapy works.
3 The presenters will demonstrate _____ laughter can help you be positive.
4 I sometimes wonder _____ people at work are so stressed.
5 They told us _____ the workshop will take place, but I've forgotten which office exactly.
6 Do you know _____ the next workshop will be held? Is it next month?

WATCH OUT!
✓ I agree with what you said.
✗ I agree with what did you say.

D 🎙 **NOW YOU DO IT** Work in pairs. Complete the sentences in your own words. Then compare with your partner. How similar or different are your ideas?

I'd like to learn about what ...   I'm happier if I know why ...   I often wonder how ...

3 READING: a magazine article

A Read the magazine article. What are two ways to be happier, according to research mentioned in the article?

HAPPINESS

WHAT IS HAPPINESS?

[1] Is it being **in a good mood**? Is it a state of contentment, or is it a feeling of excitement or pleasure? It seems that happiness is all of these things. Psychologists have defined it as a "**state of well-being**"—a combination of life satisfaction and experiencing more positive than negative **emotions**.

WHAT MAKES US HAPPY?

[2] Happiness is a very subjective state and can mean different things to different people. However, researchers have identified some basic components of happiness.

[3] One component is our physical condition, such as our level of income and state of health. There is no doubt that financial stress and illness can have a negative impact on our level of happiness. But wealth on its own isn't enough; you can be very wealthy and also very unhappy.

[4] Another component is genetic; it seems that some of us may be born to be cheerful. Some of our character traits are inherited and may include a tendency to either be more **optimistic** or to get **depressed** more easily.

[5] By far, the greatest influence on our happiness is our choice about how we feel and think. We can make a decision to be optimistic about life, or choose to focus on the negative side and be more **pessimistic**. Some recent research has found that practicing positive emotions such as gratitude, joy, hope, and kindness can have a positive effect on our general state of well-being. In other words, we can control how happy we are.

HOW CAN WE MEASURE HAPPINESS?

[6] One simple method is just to ask people how they are feeling. A recent research project used a cell phone app to track how happy people were. From time to time, the app sent a message asking the person to report how happy he or she was feeling as well as what activity the person was doing. The study found that people who are less **focused** on what they're doing tend to feel less happy. When they get **distracted**, they start to worry or think about negative things, which makes them unhappy.

WHY DO SCIENTISTS RESEARCH HAPPINESS?

[7] Researchers believe that researching happiness is very useful. The more we understand about the causes of happiness, the more we can learn about developing social or psychological traits that contribute to our general state of well-being and help us lead fuller lives.

B Read the statements and choose T (true), F (false), or NM (not mentioned).

1 It is not possible to measure happiness.   *T / F / NM*
2 Scientists disagree about the causes of happiness.   *T / F / NM*
3 Our personality influences our level of happiness.   *T / F / NM*
4 It is possible to learn how to be happier.   *T / F / NM*
5 Asking people about their state of mind is unreliable.   *T / F / NM*
6 Lack of concentration can cause negative emotions.   *T / F / NM*

C VOCABULARY: MOOD Match the definitions (a–h) with the words in bold in the text.

a) having a generally positive attitude
_____

b) preoccupied, thinking about something else
_____

c) feeling of general happiness
_____

d) having a generally negative attitude
_____

e) feelings
_____

f) unhappy
_____

g) concentrated on what you're doing
_____

h) cheerful
_____

D 🗣 **VOCABULARY: MOOD** Work in pairs and answer the questions.

1 What is your mood right now?
2 Do you consider yourself to be generally optimistic or pessimistic? Why?
3 Do you ever get depressed? If so, what do you do?

4 GRAMMAR: review of conditional forms

A 🔊 **1.19 LANGUAGE IN CONTEXT**
Listen to the conversation. What advice does Tom's uncle give?

Tom: Do you think I should take a year off before going to college? I think that if people take a year off, they're more mature when they start school, and they get more out of it. What do you think?

Uncle: That's a good question. If I had taken a year off, I would have traveled around the world. I think it can be a very good idea if you plan it properly and do something useful with it.

Tom: I know! But Mom thinks that if I travel for a year, I won't want to go to college when I come back.

Uncle: Yes, that is a risk, but if I were you, I'd go for it. Just make sure you keep your main goal in mind and don't get distracted!

NOTICE!
Underline sentences in the text that use conditional forms. How many types of conditionals can you find?

B **ANALYZE** Read the conversation in Exercise A again.

Form & Function Complete the table with examples from the text.

Type of conditional	Form	Function and Examples
third	If + past perfect, would(n't) have + past participle	To talk about unreal situations in the past. (1) _____
second	If + simple past, would(n't) + base form	To talk about things the speaker feels are unreal or unlikely in the present or future. (2) _____
first	If + simple present, will (won't) + base form	To talk about things that the speaker thinks are likely or possible in the future. (3) _____
zero	If + simple present, simple present	To talk about things that are generally true. (4) _____ (5) _____

C **PRACTICE** Match the two parts to make complete sentences.

1 You would have studied harder   a) if you were more outgoing.
2 You'll always succeed   b) if you'd had more time.
3 People are generally friendly   c) if you're polite to them.
4 You would have more friends   d) if you work hard enough.

WATCH OUT!
✓ If you had said you were sick, I would have called a doctor.
✗ If you would have said you were sick, I had called a doctor.

D 🗣 **NOW YOU DO IT** Work in pairs. Complete the sentences and tell your partner. Ask questions to get more information. Find three things you have in common.

If I had studied …, I would have …   *If I hadn't …, I wouldn't have…*   *If I were richer, I would …*

5 WRITING: a thank-you note

Writing a thank-you note for a gift or a favor is an important way to make people feel appreciated. In a thank-you note, be sure to say what you are giving the person thanks for, and explain what effect it has had, if relevant.

A Read the thank-you note and answer the questions.

1 Identify two things the writer is saying thank you for.
2 What positive changes does the writer report since the event?
3 Is this a formal or informal thank-you note? How can you tell?
4 What three words in the note increase the positive tone?
   a) i_____
   b) f_____
   c) b_____

B Choose one of the situations and write a thank-you note. Write your note using the prompts to help you.

> You received some money as a birthday gift from your aunt.
> You attended a job interview with a computer company.
> You received a goodbye gift from your co-workers when you left your job.
> You attended a dinner at your professor's home.

Dear Lucinda,

Thank you so much for your inspiring workshop at our annual professional development day last week.

It was fascinating to hear your advice on maintaining a positive attitude in the workplace. We have tried out some of your ideas and it has already had a beneficial effect on our office environment. We're all smiling more than we used to, thanks to you! And thank you so much for explaining how our work environment affects our mood. If you hadn't, we wouldn't have thought of changing things. It's a much more attractive and pleasant place to work now. We are planning to use many of your ideas in our office over the coming months.

We hope to attend one of your workshops again very soon.

Many thanks again from all of us here.

Sincerely,
Kate Dansworth
Human Resources Manager

Starting expression:
I am writing to thank you for …
I would like to express my gratitude/appreciation for …
Thank you for your wonderful hospitality/generosity/kindness.
Your gift was so thoughtful/inspiring/helpful.
Beneficial effect (if any): _____
Ending expression: _____

C Work in pairs and take turns showing your notes. Suggest ways to improve your partner's notes.

6 PRONUNCIATION: reduced forms of *would you* and *did you*

A 1.20 Listen to the questions. Notice the reduced forms of *would you* /wʊ-ʤʊ/ and *did you* /dɪ-ʤʊ/.

1	a)	What would you do?	b)	What did you do?
2	a)	Why would you go?	b)	Why did you go?
3	a)	When would you leave?	b)	When did you leave?
4	a)	How would you find out?	b)	How did you find out?

B 1.21 Listen and choose which question you hear from each pair in Exercise A.

C Work in pairs and practice. Say one question from each pair in Exercise A. Your partner will identify which one they hear.

7 SPEAKING: talking about having a positive attitude

A  Work in groups. Discuss what you think each of these sayings means. Does each one express a positive or negative attitude?

EVERY CLOUD HAS A SILVER LINING

 THINK OF the glass as HALF FULL, NOT HALF empty.

 ➡ Always expect ⭐ THE WORST ⭐ and then • YOU'RE NEVER disappointed.

B 🔊 **1.22** Listen to the person talking about a workshop he attended. Check the things that helped him.

- [ ] talking about a problem
- [ ] thinking positively
- [ ] talking to an expert
- [ ] learning techniques for relaxation
- [ ] remembering a similar experience

C Think of a time when you experienced a difficult situation at school or at work. Complete the notes.

What was the difficult situation?	
How did it make you feel?	
What did you do about it?	
If things had been different, what might have happened?	

D 🧍 **Independent Speaking**
Work in pairs. Tell each other about the situation you made notes on in Exercise C. Then ask your partner to tell your problem back to you. Try to offer positive advice and suggestions on what you could have done differently.

HOW TO SAY IT 🔊

I'd like to tell you about what happened when …
It was difficult for me because …
If I hadn't …, he/she/they wouldn't have …

lifeSkills

BEING A POSITIVE TEAM MEMBER

- Focus on finding solutions rather than blaming people for problems.
- Listen to other team members with a positive attitude.
- Present your point of view in a positive way.

A Read about the following situation. What is the problem? Underline the issues.

Sportsense is a company which produces sports and fitness equipment. Their latest project, developing a new range of fitness equipment, has run into serious problems. It's very behind schedule, and the costs seem to be increasing. There also seem to be personal problems among some of the team members. If something isn't done very soon, the project may fail.

B Look at pairs of sentences. For each pair, write P next to the one that focuses on the problems, and S next to the one that focuses on solutions.

1. a) _____ The project is behind schedule because we had a lot of problems the manager didn't expect.
   b) _____ The project faced some unexpected challenges, but I'd like to suggest something.

2. a) _____ It may be possible to work with the supplier to control the increasing costs.
   b) _____ Someone chose the wrong supplier, so costs are increasing.

3. a) _____ Some of the team members don't get along with the others and there are constant arguments.
   b) _____ We should arrange team-building exercises to improve relationships within the team.

4. a) _____ The design is very creative, but maybe we need to simplify it so that we can finish this project on schedule.
   b) _____ If the designers hadn't made such a complicated design, we would have finished this project by now.

C Work in groups. Choose one of the following roles for each member of the group. Prepare for a meeting to discuss the project. Make notes of positive ways to present your problems, together with possible solutions.

Project Leader

You are responsible for the whole project. It is your job to make sure everything is done on time and within budget. You are worried that the project is behind schedule, costs are increasing, and there are personal problems between some members of the team. You think there are communication problems among the team members.

Research and Development Manager

You are responsible for the designs of the equipment. It is your job to make sure they are safe and develop fitness. You have fallen behind schedule because there aren't enough people working in your department. You feel that the marketing department hasn't given you a clear idea of what they want and that they should have done more market research.

Logistics Manager

You are responsible for supplies. It is your job to make sure everyone has the materials they need at the right cost. You feel that the design department is being too ambitious and should try to cut costs. You also think that everyone needs to stick to the schedule more because delays increase costs.

Sales and Marketing Manager

You are responsible for selling the equipment. It is your job to make sure the company sells as many pieces of equipment as possible. You feel that the current designs won't appeal to enough people. You would like to have new designs as soon as possible so that you can do more market research.

D Work in your groups and role-play the meeting. Listen to others carefully and make positive comments when appropriate. You should finish the meeting with an action plan, which is a list of ways to make the project more successful.

HOW TO SAY IT

That's a good suggestion, and we could …

That's a good point. I'd like to add that …

I take your point. From my point of view, …

Thanks for bringing that up.

E Report your ideas to the class. Explain how you are now planning to deal with the problems.

F Work in groups and discuss the questions.

1 Do you feel you now have a better understanding of what it means to be a positive team member? In what ways?

2 Which aspects of being a positive team member come naturally to you? Which aspects do you think you need to work on?

REFLECT … How can the skill of being a positive team member be useful to you in **Study & Learning** and **Self & Society**?

RESEARCH …

What else makes someone a good member of a team? Look at a few websites that discuss this idea. Make a note of what you discover and report back to the class. Do all the websites you have looked at agree?

Language wrap-up

1 VOCABULARY

Complete the paragraph with the words from the box. (12 points)

> appreciate   content   depressed   distracted   emotions   enjoyment
> mood   optimistic   pessimistic   pleasures   wealth   well-being

Do you sometimes feel sad or **(1)** _____? Do you often experience negative
(2) _____? Do you have a generally **(3)** _____ outlook on life? If you
answered yes, then this workshop is for you. Thought Power is a new technique that
helps put in you in a good **(4)** _____ and recover your **(5)** _____ of life.
Happiness doesn't depend on material **(6)** _____. We can all become more
(7) _____ with our lives by focusing on the positive and not being **(8)** _____
by negative thoughts. Learn to be more **(9)** _____ and improve your state of
(10) _____. It's easy to **(11)** _____ the simple everyday **(12)** _____ of life
by using this simple technique. Try it and see!

> **10–12 correct:** I can use words for describing life satisfaction and mood.
> **0–9 correct:** Look again at Sections 1 and 3 on pages 46, 48, and 49.   **SCORE:**   /12

2 GRAMMAR

A Complete the sentences with noun clauses as objects using the prompts and the question words in parentheses. (4 points)

1   I went to a laughter workshop last year. (*when*)
    I want to tell you about _____.
2   Something happened at work the other day. (*what*)
    Did I tell you about _____?
3   You aren't happy. (*why*)
    I can't understand _____.
4   Stress can affect our state of well-being in many ways. (*how*)
    The instructor explained _____.

B Choose the correct options to complete the text. (8 points)

"Did you hear about Megan? I saw her by chance. I was in a store, and if I **(1)** *had / hadn't*
turned around when I did, I **(2)** *won't / wouldn't* have seen her. She told me she was
looking for a new job. She got fired because she was two hours late one morning! Just
imagine that! If she **(3)** *were / would be* more punctual, she **(4)** *would / wouldn't* still have
her job. I can't understand it!
Well, she was really depressed, so I encouraged her to be more optimistic. If you
(5) *have / will have* a positive attitude, it usually **(6)** *helps / will help* you find a solution
to a problem. She seemed happy to hear that. Anyway, if I **(7)** *will have / have* time
this weekend, I **(8)** *will invite / invited* her over for dinner. I'm sure with a little support,
she'll be able to find something else very soon."

> **10–12 correct:** I can use noun clauses as objects and use a variety of conditional structures.
> **0–9 correct:** Look again at Sections 2 and 4 on pages 47 and 49.   **SCORE:**   /12

SPEAKING WORKSHOP

Expressing personal preference

A 🎧 **1.23** Read the question and listen to one man's response. Make notes under the headings below. Compare your notes with a partner.

Some people think that money is the key to happiness. Others think that family and friends are more important. What do you think? Explain why and give an example to support your answer.

Which option does the speaker select?

Reason 1:

Example:

Reason 2:

Example:

Conclusion:

B Listen again and match the two parts to make correct phrases.

1	Although	a)	of all
2	There are	b)	give you an example
3	First	c)	what I've been saying
4	Let me	d)	two main reasons
5	To sum up	e)	many people believe that …

C Read the question. Prepare your response. Complete the notes. Use the expressions in Exercise B.

Some people think that happiness is a matter of good luck. Others think it is something you can create and control. What do you think? Explain why.

Which option do you select?

Reason 1:

Example:

Reason 2:

Example:

Conclusion:

D 🎧 Work in pairs. Speak to your partner. Make sure to cover all the points in your outline.

HOW ARE YOU DOING?

○ I stated my opinion clearly.
○ I supported my opinion with at least two reasons and examples.
○ I used a variety of discourse markers.

UNIT 5 SOMETHING IN THE WATER

IN THIS UNIT YOU

- ⚙ learn language to talk about marketing and environment-related issues
- ⚙ read about designer bottled water
- ⚙ talk about ways to help a charity
- ⚙ listen to an interview with a charity spokesperson
- ⚙ write an opinion in an online debate about bottled water
- ⚙ learn about developing empathy
- ▶ watch a video about solutions to problems with water and sanitation

READING
inferring opinion
What do you think the expression "read between the lines" means?

SPEAKING
suggesting alternatives
When was the last time you helped someone make a decision? What phrases can you use to suggest alternatives?

LIFE SKILLS

SELF & SOCIETY

developing empathy When you see someone less fortunate than yourself, how do you feel? Why might imagining how someone feels in a situation be important?

A 🗣 Work in groups. Look at the pictures of different ways to collect or process water. Which ones are you familiar with? Which are new to you? Which of the systems are already in use in your country, and where?

1

When fog hits large nets, it condenses into water and falls into pipes for collection in large tanks.

fog nets

2

Salt water from the ocean is processed to take out the salt and produce fresh water.

desalination plant

3

A dam is built on a river to form a reservoir.

dam

4

Ponds are built at the bottoms of mountains or hills to collect water when it rains.

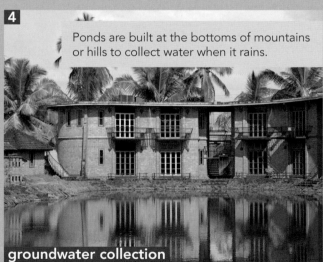

groundwater collection

B 🗣 Work in groups and discuss the questions.

1 In what countries or geographical areas within a country would each of the water systems in the pictures be most appropriate?
2 What advantages and disadvantages do you think each of the systems has?
3 Do any areas in your country have problems with a lack of water? If so, which of the systems in the pictures do you think would work the best in those areas? Why?

5

Rainwater on the roofs of houses is collected in barrels.

residential rainwater collection barrels

A LANGUAGE IN CONTEXT Read the article. What is a monsoon season? What problems can it create?

PAKISTAN UNDER WATER

In August 2013, large areas of Pakistan were under water as the country suffered from severe flooding yet again. The floods <u>were caused</u> by unusually heavy monsoon rains.

Over 200 people <u>were killed</u>, and it <u>is estimated</u> that 80,000 houses and 1.5 million acres of crops were damaged or destroyed. Approximately 1.5 million people were affected in some way by the disaster.

When the 2013 floods occurred, much of the damage caused by the previous year's flooding had not yet been repaired, which increased their impact. However, several years of severe flooding had improved the response to the disaster.

Since 2013, many houses, buildings, and roads have been rebuilt, but the focus needs to be on reducing the risk of damage in the event of extreme weather in the future. Dams and other water channels are being constructed to help control large amounts of rainwater, and people are being advised not to build in very low-lying areas or near rivers and canals. However, a lack of funding remains an issue.

B ANALYZE Read the article in Exercise A again.

NOTICE!
Look at the underlined examples of the passive in the text. How do we form the passive?

Function Check the phrases that state how the passive is usually used.
- ☐ when the action is more important than the person doing the action
- ☐ when we do not know the person doing the action
- ☐ when the person doing the action is as important as the action

Form Complete the table with the correct rule for each tense.

Tense	Form	Example
present progressive passive	**(1)** _____ + _____ + past participle	*Dams and other water channels are being constructed …*
present perfect passive	**(2)** _____ + _____ + past participle	*… many houses, buildings, and roads have been rebuilt …*
past perfect passive	**(3)** _____ + _____ + past participle	*… the previous year's flooding had not yet been repaired …*

C PRACTICE Complete the sentences with the correct passive form of the verbs in parentheses. In some cases, more than one form is possible.

1 My town _____ (*hit*) by heavy rains every year, and sometimes we have terrible floods.
2 About 50 people _____ (*kill*) in floods here in the past five years.
3 We had a flood six months ago, but most people _____ (*evacuate*) before the flood started.
4 Thousands of buildings _____ (*destroy*) by the flood.
5 The devastation was particularly bad because many buildings _____ (*damage*) already by last year's floods.
6 Most of the businesses downtown _____ (*repair*) by now.
7 The shopping mall _____ (*rebuild*), and it will reopen in a year.
8 A system of canals _____ (*construct*) to catch rainwater, and they'll finish the project next year.

WATCH OUT!
- ✓ Thousands of people were affected by the flood.
- ✗ Thousands of people were affecting by the flood.

D NOW YOU DO IT Work in pairs. Make notes on a water-related disaster using the prompts below. Then tell another pair about it.

- event
- area affected
- damage caused
- lives lost
- reconstruction done
- things still being done

2 READING: inferring opinion

⚙ Inferring means using the information we are given to guess further details, connections, or opinions. By thinking carefully about what you're told, you can "read between the lines."

A What's the most you've ever paid for a glass or bottle of water? Where was it?

B Read the text about a brand of bottled water. Would you want to buy Bling H2O? Why or why not?

Would you pay $55 for bottled water?

by John Fuller

[1] Believe it or not, there is such a thing as a bottle of water that costs $55. Kevin Boyd, a writer and producer from Hollywood, has developed a "luxury" bottled water called Bling H2O that costs an average of $55. Depending on the size, prices can range anywhere from $25 to as much as $75. So what makes Bling H2O worth the money? Is the water treated differently from the bottled water you buy at the gas station? Does it at least come with vitamins?

[2] Unfortunately, you won't find any vitamins in Bling H2O. The water inside, however, does receive more treatment than what's inside an average $2 plastic bottle. According to Bling H2O's website, the water is bottled from natural springs in Dandridge, Tennessee. The company claims to use a "nine-step purification process that includes ozone, ultraviolet, and microfiltration."

[3] And don't forget the bottles themselves, which are available in limited-edition frosted glasses and covered with Swarovski crystals. Even Bling H20's website admits that the product is as much about image as it is taste. The company originally handed out the water only to actors and athletes—celebrities such as Jamie Foxx and Ben Stiller have been spotted showing off shiny bottles, and Paris Hilton allegedly feeds the water to her dog. Now, the water is available to the public and showing up in fancy New York restaurants. The makers of Bling H2O also market the bottle as reusable and refillable—you can flaunt it around town and show how trendy and environmentally friendly you are.

[4] Blind taste tests in New York City put Bling H2O up against regular bottled water and Manhattan tap water. The reactions proved to be inconsistent and unpredictable—most people proclaimed Manhattan tap water as the best-tasting, while Bling H2O was believed to be simple tap water.

C 🗣 Work in pairs. Discuss the questions.

1 Overall, do you think the writer has a positive or negative opinion of Bling H2O? How can you tell?
2 What can you infer from how the following words or phrases are used?
   a) believe it or not (para 1)   **b)** luxury (para 1)   **c)** claims (para 2)

D VOCABULARY: MARKETING Complete the statements with the correct forms of the words and phrases from the box.

> to be as much about … as   to make … worth   to market … as
> to put … up against   ranging from … to

1 Companies shouldn't _____ water _____ something special.
2 Companies should be required _____ their products _____ other products for people to compare.
3 We sell a number of products _____ high-end items _____ absolute bargains.
4 A fancy package doesn't _____ bottled water _____ the money you pay for it.
5 My decision to buy a product _____ image _____ the product itself.

E 🗣 VOCABULARY: MARKETING Work in groups. Discuss whether you agree or disagree with the statements in Exercise D.

3 WRITING: contributing to an online debate

A Read the topic for the online debate. What does the word "really" suggest?

B Read these contributions to the debate. What is each writer's general opinion of bottled water?

WELCOME TO

News 24/7
ONLINE

In response to last week's article about bottled water, we're asking you to contribute your thoughts to the following debate:

"Should we really drink bottled water?"   Monday, March 27, 11:40 EST

I'm amazed that so many people here in France drink bottled water. France is the number one consumer of bottled water in the world, and that is ridiculous. We have perfectly good, clean public drinking water, so why don't people drink it? I don't think it's worth spending money on bottled water just to be trendy.

August 28, 12:34 posted by: jacques

I agree with Jacques that in countries that have good, safe public drinking water, people shouldn't buy so much bottled water. Producing so many plastic bottles is bad for the environment, and buying bottled water is expensive, at least in my country. However, the public water in some countries is not very safe to drink, so people have to drink bottled water.

August 29, 8:11 posted by: bebe12

Bottled water is marketed as an almost magical product, and companies claim that if we want to be healthy and beautiful, we should drink only bottled water. However, in some countries, good public water systems have not been built and people have to drink bottled water. If bottled water is made affordable in those countries, then I think it becomes an important product for saving lives.

September 2, 3:42 posted by: kofi

C 🎧 What do you think about drinking bottled water? Make some notes about whether you are primarily in favor of or against drinking bottled water. Write a paragraph to contribute to the debate. Then work in small groups and compare your ideas.

4 PRONUNCIATION: word stress in adjective + compound noun phrases

A 🎧 **1.24** 🎧 Listen to the phrases and notice that the main stress is on the second word in each phrase. Then work in pairs and practice saying the phrases.

clean drinking water	trendy water bottles	underground water tanks
public water systems	large fog nets	new marketing techniques

B 🎧 **1.25** 🎧 Work in pairs and practice the sentences. Be sure to stress the second word in each underlined phrase. Then listen and check.

We all want good <u>public water systems</u> with <u>clean drinking water</u>.
<u>New marketing techniques</u> include designing <u>trendy water bottles</u>.
<u>Underground water tanks</u> and <u>large fog nets</u> are two ways to collect water.

5 GRAMMAR: expressions of purpose

A LANGUAGE IN CONTEXT Read the FAQs about water. Which, if any, of the facts surprise you?

FAQs

Q: How long can humans survive without water?
A: Well, not for very long! Because we need water <u>to control all of our body's functions</u>, scientists estimate that the average person can survive for only about three or four days.

Q: Is it dangerous to drink too much water?
A: Yes, very! In order to be healthy, we should drink plenty of water, but drinking too much too fast can cause death from "water intoxication." So as not to suffer from this dangerous condition, never participate in a water-drinking contest!

Q: How much water does the average person use per day?
A: The average U.S. citizen uses between 300 and 400 liters of water daily. Not surprisingly, most of the water used is for washing and flushing the toilet!

Q: Is it best to drink pure water during high-intensity exercise?
A: Not really. When you sweat during exercise, you lose electrolytes such as calcium and potassium. If you're doing very heavy exercise and sweating a lot, it's better to drink a sports drink so that electrolytes are replaced.

> **NOTICE!**
> Look at the underlined phrase in the text. What does this phrase express?

B ANALYZE Read the FAQs in Exercise A again.

Form & Function Complete the table with examples from the text.

Expression of purpose	Formality	Function	Example
for + gerund (*–ing*)	neutral	to express the use or purpose of a thing, especially when the thing is the subject of the verb: *A knife is for cutting.*	**(1)** _____
to + base form *in order (not) to /* *so as (not) to* + base form	neutral more formal very formal	to express why someone does or uses something: *The store was closed to / in order to / so as to allow the workmen access.*	**(2)** _____ **(3)** _____ **(4)** _____
so (that) + noun + clause	neutral	to express why someone does or uses something: *The store was closed so that the workmen could have access.*	**(5)** _____

C PRACTICE Choose the correct options to complete the sentences.

1 We did an experiment in class *in order / for* to understand how water is used by plants.
2 They add a special chemical to the water in the pool to *keep / keeping* it clean.
3 Drink lots of water so as not *get / to get* dehydrated.
4 Water therapy is great for *help / helping* stressed-out people to relax.
5 Water houseplants regularly *so that / in order* they will not die.
6 Some companies claim bottled water has health benefits *for / so as to* be able to charge a higher retail price.
7 I use tap water *to / for* refill my reusable water bottle when I go to the gym.
8 The city has initiated new restrictions *so as / so that* to save water.

> **WATCH OUT!**
> ✓ I went swimming to relax.
> ✗ I went swimming for relax.

D NOW YOU DO IT Work in pairs. Discuss the questions. Use expressions of purpose.

1 Do you prefer drinking bottled water or tap water? Why?
2 How many different uses for water can you think of?
3 How many reasons can you think of for why it is important to clean up polluted lakes and rivers?

6 LISTENING: to an interview

A 🎧 **1.26** Listen to a radio interview with a spokesperson for Water Watch. Then answer the questions.

1 What is the primary purpose of Water Watch?
2 What are two of the charity's other goals?
3 Why do many girls in Africa not have access to an education?
4 Apart from money, what else is the charity appealing for?

B Listen to the interview again. Complete the notes with the numbers you hear.

1 Number of people in the world without access to clean water:

_____

2 Amount of money needed by Water Watch:

_____

3 Approximate number of households in the U.S.A.:

_____

4 Minimum donation per household to reach target:

_____

5 Number of volunteers already working for the charity:

_____

C 🎙 **VOCABULARY: ENVIRONMENTAL ISSUES** Work in pairs. Match the bold words and phrases (1–8) with their correct definitions (a–h). Use a dictionary if necessary.

1 … help in the fight against **water poverty** …
2 … to improve **hygiene**, education, and the standard of living …
3 … because of diseases caused by **water pollution**.
4 … no child should die from a **disease** that's easily preventable.
5 **Climate change** has made a bad situation much worse.
6 Some areas are experiencing severe **drought** …
7 **Famines** can be caused by too little water or too much water.
8 In areas that do experience a regular rainy season, there have been **floods** …

a) the practice of keeping yourself and the things around you clean
b) the process of damaging water with chemicals and/or other substances
c) the condition of not having enough clean water for drinking, cooking, or sanitation
d) a serious illness that affects people or animals
e) large amounts of water that cover areas that were dry
f) a serious lack of food so that many people become sick or die
g) long periods with little or no rain
h) the change that affects the world's weather so that it is becoming warmer

D 🎙 **VOCABULARY: ENVIRONMENTAL ISSUES** Work in pairs. Discuss these questions.

1 Do any of the environmental issues from Exercise C exist in your country?
2 If so, who should be responsible for solving the problem and how?
3 Do you think you have a responsibility to help people in a different country? Why or why not?

HOW TO SAY IT 🎙

In some parts of the country …

In order to prevent water pollution / disease/drought, etc., I think the government/charities/individuals should …

7 SPEAKING: suggesting alternatives

⚙ When you want to help someone make a decision about something or offer them advice, you can use certain phrases to suggest different alternatives to them.

A 🗣 Work in pairs. Look at these pictures from advertising campaigns for different charities (1–3) and match them with the texts (A–C). Say what environmental issue each advertisement aims to address.

A
YOU WOULDN'T GIVE THIS WATER TO A CHILD TO DRINK

But millions of people worldwide have to …
Please give generously to support Pure Water Action and help prevent the spread of diseases caused by water pollution.

B
THIS LAND HAS FED SAID'S FAMILY FOR GENERATIONS

With your help, it still can. A donation to Food for Thought of just $5 per month could help prevent famine in Africa.

C
Humans can't survive without water. Or with too much. To help fund research into the effects of climate change, call 1–800–CLIMATE or 1–800–555–6283 to give what you can.

B 🎧 1.27 Listen to the discussion about helping one of the charities in Exercise A. Check the phrases used for suggesting alternatives.

☐ What if we do … instead?
☐ There's always …
☐ What about …?
☐ We could try …
☐ I'd suggest …
☐ Another option/idea would be to …
☐ Have you considered giving … a try?

C 🗣 Work in pairs and follow the instructions. Then report to the class.

- Choose one of the charities in Exercise A that you'd like to support.
- Discuss things you could do to help support it.
- Suggest different alternatives as necessary.
- Give reasons for your choice.

lifeSkills

DEVELOPING EMPATHY

- Think of an experience that you have had that is similar to another person's situation.
- Compare the difficulty of your experience with that of the other person.
- Imagine how you would feel in the other person's situation.

A 🔊 Work in pairs. Make a list of all the different ways you use water in one day. Then try to estimate how much water you use per day in liters. The following information might help. Compare your water usage with your classmates'.

> taking a shower = approx. 25 liters per minute
> taking a bath = approx. 150 liters per bath
> brushing teeth = 6 liters per minute
> flushing the toilet = approx. 6 liters per flush
> washing clothes = 50 liters per load
> cooking and drinking = approx. 5 liters per day

B 🔊 Work in groups. Discuss what kinds of water problems you've experienced in your home or community. Say how you felt.

empathy /ˈempəθi/ **(n.) [non-count.]** the ability to understand how someone feels because you can imagine what it's like to be them. When you empathize with someone, it makes it easier for you to communicate with them, even if their experience of something is very different from yours.

HOW TO SAY IT 🔊

Last spring/summer, etc. we had a drought/flood, and …
One winter our pipes froze, so …
It's not easy being without water because …

C  **Work in pairs. Read the information about Shartati and her family. Estimate how much water you think she and her family use per day. Use the notes in Exercise A for comparison.**

This is Shartati and one of her daughters. She has five children ranging in age from six months to nine years old. They live in a village in northern Ethiopia. Shartati's husband is a farmer.

D **1.28** **Listen to Shartati talking about her daily routine. How accurate were your guesses about her family's water usage?**

E **Work in groups. Discuss the questions.**

1 Think about the water problems you discussed in Exercise B. How serious are or were your problems compared with Shartati's difficulties in getting water?
2 Look back at the water usage you calculated in Exercise A. What things would you need to give up if you were able to use only the amount of water that Shartati's family uses?
3 With your answers to 1 and 2 in mind, imagine yourself in her situation. How would you feel?
4 How might the world be different if people took more time to empathize with others?

F **Work in groups. Discuss the questions.**

1 Do you find it easy to empathize with people you don't know? Why or why not?
2 Did the process you followed in Exercise E help you empathize with Shartati? Why or why not?

REFLECT ... How can developing empathy be useful to you in **Study & Learning** and **Work & Career**?

RESEARCH ...

Find out about a water problem in an area of your country or in another country and prepare a short report on it. Make suggestions for how to deal with it. Present your report to the class and discuss your suggestions.

Language wrap-up

1 VOCABULARY

A Complete the text with the correct form of phrases from the box. (5 points)

> to be as much about … as …   to make … worth …
> to market … as …   to put … up against …
> to range from … to …

B Choose the correct options to complete the text. (5 points)

Water-related disasters can cause many problems even after the event is over. When a tsunami hit Indonesia in 2004, many villages in coastal areas were washed away by the **(1)** *floods / drought*. But the disaster had other consequences: **(2)** *water poverty / diseases* spread rapidly due to poor levels of **(3)** *water pollution / hygiene*. It was also difficult to find clean sources of drinking water because of **(4)** *climate change / water pollution* and a lack of medical supplies. Disasters like this one can even cause **(5)** *famine / water poverty* because of the loss of animals and crops.

> The most refreshing and convenient water money can buy, delivered to your door! When we **(1)** _____ Water 2U _____ our competitors, nine times out of ten people preferred our water. That's because we **(2)** _____ quality _____ service. Is it expensive? It depends on your perspective. Our prices **(3)** _____ $15 _____ $25 per bottle, but we think the quality and service **(4)** _____ our water _____ the price! We don't **(5)** _____ our water _____ anything it's not. If you don't like it, we'll give you your money back!

> **8–10 correct:** I can use marketing vocabulary and words to describe environmental issues.
> **0–7 correct:** Look again at Sections 2 and 6 on pages 59 and 62.
> **SCORE:**   **/10**

2 GRAMMAR

A Rewrite what these people said in the passive. (5 points)

1 "Climate change has seriously affected the environment."
   "The environment _____."
2 "The water company cut off our water supply last week."
   "Our water supply _____."
3 "Before we bought the house, a flood had damaged the basement."
   "Before we bought the house, the basement _____."
4 "They're charging me $10 for this bottled water!"
   "I _____."
5 "They limit water usage in some areas."
   "Water usage _____."

B Complete the sentences with a suitable expression of purpose. More than one answer may be possible. (5 points)

1 I use tap water _____ cooking, but not drinking.
2 So _____ avoid wasting water, turn off the faucet when you brush your teeth.
3 Take an umbrella _____ you don't get wet!
4 _____ not to have a big water bill, water your lawn only once a week.
5 We use rainwater _____ clean the patio.

> **8–10 correct:** I can use the passive and expressions of purpose.
> **0–7 correct:** Look again at Sections 1 and 5 on pages 58 and 61.
> **SCORE:**   **/10**

WRITING WORKSHOP

A Read the writing assignment and a student's answer. Do you think the student has answered the question? Why or why not?

> The table below shows the consumption of bottled water in the U.S.A. over a ten-year period. Write a report of about 200 words to summarize the information, reporting the main features and making comparisons where relevant.

U.S. Bottled Water Market

Per capita consumption		
Year	Gallons per capita	Annual % Change
1	21.6	
2	23.2	7.5%
3	25.4	9.7%
4	27.6	8.4%
5	29.0	5.3%
6	28.5	-1.8%
7	27.6	-3.2%
8	28.3	2.7%
9	29.2	3.1%
10	30.8	5.3%
11	32.0	4.0%

Their source: **Beverage Marketing Corporation**

The table shows changes in the annual **per capita** consumption of bottled water over a ten-year period in the U.S.A. We can clearly see that consumption **rose sharply** between Year 1 and Year 5, but that it fell in Years 6 and 7. It started to rise again in Year 8, and it **rose steadily** from Years 8 to 11. By the end of the period, Americans were consuming **over 10 gallons more** bottled water per person per year than they had in the first year.

In Year 1, Americans consumed **an average of** 21.6 gallons of bottled water each. The figure rose each year over five years, with the **sharpest rise** in Year 3 (9.7%). Consumption continued to rise over the next two years. However, in Years 6 and 7, it **dropped drastically**, with a **decrease** of 1.8% and 3.2% **respectively**. In Year 8, consumption began to rise again, but it rose much more slowly in the last four years than it had in the first four.

Overall, we can clearly see that the consumption of bottled water in the U.S.A. increased **over a decade** although **the rate of change** was much lower at the end of the decade than at the beginning.

B 🔊 Look back at the model answer and discuss the questions as a class.

1 What do the phrases in bold mean? Discuss any you are not sure about.
2 What kind of information does the first paragraph give? How is it different from the second paragraph? What is the purpose of the third paragraph?

C Make notes for a report based on the data in the following table.

Global Bottled Water Market

Year 2 Rank	Countries	Millions of Gallons		% change
		Year 1	Year 2	
1	U.S.A.	8,255	9,107.3	2.0%
2	China	4,163.3	7,686.4	13.0%
3	Mexico	5,359.9	7,520.7	7.0%
4	Brazil	3.301.6	4,500.9	6.4%
5	Indonesia	2,155.9	3,760.6	11.8%
6	Thailand	1,426.2	3,118.8	16.9%
7	Italy	3,115.5	3,034.7	-0.5%
8	Germany	2,808.9	2,954.2	1.0%
9	France	2,285.3	2,291.0	0.0%
10	Spain	1,524.0	1,514.6	-0.1%
	Top 10 subtotal	34,395.6	45,489.3	5.8%
	All others	12,606.8	15,880.7	4.7%

Their source: **Beverage Marketing Corporation**

D Write your report, using the model in Exercise A and your notes from Exercise C. Write about 200 words.

HOW ARE YOU DOING?

- ○ My first paragraph gives general information about what the table shows.
- ○ My second paragraph gives statistics to support the information in the first paragraph.
- ○ My third paragraph gives a summary of the main trends shown in the table.

UNIT 6 LIVING TRADITIONS

IN THIS UNIT YOU

- ⚙ learn language to talk about traditions and personal rituals
- ⚙ listen to interviews with members of the public expressing opinions on traditions
- ⚙ write a blog post about a family tradition
- ⚙ read about a tradition involving an animal
- ⚙ talk about personal rituals
- ⚙ learn about managing distractions
- ▶ watch a video about everyday rituals

WRITING *avoiding run-on sentences*

What do we use commas for? Make a list of as many uses as you can think of.

LISTENING *for main ideas*

In which situations might it be important to understand the main ideas without worrying too much about the details?

LIFE SKILLS

STUDY & LEARNING

managing distractions How easily are you distracted when you are trying to work or study?

- ● I find it hard to concentrate, and I get distracted by texts, Twitter, etc.
- ● Sometimes I get distracted, but mostly I can concentrate enough to get things done.
- ● I'm never distracted from the work I need to do.

A 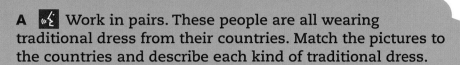 Work in pairs. These people are all wearing traditional dress from their countries. Match the pictures to the countries and describe each kind of traditional dress.

Albania   Ecuador   Kenya   Morocco   Norway   Wales

B Discuss the questions.

1   Describe traditional dress from your country. Are there different traditional dresses?
2   What other traditions (festivals, events, family traditions, etc.) are there in your region/country? Do you think they are relevant to the modern world? Explain why or why not.

1 GRAMMAR: *be used to / get used to*

A »🎧 **1.29 LANGUAGE IN CONTEXT** Listen to the conversation. What traditions are mentioned?

Harry: So, Brandon, I'm going to be in the U.S.A. for Thanksgiving this year. Are there any traditions or customs I should know about before I go?

Brandon: Well, the main tradition is that everyone gets together with the whole family and has Thanksgiving dinner. There's lots of traditional food, like turkey and sweet potatoes.

Harry: I'm used to big family meals, but I'm not used to eating that kind of food, so that'll be interesting! Anything else?

Brandon: Everyone watches the Macy's Thanksgiving Day Parade on TV. That's a really important tradition. And one unusual tradition is that the President pardons a turkey.

Harry: Excuse me?

Brandon: The President goes on TV, and there's a ceremony with a live turkey. That turkey is allowed to live, instead of being eaten for Thanksgiving dinner. It's a kind of joke tradition, really.

Harry: I'll never get used to the President pardoning a turkey, and I'm not sure I'll ever get used to the American sense of humor, either!

Brandon: You'll have to get used to a lot more than that in my country, believe me!

B **ANALYZE** Read the conversation in Exercise A again.

Form Complete the table with examples from the text.

Form	Example
be + used to + –ing / noun	(1) _____
	(2) _____
get + used to + –ing / noun	(3) _____
	(4) _____
	(5) _____

Function Choose the correct options to complete the rules.

1 We use *be* / *get used to* to talk about things we may or may not already be familiar with.
2 We use *be* / *get used to* to talk about the process of becoming familiar with something.

C **PRACTICE** Complete the sentences with the correct form of *be used to* or *get used to*. Use negative forms where appropriate.

1 I can't _____ living overseas. The customs are just so different here.
2 It's traditional to take care of old people in my country, so people _____ it.
3 I _____ eating with chopsticks when I lived in Vietnam for a year.
4 If you _____ spicy food, you might find some of our dishes too hot!
5 Did you _____ speaking English all the time while you were there?
6 Don't worry about the local traditions—you _____ them in no time!

D 🎙️ **NOW YOU DO IT** Work in pairs. Think of a time when you were in a new situation (e.g., a new school, a new neighborhood, etc.). Ask and answer the questions.

1 What things did you have to get used to in your new situation?
2 Are you completely used to them now?
3 Did it take you long to get used to them?
4 What helped you get used to them?
5 Was there anything you couldn't get used to?

> **NOTICE!**
> Underline all the examples of *used to* in the conversation. What part of speech follows each one?

> **WATCH OUT!**
> ✓ I'm used to cooking Thanksgiving dinner for everyone.
> ✗ I'm used to cook Thanksgiving dinner for everyone.

70

2 LISTENING: for main ideas

⚙ If you know what the topic is before listening, try to predict some of the things the people will talk about and the vocabulary they will use. While listening, pay attention to clues such as verbs of attitude (*love, dislike*, etc.), adjectives (*wonderful, horrible*, etc.), signal words and phrases (*because*, etc.), and tone of voice.

A Read the description in an online program guide. Answer the questions below.

This week on KTMU

Monday, 2:00–2:30 p.m.: *Vox Pop*

Interviewer Katie Miles hits the streets to ask people their opinions on the importance of traditions in society. Should we work hard to maintain our traditions, or should we allow them to change or disappear over time? Hear what people on the street have to say on the subject.

1 What specific traditions do you think people might mention? What vocabulary would you expect to hear related to those traditions?
2 What reasons might people give for maintaining traditions?
3 What reasons might they give for not maintaining traditions?

B 🎧 **1.30** Listen to the interviews. For each interviewee, check the box if the person thinks it's important for traditions to be maintained and put an X if not. Then underline the sentence that best states the main idea.

Interviewee 1 ☐
a) Most young people don't know about traditions.
b) Old people want to keep traditions.
c) Traditions are not relevant to young people.

Interviewee 2 ☐
a) Traditions are important to society.
b) Each generation changes traditions in some way.
c) Graduation ceremonies are different each year.

Interviewee 3 ☐
a) Traditions are important and should not be lost.
b) Kids don't like the city history festival.
c) Some kids are interested in traditions.

Interviewee 4 ☐
a) Many young people find traditions boring.
b) Traditions support family and society identity.
c) A traditional wedding is best.

C Listen again. Make a note of the reasons the interviewees give for their opinions.

Interviewee 1: _____

Interviewee 2: _____

Interviewee 3: _____

Interviewee 4: _____

D 🗣 Work in groups. Say which of the opinions expressed you agree with and why.

3 READING: a book excerpt

A 🔊 Work in pairs. Look at the picture and discuss what role you think the dog might have. Then read and check your ideas.

AGGIE ⭐ TRADITION

Texas A&M University differs from other universities in that it has a School of Military Science. Aggies (A&M students) who want to receive military training as well as a college degree join the Texas A&M Corps of Cadets. Freshman Corps members are called "fish," and during their first year, they participate in a number of initiation rituals. Some of the most famous rituals are associated with the university's mascot, a collie dog named Reveille.

B 🔊 Work in pairs. Read the excerpt. How is Reveille treated at the university? Why do you think this is?

Miss Reveille, ma'am

¹ Reveille is certainly more of a princess than a pooch. Her custom-made blanket, which drapes across her back and snaps under her belly, is adorned with five diamonds, symbolic of her status as the highest-ranking member of the university's Corps of Cadets.

² She has access to any building on campus, attends virtually every football game and many other sporting events, travels in style, lives and sleeps in the Corps dorms, attends classes, and occasionally determines when those classes should end. From the days of the original Rev, she has been called the "Queen" or the "First Lady of Texas A&M."

³ One of the things that makes Reveille particularly unusual among all the other college mascots is that she attends class with the student body of Texas A&M.

⁴ According to A&M tradition, when Reveille barks in class, the professor is supposed to pack up the lesson plan and give the class a walk. Even today, many of the professors—especially those with A&M ties or an appreciation of Aggie traditions—still honor the walk-for-bark tradition.

⁵ Fish are not allowed to let their eyes linger on Reveille, and they must greet her with a respectful, "Howdy, Miss Reveille, ma'am," when she is in their presence. The greeting is preferably performed while looking away from her and after the freshmen have slammed their backs against a wall in a show of respect for the highest-ranking member of the Corps of Cadets. After the greeting, fish are expected to run in another direction from her, so she will not be forced to linger in the presence of a "lowly" fish.

Taken from *Reveille: First Lady of Texas A&M*

C VOCABULARY: INSTITUTIONAL TRADITIONS Match the words (1–6) with their definitions (a–f).

1	initiation (*n.*)	**a)**	a process or ceremony in which someone becomes a member of a group
2	symbolic (*adj.*)	**b)**	1. a formal ceremony; 2. something that you do regularly and always in the same way
3	high-ranking (*adj.*)	**c)**	an animal, person, or object used as a symbol of a team or organization
4	freshman (*n.*)	**d)**	a first-year student in a high school or college
5	ritual (*n.*)	**e)**	in a position of importance in an organization
6	mascot (*n.*)	**f)**	representing something important; it might be an idea or something that cannot be touched

D 🔊 **VOCABULARY: INSTITUTIONAL TRADITIONS** Work in groups. Discuss the questions.

1 What other examples of mascots can you think of? Do you know of any other mascot traditions?
2 Are there any rituals or traditions at your school or college? Do freshmen have to show respect to older students in specific ways?
3 Why do you think some organizations have initiation rituals?

4 GRAMMAR: verb + object + infinitive

A 🎧 1.31 LANGUAGE IN CONTEXT
Listen to the conversation. How does the woman's new job compare to a traditional job?

Keith: So, how's your new job?

Lorena: Oh, it was strange at first, but I'm getting used to it! They <u>allow</u> people to arrive at any time they want, and they don't ask us to work exactly eight hours. I end up working more hours because there's no specific quitting time! They say they don't force people to work if they aren't feeling creative. They even ask us not to work at our desks all day. They encourage us to move around, talk to people, and work in different places. If someone needs you to do something, they text you. It's nice, I guess, just not what I'm used to.

B ANALYZE Read the conversation in Exercise A again.

> **NOTICE!**
> Find and underline all the verbs that are followed by an object of that verb and then an infinitive (one has been done for you as an example). Where do *not* and *don't* go in these types of structures?

Form Complete the table with examples from the text.

verb + noun + infinitive	negative verb + noun + infinitive	verb + noun + *not* + infinitive	verbs
They allow (1) _____ at any time they want.	They don't ask (2) _____ exactly eight hours.	They even ask (3) _____ at our desks all day.	*advise, allow, ask, encourage, expect, force, get, invite, need, order, permit, persuade, tell, want, warn, would like*

Function Which statements are true?
The structure verb + object + infinitive is used to report …

- ☐ advice
- ☐ requests
- ☐ warnings
- ☐ encouragement
- ☐ commands
- ☐ emotions

> **WATCH OUT!**
> ✗ They tell us don't work at our desks all day.
> ✓ They tell us not to work at our desks all day.

C PRACTICE Rewrite the sentences with the verbs in parentheses.

1 In the military, people have to show respect for higher-ranking members.
   The military _____. (*force*)

2 Many colleges tell freshmen that it is a good idea to join an organization.
   Many colleges _____. (*encourage*)

3 Doctors say that people shouldn't look at a computer screen for too long.
   Doctors _____. (*warn*)

4 I have to ask someone for help with this project.
   I _____. (*need*)

5 At some colleges, freshmen don't have permission to live off campus.
   Some colleges _____. (*allow*)

6 Our boss says it isn't a good idea to eat lunch at our desks.
   Our boss _____. (*advise*)

D 🗣 NOW YOU DO IT Work in pairs. Discuss the advantages of these traditional and nontraditional ways of working. Can you think of any others? Choose the ways of working that you think suit, or would suit, you best.

Traditional	Nontraditional
working in an office	working from home
working office hours	setting your own schedule

5 PRONUNCIATION: stress in words with –tion/–sion

A 🎧 **1.32** Listen to the words and notice the way the stress falls on the syllable before the endings –tion and –sion. Practice saying the words.

tradition   initiation   institution   permission   distraction   graduation

B 🎧 **1.33** 👥 Listen to the text. Work in pairs and take turns reading it. Pay particular attention to words ending in –tion or –sion.

There's an initiation ritual at our institution which is a very old tradition. All the freshmen have to take a test while the sophomores make noise and throw water at them. You have to try and ignore all the confusion and the distractions, and it takes all your powers of concentration! It's a fun occasion and a real celebration!

6 SPEAKING: talking about personal rituals

A 👥 Work in pairs. Say whether you think most people follow rituals in their daily lives. Then read the paragraph to see if it supports your opinion.

When you think of rituals, you probably think of traditions at weddings or activities at club initiations. But there is another type of common ritual—personal rituals. For example, an athlete may do things in a certain order on the day of a game, or a singer may always greet an audience in the same way. Personal rituals can be very simple; for example, maybe you always sit in a favorite chair to have your morning coffee, or maybe you write down the things you have to do every day and cross them off your list as you do them. Other rituals are a little more unusual or even obsessive. There are people who can't sleep if they haven't put away everything in their bedroom or cleaned out their email inbox. Other people count exactly how many times they chew their food before swallowing. Whether they are simple or complex, personal rituals are a part of everyone's life.

B VOCABULARY: PHRASAL VERBS FOR PERSONAL RITUALS
Complete the sentences with the correct forms of the verbs from the box. One of the words can be used more than once.

clean   cross   go   line   plan   put   write

1   Every spring, I _____ out all my closets and organize the house from top to bottom.
2   To get organized, I _____ down everything I have to do; then I _____ things off my list when I have done them.
3   I don't make a list, but every morning I mentally _____ over the things I have to do.
4   I _____ through my closet on the weekend and _____ out what I'm going to wear for the whole week.
5   I always _____ on my clothes in the same order every day—socks first!
6   Before an exam or a test, I always _____ all my pens up in a certain order on the desk.

C 🎧 **1.34 VOCABULARY: PHRASAL VERBS FOR PERSONAL RITUALS** Listen to three people talking about their personal rituals. What rituals do they mention?

D Think about your personal rituals. Make notes about the things you do and why you do them.

E 👥 Independent Speaking Work in pairs. Tell your partner about your rituals.

7 WRITING: avoiding run-on sentences

A common error in writing is to connect two independent clauses with a comma. These are called run-on sentences. It is important to check your work and correct any run-on sentences.

A Read the sentences below. Check the ones that are correct. Correct the run-on sentences.

1 I look forward to having breakfast with my family every morning and going over our plans for the day. ☐

2 Some of our family traditions are normal, some of our traditions might seem strange to other people. ☐

3 Some families are used to doing things in a certain way, they don't like to change. ☐

4 When it's a holiday, we all get together and have a big family meal. ☐

5 One tradition in my family is Sunday dinner, we all relax and talk about our week. ☐

6 Every summer we have a family sports tournament, in which we all compete against each other! ☐

B Read the blog post. Underline any run-on sentences. Suggest ways to correct them.

I think family traditions are really important! One in our family is the summer picnic, we organize one every year. Everyone makes sure they have the day off work and the whole family helps prepare. Mom tells everyone to get things ready, she's the one in charge! Everyone has a job and there's lots of activity and noise. Even the little ones have things to do, they love getting involved. Other people think maybe it's someone's birthday or a special occasion, but it never is. It's just our family day, it's very special to all of us because it means we're making time for each other. And the things that happen at the picnic usually keep us laughing for the rest of the summer!

What about you? Do you have any family traditions? Are they important to you? Let us know!

Share   Comment   Next post

C Work in pairs. Talk about any family traditions you have. Explain where they come from and what they mean to you.

D Write a comment on the blog post describing your family tradition(s). Check your work for run-on sentences. Ask a partner to read your comment and point out any run-on sentences you have missed.

lifeSkills

MANAGING DISTRACTIONS

- Recognize your main distractions.
- Find out ways to change habits and choose ones that work for you.
- Make a plan for managing distractions.

A Read the webpage and take the quiz about electronic distractions.

HOME COURSES FACULTY GRADUA
PROGRA

STUDENT SUPPORT SERVICES
EFFECTIVE STUDYING

Many students are able to remain completely focused while they are studying for class, but most of us allow ourselves to be distracted from a task at least some of the time. Our brain seems to let us know when we need a break, so we stop what we're doing to make a phone call, talk to someone in person, eat something, have coffee, or whatever.

This has always been true, but in the 21st century there are more potential distractions than ever before. We are constantly bombarded with emails, text messages, tweets, instant messages, and other electronic distractions.

An important part of being an effective student is to learn to manage those distractions to get the best out of the time you spend studying. Complete our quiz to get an idea of where you might have problems dealing with distractions.

Check the statements that apply to you. Then estimate how much time you spend every day doing each activity you checked.

When I am studying/ working ...	YES	NO	MINUTES/ HOURS PER DAY
I check my personal email.	●	●	
I answer my cell phone.	●	●	
I answer text/instant messages.	●	●	
I chat online.	●	●	
I use social networking sites.	●	●	
I read messages on Twitter, etc.	●	●	
I surf the internet.	●	●	

B 🔊 **Work in pairs. Compare your answers to the quiz. Which of you is more easily distracted? Then discuss the questions.**

1. What are your three main electronic distractions? How much time do you spend doing each one every day?
2. What effect do these distractions have on your life? Do they make you less effective when you are studying?

C 🔊 **Read the rest of the webpage. Work in pairs and discuss the suggestions you think the website goes on to make. Make a list of your ideas and then compare it with another pair.**

Most people have personal rituals associated with their study habits. For example, some people can't even think about starting to study if their desk isn't organized. Others are used to studying with music on, and they say it helps them stay relaxed while they work. Still others always end their day by answering email. These are the normal types of routines that make us feel comfortable. The problem is when rituals or routines become distractions. For example, studies show that most people check their email at least once every 15 minutes. This type of constant distraction disrupts concentration and can make a task longer and more difficult. For many people, email has become more of a bad habit than a useful tool.

If you allow yourself to become distracted too easily, you will have to work to break the habit. Click here to read our top suggestions.

D 🔊 **Work in pairs. Identify your three main distractions. Help each other make a plan for managing those distractions. You can use suggestions from Exercise C or any other suggestions. Write down the changes you plan to make in each area.**

A: *I always answer text messages immediately, even if they're not urgent. I'm constantly interrupting what I'm doing to go through my messages. I feel nervous if I don't check them.*

B: *Well, why don't you check them once an hour? You can answer any that are important and answer the rest after work.*

A: *Yeah, I'm going to force myself not to check them every ten minutes!*

E 🔊 **Work in groups. Discuss the questions.**

1. What have you learned about distractions and avoiding them?
2. How will you manage distractions in the future?

HOW TO SAY IT 🔊

You need to get used to …
I would advise you to …
Don't you get tired of …?
It might be a good idea to …
Get someone to help you …

REFLECT … How can the skill of managing distractions be useful to you in **Work & Career** and **Self & Society**?

RESEARCH …

Research techniques to help you avoid distractions (e.g., the Pomodoro Technique). Choose one technique and in your next class, be ready to explain how this technique works. Consider using it, or the ideas behind it, the next time you study.

Language wrap-up

1 VOCABULARY

Complete the text with the correct forms of the words from the box.
(10 points)

cross off   freshmen   go over   initiation   line up
mascot   plan out   ritual   symbolic   write down

To: j.patterson@ug.mac.wd

From: kylie@mastermail.mac.wd

Subject: Hey

I can't believe it—I'm actually going to be a University of Georgia student! On Saturday I went to a party for new students. It was kind of a combination welcome party and **(1)** _____, and all the **(2)** _____ had to wear costumes. Wearing a silly costume is a University of Georgia **(3)** _____ and it's **(4)** _____ of our low status at the school, but it's fun, too! I went dressed as a chicken because that's the university **(5)** _____! The party was good because I've been kind of nervous about starting classes next week. I've **(6)** _____ everything I have to do before next week, and the lists are all over my room. Every day I **(7)** _____ the things I've done, but the lists never seem to get smaller! I've walked around the campus to **(8)** _____ the fastest ways to get from one class to another, and I've **(9)** _____ my class schedule mentally lots of times to memorize it. I've bought all my books and have them **(10)** _____ on my desk.

8–10 correct: I can describe institutional traditions and use phrasal verbs for personal rituals.
0–7 correct: Look again at Sections 3 and 6 on pages 72 and 74.   SCORE: /10

2 GRAMMAR

Choose the correct options to complete the email. (12 points)

To: kylie@mastermail.mac.wd

From: j.patterson@ug.mac.wd

Subject: Re: Hey

Hey, Kylie, I'm arriving in Georgia on Thursday to move into my dorm before classes start. I just can't **(1)** *be / get* used to the idea that I'm finally going to be living away from home! Did your parents finally persuade **(2)** *to live / you to live* at home? My parents want me **(3)** *stay / to stay* in the dorm for at least a year. Anyway … you sound a little nervous. I was, too, but my brother told me **(4)** *not to / don't* worry. He's a sophomore at the college, so he's totally **(5)** *use / used* to the place. I think I'm going to need **(6)** *he / him* to show me around! He said that the first week is pretty light. They don't **(7)** *expect / persuade* freshmen to do lots of homework, and they kind of allow you **(8)** *settle / to settle* in. They encourage freshmen **(9)** *to go / going* out and **(10)** *be / get* used to the campus and the city. I was going to take six classes, but my brother warned me not **(11)** *take / to take* such a heavy load my first semester, so I'm taking the normal five-class load. Anyway, once I'm settled I'll invite **(12)** *to stay / you to stay*! See you soon!

10–12 correct: I can use *be/get used to* and verbs followed by object + infinitive.
0–9 correct: Look again at Sections 1 and 4 on pages 70 and 73.   SCORE: /12

A ▶ **1.35** 🎤 Listen to someone comparing these two pictures and answering the question. Make a note of the main points the speaker makes. Work in pairs and compare your notes.

Why might these traditions be important to these people?

B Listen again for phrases the speaker uses to compare the pictures. Write a word or short phrase in each blank.

1 _____ pictures show …
2 _____ the first picture is of a traditional meal, …
3 One thing the pictures have _____ …
4 In the first one it's a family, _____ in the second …
5 The pictures are _____ because …
6 _____ the first picture, the second picture shows …

C 🎤 You are going to compare the pictures and answer the question from Exercise A. First, complete the table with your own ideas. Work in pairs and compare your ideas.

What do the pictures have in common?	How do the pictures differ from each other?
They both show traditional activities.	*A is a family meal, B is a traditional dance.*
These traditions might be important to these people because _____ _____ .	

D 🎤 Work in groups and discuss the question in Exercise A.

HOW ARE YOU DOING?

⚪ I used good phrases to say what the pictures have in common.
⚪ I used good phrases to say how the pictures differ.
⚪ I answered the additional question after comparing the pictures.

UNIT 7 DESIGNED TO PLEASE

IN THIS UNIT YOU

- ⚙ learn language to talk about design
- ⚙ read about 3D printing in design
- ⚙ talk about interior design
- ⚙ listen to a conversation about celebrity designers
- ⚙ write a biography about a designer
- ⚙ learn about showing initiative
- ▶ watch a video about supermarket design

READING
inferring factual information

Why is it important to be able to infer facts when you are reading? Give an example from something you have read recently.

SPEAKING
distancing language

Give some examples of situations when you would need to make a very polite request. What kind of language would you use?

LIFE SKILLS
WORK & CAREER

showing initiative Employers often look for employees who can show initiative at work. What is initiative? What are some different ways to show initiative? Why is it sometimes difficult to show initiative?

A 🗣 Work in pairs. Discuss the questions.

1 Is design important in our lives? Why or why not?
2 Discuss each of the types of designs and how their design affects our lives. Then number the different types in order of importance from 1 (most important) to 5 (least important).

☐ **fashion design**

☐ **architecture and interior design**

☐ **gadgets and technology design**

☐ **graphic design**

☐ **food design**

B 🗣 Work in groups. Discuss the questions.

1 Who or what influences our choices in design? Are the influences different for each type of design?
2 What makes a design fashionable?

As well as inferring a writer's attitude or opinion, you can often infer facts. Making deductions about what must be true or can't be true will help you understand facts that are not stated explicitly.

A Read the article. How is 3D printing changing the design process?

Revolutionizing the design process

[1] From T-shirts to sneakers, many websites now make it possible for consumers to customize their own products, but developments in printing technology are making it easier than ever for consumers to get involved in the design process.

[2] 3D printing is a technology that allows designers to **manufacture** products from digital **templates** using layers of plastic, paper, and many other types of materials.

[3] One area where 3D printing is already gaining ground is jewelry. Not only can independent jewelry designers more easily manufacture their own designs, customers can also create their own **unique** designs for a piece of jewelry for themselves, or a romantic **personalized** gift for a partner. This approach allows companies to keep costs low, since the pieces are manufactured only when requested by the customer. It may also allow consumers to purchase cheaper versions of **top quality** jewelry products using more **affordable** materials.

[4] Another area where 3D printing is making interesting progress is in the kitchen. It is now possible to print multicolored candy in intricate designs with layers of flavored sugar. Elaborate shapes can also be made from chocolate and pasta. Imagine a wedding cake with **miniature** chocolate figures of the happy couple, or pasta shapes for a birthday or anniversary in the shape of your friend or relative's name!

[5] As the cost of 3D printers decreases, they will be more commonplace in people's homes. One **innovative** company has created a range of 3D-printed shoes for women that can be made at home overnight. Consumers can download digital files from the internet and print them out in the size and color of their choice.

[6] Footwear jewelry, eyewear, toys, clothing, and furniture—3D printing technology is revolutionizing the way we think about design. With 3D printing, everyone has the potential to become a great designer.

B Read the article in Exercise A again. From which paragraphs (1–6) can you infer the following? There may be more than one answer for each.

1 3D printing allows consumers to have more influence over design. _____
2 It is easy to buy customized products online. _____
3 3D printing is much more versatile than 2D printing. _____
4 It is expensive to buy 3D printers right now. _____
5 3D printing can save money for consumers. _____

C VOCABULARY: DESIGN Complete the sentences below with the words in bold from the article.

1 The machine followed a _____ provided by the designer.
2 The new shoes are made from cheaper materials and are therefore more _____.
3 You can create _____ fashion items that no one else is wearing.
4 Printers allow people to _____ products at home.
5 You can design a _____ model of yourself in sugar or chocolate.
6 Customers can buy _____ products by adding their own name and logo.
7 Some of our _____ jewelry items cost thousands of dollars.
8 New technology is allowing people to create designs full of _____ ideas.

D VOCABULARY: DESIGN Work in pairs and answer the questions.

1 Is it important to you to have unique or personalized things? Why or why not?
2 Do you think it's more important for products to be affordable or top quality? Why?
3 What innovative product would you like to manufacture with 3D printing?

2 GRAMMAR: possessive apostrophe

A LANGUAGE IN CONTEXT Read the article. Why was the designer clothing sale so popular?

CELEBRITIES' DESIGNER CLOTHING SALE

Celebrities Victoria and David Beckham, both well known for their trendsetting fashion sense, recently donated 500 items of clothing for a charity event. The sale included several of <u>Victoria's and David's designer suits</u> and 100 pairs of Victoria's designer shoes.

"It's a bargain-hunter's dream," said one customer. "It's amazing to own something from <u>Victoria and David's designer collection</u>."

Some popular items included T-shirts from Victoria's Spice Girls days, personalized with her nickname Posh, as well as tank tops decorated with the couple's sons' names: Brooklyn, Romeo, and Cruz. In spite of the one item per customer policy, most of the Beckhams' designer jackets, belts, and other items sold out soon after the store's opening.

NOTICE!
Look at the underlined phrases. Which things are owned by both Victoria and David together? Which things do they own separately?

B ANALYZE Read the article in Exercise A again.

Form Complete the table with examples from the text.

possessive apostrophe

Singular	(1) _____ , (2) _____
Plural	(3) _____ , (4) _____
Compound (two nouns joined by *and*) 1 separate ownership 2 joint ownership	(5) _____ and _____ (6) _____ and _____
Double (two consecutive nouns)	(7) _____
With gerund (to describe an action done by someone or something)	(8) _____

WATCH OUT!
- ✗ She mainly designs womens' clothes.
- ✓ She mainly designs women's clothes.

C PRACTICE Rewrite the sentences with possessive forms.

1 My friends have a new art gallery. It's beautiful.

_____

2 The couple has a daughter whose design won first prize in the competition.

_____

3 Patricia and Jenny have a friend whose father works in the fashion industry.

_____

4 Lorraine and Julia each have designer shoes that cost a fortune.

_____

5 Fashions for women are in shades of green and gray this fall.

_____

6 Teenagers are changing their fashion-buying habits.

_____

D NOW YOU DO IT Work in pairs. Discuss the questions.

1 Would you like to own a celebrity's item of clothing? Why or why not?
2 What do you think about celebrities promoting charities? What are the positives? Are there any negatives?

A 〔(·¿〕 Work in pairs. Identify these people if you can, and say what they are famous for. What do you think about their fashion styles?

B 〔»🎧〕 **1.36** Listen to a radio call-in show. Decide if the following statements are true or false. Choose T (true) or F (false).

Tony …
1	likes celebrities who become designers.	T / F
2	thinks being good in one area makes you good in other areas.	T / F

Marianne …
3	says celebrities make good designers because they understand fashion.	T / F
4	thinks it's important that celebrities create their designs themselves.	T / F

C VOCABULARY: PHRASAL VERBS Match each phrasal verb in bold (1–6) with a definition (a–f).

1 What do you think of celebrities who **bring out** their own ranges of products?

2 … it seems that anyone whose career **takes off** decides to produce a line of clothes …

3 … but does that mean they can **come up with** good ideas?

4 I think a lot of the time they don't even **draw up** the designs themselves.

5 … it takes real talent to create new designs that **catch on**, …

6 Millions of young women **look up to** them for what they've achieved.

a) become successful or popular very quickly

b) create plans, designs, etc.

c) admire

d) produce and start to sell a new product

e) become popular or fashionable

f) think of an idea or a plan for the first time

D 〔(·¿〕 **VOCABULARY: PHRASAL VERBS** Work in pairs. Complete the questions with a phrasal verb from Exercise C. Then answer the questions.

1 Do you _____ any celebrity designers? Why or why not?

2 Do you think it takes talent to _____ clothing designs that catch on? What kind of talent do you need?

3 Should a celebrity whose career _____ bring out their own line of clothes, or are there too many celebrity designers already?

4 Does it matter if celebrity designers don't _____ the designs themselves? Is it cheating the public?

4 GRAMMAR: past perfect vs. past perfect progressive

A LANGUAGE IN CONTEXT Look at the picture and say what you know about this famous person. What is she famous for? Then read the biography and check your answer.

JENNIFER LOPEZ

Designer Profile
by Jane Merchant

Jennifer Lopez had been working as an actress for over a decade and she had already appeared in seven movies by 1997, the year she starred in *Selena*. Her career took off with that role, and today she is internationally famous. Many people look up to her because she has managed to turn her success as a singer and actress into two very successful brands of designer goods, JLo and Sweetface.

B ANALYZE Read the biography in Exercise A again.

Form & Function Complete the table with information from the text.

NOTICE!
Underline the events that happened before 1997. How do we know they happened before that date?

Tense	Form	Function	Examples
past perfect	**(1)** _____ + past participle	describes a completed event, action, or state that took place before an event, action, state, or time in the past	*She had appeared in seven movies by 1997.*
past perfect progressive	**(2)** _____ + _____ + –ing	emphasizes the duration of an event, action, or state that continued up to another event, action, state, or time in the past	*She had been working as an actress for over a decade.*

C PRACTICE Complete each sentence with the verb in parentheses in the past perfect or past perfect progressive.

1 When I saw Scott, he _____ (*work*) all day and he was very tired.
2 I _____ (*finish*) eating dinner when the doorbell rang.
3 By 2012, he _____ (*appear*) in over 100 movies.
4 Tom couldn't tell me what the problem was because he _____ (*run*) and was out of breath.
5 I was late for the meeting and they _____ (*start*) by the time I got there.
6 He _____ (*design*) clothes for some time before the look caught on.
7 She _____ (*consider*) a career as a designer for a long time before she finally decided to do it.
8 By the time she was 30, her career _____ (*take off*) and she was famous.

WATCH OUT!
✗ By 2001, she had been bringing out her own fashion line.

✓ By 2001, she had brought out her own fashion line.

D NOW YOU DO IT Work in pairs. Look at the notes about Justin Timberlake and use the prompts and your own ideas to talk about his life using the past perfect and past perfect progressive.

By 2002, he … (sing)
By 2006, he … (release)
By 2010, he … (appear)
By 2012, he … (date)

started singing with 'N Sync	released his first solo album	released his second solo album	appeared in several movies
1995	2002	2006	2006–10

2005	2007	2012
brought out William Rast clothing line	started dating actress Jessica Biel	married Jessica Biel

5 SPEAKING: distancing language

When we want to make a request or suggestion in a polite way, we often use certain phrases with past tenses. These distance our request or suggestion from the present and make it less direct.

A))) 1.37 Listen to the conversation. Austin is an interior designer. Work in pairs. Discuss what his job involves.

Celine: Thanks for agreeing to help me decorate, Austin. I had been planning to ask you for a while. I was wondering if you could come up with some suggestions for this room.

Austin: Well, I was thinking you might use a very bright color scheme in here, maybe bright yellow and green.

Celine: That's a great idea! I was hoping you might also be able to help me choose furniture.

Austin: Of course. I wanted to suggest looking through some magazines together and checking out some ideas.

Celine: Fantastic! I'll make some coffee and we can get started.

B Work in pairs. Look at the conversation again and answer the questions.

1 What two phrases are used to introduce requests?

_____

_____

2 What two phrases are used to introduce suggestions?

_____

_____

C Rewrite the requests and suggestions with the words in parentheses.

1 I hope you will help me. (*hoping*)

_____

2 You should paint the walls green. (*thinking*)

_____

3 Can you help me paint my bedroom? (*wondering*)

_____

4 We should look on the internet for ideas. (*wanted*)

_____

D Work in pairs. Do the role-play. Use distancing language as in the conversation in Exercise A.

Student A:

You have just rented a room in a house, and you are moving in soon. You have asked a friend of yours to come up with some ideas to help you make it more comfortable. Talk about the kinds of things you would like and ask your friend for suggestions.

Student B:

Your friend has asked you to help draw up a plan for their new room. Ask what kind of interior design your friend likes and suggest ways in which they might make the room more comfortable.

6 PRONUNCIATION: 's after names that end in /s/, /ʃ/, or /z/

A 🎧 **1.38** People's names that end in /s/, /ʃ/, or /z/ add an extra syllable when used with 's. Listen and repeat.

Josh's apartment   Max's studio   Liz's camera   Chris's shoes

B 🎧 **1.39** Practice saying the names. Which ones add an extra syllable? Listen and check.

Pat's brother   Chaz's friend   Rick's car   Beth's sister   Ros's teacher

7 WRITING: a biography

A 🗣 Work in pairs. Look at the two hotels by the interior designer Anouska Hempel. Explain which design you prefer and why, and what you think it would be like to stay there.

Warapuru Hotel, Brazil

Blakes, London, England

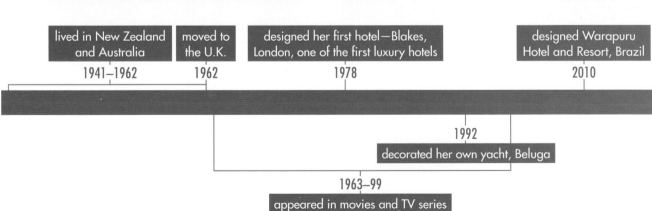

lived in New Zealand and Australia	moved to the U.K.	designed her first hotel—Blakes, London, one of the first luxury hotels	designed Warapuru Hotel and Resort, Brazil
1941–1962	1962	1978	2010

1992
decorated her own yacht, Beluga

1963–99
appeared in movies and TV series

B Read the notes about Anouska Hempel and answer the questions.

1 What had Hempel been doing before 1962? _____
2 What had she done by 1978? _____
3 By 1999, how long had she been acting? _____
4 What had she designed by the end of 2010? _____

C Write a short biography of Anouska Hempel in your notebook. Use your answers to the questions in Exercise B to help you start.

Before she moved to the U.K. in 1962, Hempel had been …

lifeSkills

SHOWING INITIATIVE

- Understand ways of showing initiative.
- Identify opportunities to show initiative.
- Be proactive and find practical solutions.

initiative /ɪˈnɪʃətɪv/ **(n.)** the ability to decide in an independent way what to do and when to do it. When you show initiative, you make decisions without being told what to do. You need to have the ability to analyze the situation, weigh the pros and cons, and come up with solutions that are effective.

A Work in small groups. Read the definition of *initiative*. Can you think of a time when you showed initiative? Explain what happened.

B Work in pairs. Read paragraphs 1–4 and decide which of the people show initiative. For those who don't show initiative, suggest what they could have done differently.

1

Lauren takes a call from an important client. Her manager is out of the office, and the client says it's very important. Lauren suggests that the client call back later, when her manager might be in the office.

Does Lauren show initiative?   ☐ yes   ☐ no
If not, what could she have done differently?

_____
_____
_____

2

Megan works in a department store. She sees many young mothers trying to shop with children and she notices that the children soon get bored and want to leave the store. She suggests to her manager that they create a play area for children. The manager agrees and makes Megan responsible for the play area.

Does Megan show initiative?   ☐ yes   ☐ no
If not, what could she have done differently?

_____
_____
_____
_____

3 Nathan's boss hasn't arrived at work yet and he can't get in touch with her. Nathan knows that his boss has an important meeting that morning so he decides to contact the other people who are coming to the meeting and rearrange it for an hour later.

Does Nathan show initiative? ☐ yes ☐ no
If not, what could he have done differently?

_____
_____
_____
_____

4 Justin works in a pizza parlor. He notices that the place is very quiet on weekday mornings. He finds himself standing around a lot at those times. He gets bored until the manager gives him a task to do.

Does Justin show initiative? ☐ yes ☐ no
If not, what could he have done differently?

_____
_____
_____
_____

C 🎧 **1.40** Listen to this man describing his situation at work. What is he worried about?

D 👥 Work in pairs. Make an action plan for the man. Decide what he should do over the next few weeks.

volunteer to attend the conference

E 👥 Report back to the class. Tell them what you suggest the man should do. Compare the ideas you hear with your own ideas.

F 👥 Work in groups. Discuss the questions.

1 Do you think you would find it easy to show initiative? Why or why not?
2 Are there any possible risks of showing initiative? Explain what they might be and what you might do about them.

HOW TO SAY IT

He should put himself forward for …
If he volunteered to …, then he could …
One thing he might consider is …
He could show initiative by …
His boss would be impressed if …

REFLECT … How can the skill of showing initiative be useful to you in **Study & Learning** and **Self & Society**?

RESEARCH …

Find out about performance reviews. What are they and how do people feel about them? What kind of questions do you need to be prepared for?

Language wrap-up

1 VOCABULARY

Complete the paragraph with words from the box. (12 points)

> affordable bring catch come up innovative manufacture
> miniature personalized take template top quality unique

Myamazingdesign.com is an **(1)** _____ new website for anyone who has ever dreamed of being a fashion designer. Simply **(2)** _____ with a **(3)** _____ idea for a new fashion trend in clothing or accessories and send your design to us. The design can be **(4)** _____ with your name or logo. We will **(5)** _____ a **(6)** _____ 3D model of your design and send you the model as well as a digital **(7)** _____ that can be used to create a full-scale model. All the designs will be shown to the very best **(8)** _____ designers in the field. The low cost makes it an **(9)** _____ way to find out if your designs are going to **(10)** _____ off. Who knows? Maybe your idea will **(11)** _____ on and you'll **(12)** _____ out your own fashion range. Your career in fashion design starts here!

> **10–12 correct:** I can use words and phrasal verbs connected to design.
> **0–9 correct:** Look again at Sections 1 and 3 on pages 82 and 84. **SCORE:** /12

2 GRAMMAR

Read the paragraph. Correct the mistakes with apostrophes and complete the sentences with the verbs in the past perfect or past perfect progressive. Write your answers on the lines below (12 points).

Stella McCartney is a British fashion designer as famous for her innovative designs as for her **(1)** *fathers'* celebrity status. Daughter of the former **(2)** *Beatles's* bass player and singer, Paul McCartney, her childhood was spent traveling around the world with her **(3)** *parents's* band *Wings*. By the time she was a teen, Stella **(4)** _____ (already design) her first jacket. Before bringing out her own fashion label in 2001, she **(5)** _____ (work) for famous designers in Paris and Milan for over two years. By 2003, she **(6)** _____ (open) 53 stores worldwide and **(7)** _____ (launch) her own perfume. Influenced by her **(8)** *mother* campaign against animal cruelty, Stella refuses to use animal fur or leather in her fashions. Many people admire **(9)** *Stellas* brand name which promotes ethical and sustainable fashion. She **(10)** *create* fashionable and ethical clothing for many years before she was appointed designer of the British **(11)** *athlete's* uniforms in the London Olympics in 2012. It was the first time a fashion designer **(12)** _____ (be) responsible for the design of the British Olympic and Paralympic Team uniforms.

(1) _____   (5) _____   (9) _____

(2) _____   (6) _____   (10) _____

(3) _____   (7) _____   (11) _____

(4) _____   (8) _____   (12) _____

> **10–12 correct:** I can use possessive apostrophes, the past perfect, and the past perfect progressive.
> **0–9 correct:** Look again at Sections 2 and 4 on pages 83 and 85. **SCORE:** /12

WRITING WORKSHOP

Writing a review

A Look at the pictures and read the review. Which place is being reviewed?

Jeff Conley

★ 5 reviews

🏅 2 helpful votes

I stayed at the da Vinci Hotel in London for three days last April because I wanted to visit some popular art exhibitions in the city. The hotel's exterior has the appearance of an old-fashioned 18th century town house, but inside it is full of surprises. Each room is designed in the style of a different artist so that whatever room you choose to stay in, you will have a unique experience. I chose the van Gogh Room, which was decorated to look like one of van Gogh's most famous paintings, *Bedroom in Arles*. This was done so effectively that I felt as if I had traveled back in time to when he painted it in 1888. The room was simply furnished and the dominant colours were yellow and bright blue, reminding me of the sunflowers and the sky of the south of France. It was delightful to be surrounded by furnishings of such unique character and atmosphere.

I also enjoyed eating in the hotel's restaurant, which offered an innovative combination of Italian and Japanese cuisine. It was disappointing to find that breakfast was not included in the price; however, the service was friendly. The hotel is conveniently located near art museums and galleries. The main drawback was the traffic noise because my room overlooked a busy street, but this is difficult to avoid in central London.

B Complete the phrases with words from the text in Exercise A.

Expressing approval

You will have a _____ experience.

It was _____ to be surrounded by …

I also _____ eating in …

Expressing disapproval

It was _____ to find that …

The main _____ was …

C Either choose a hotel from the picture on page 87 or a hotel that you have stayed at in the past. Make some notes under the following headings before you start to write: *room, location, food, service.*

D Write your review. Remember to include some positive and some negative points. Write about 200 words.

HOW ARE YOU DOING?

○ I used phrases to express my opinion.

○ I described several aspects of the hotel, including the design.

○ I balanced positive and negative comments.

UNIT 8 A FAIR DEAL?

IN THIS UNIT YOU

- ⚙ learn language to talk about social problems and solutions
- ⚙ listen to a lecture about fair trade
- ⚙ write about international aid
- ⚙ read about celebrities involved in humanitarian work
- ⚙ talk about social problems
- ⚙ learn about rights and responsibilities
- ▶ watch a video about a scheme for lending money to small businesses in the developing world

LISTENING
for main ideas
What phrases help you identify the main ideas in a lecture or a talk?

WRITING
sentence variety
Why is it important to use a variety of grammatical structures in your writing?

LIFE SKILLS

SELF & SOCIETY

understanding rights and responsibilities
We all have rights and responsibilities as citizens, parents, children, students, and workers. Why is it important to be aware of these rights and responsibilities?

A 🗣 Work in pairs. Discuss the questions.

1　What does the infographic show? What information does it give us?
2　What other types of social inequality exist? Use the pictures to help you.

Global Wealth Distribution

RICHEST

↕ Each horizontal band
represents an equal fifth
of the world's people

POOREST

World population	World income
■ Richest 20%	82.7%
■ Second 20%	11.7%
■ Third 20%	2.3%
■ Fourth 20%	1.9%
■ Poorest 20%	1.4%

http://businessideaslab.com/wp-content/uploads/2013/08/wealth_distribution_in_the_world.png

B 🗣 Work in groups. Discuss the questions.

1　Do any types of social inequality exist in your country? If yes, what are they?
2　What are some ways we can try to reduce social inequality?

1 GRAMMAR: *would rather* and *would prefer*

A 🎧 **2.01 LANGUAGE IN CONTEXT** Listen to the conversation. Is Kate in favor of donating to charities? Why or why not?

Kate: I think we should get more involved in campaigning for social justice and equality.

Josh: Do you mean donating money to charity or something?

Kate: No, not really. I'd rather we didn't just donate money. I'd rather we took some positive action ourselves instead. You know, like collecting clothing for the homeless, or starting a food bank.

Josh: So does that mean you'd rather not work through a charity?

Kate: Yes, I think I'd prefer not to do that. I'd rather get directly involved and start our own campaign.

Josh: Yes, I'd prefer to do that, too. I think most people would prefer charities to organize campaigns, but it would be cool to start our own!

> **NOTICE!**
> Underline examples of *prefer* and *rather*. What kind of verb forms follow each one?

B ANALYZE Read the conversation in Exercise A again.

Form & Function Complete the table with examples from the text.

Function	Form	Example
express the subject's preference about their own actions	*would rather* (*not*) + base form	(1) _____ (2) _____
	would prefer (*not*) + infinitive	(3) _____ (4) _____
express a preference about the actions of the subject and someone else, or someone else alone	*would rather* + subject + (negative) base form in past tense	(5) _____ (6) _____
	would prefer + object + (*not*) + infinitive	(7) _____

C PRACTICE Choose the correct options to complete the sentences.

1 I'd rather *start / to start* my own campaign.
2 I'd prefer *get / to get* involved directly.
3 They'd prefer us *donate / to donate* money to a charity.
4 We'd rather they *didn't organize / not organized* the campaign.
5 You'd prefer *not to work / not work* for a charity.
6 I'd rather *didn't raise / not raise* money on my own.

> **WATCH OUT!**
> ✓ I'd rather start a food bank.
> ✗ I'd rather to start a food bank.

D NOW YOU DO IT Work in pairs. Your school is planning a charity event. Discuss what kind of event would be most effective and easy to organize. Say which one(s) you would prefer to do and why.

- fashion show
- charity run
- bake sale
- clothing drive
- basketball game

2 READING: biographical profiles

A Read the profiles on page 95. Answer the questions.

1 Who works to help people who have had to leave their home country? _____
2 Who works to help promote education? _____
3 Who also works to protect animals? _____

B Work in pairs. Look at the details mentioned in each biography and write A (Angelina), S (Shakira), B (both), or N (neither). Discuss the evidence for your choices.

date and place of birth ___	causes they support ___	awards/recognition they received ___
occupation ___	charities they are involved in ___	reason why they became ___
what they studied ___	how they raise money ___	interested in humanitarian issues ___
how they became famous ___		

ANGELINA JOLIE

[1] Angelina Jolie was born on June 4, 1975 in Los Angeles, California. Her parents were both movie actors and she began acting at a young age, studying at the Lee Strasberg Theater Institute at the age of 11. She later majored in film studies at New York University. At 16, she took up a career in modeling. She started acting in movies in the 1990s and in 1999 won an Oscar for Best Supporting Actress in the movie, *Girl Interrupted*. She has since become one of Hollywood's top names, having starred in over 30 movies.

[2] Off-screen, Angelina Jolie devotes considerable time and money to **humanitarian** causes. One of her main interests is helping internationally displaced persons. She began visiting **refugees** in camps around the world to draw attention to their needs. She was appointed as a Goodwill **Ambassador** for the United Nations High Commissioner for Refugees (UNHCR). She also received the Global Humanitarian Action Award from the United Nations Association of the U.S.A. for her activism on behalf of refugee rights. In addition to forming the Jolie-Pitt **Foundation**, whose aim is to help eradicate **poverty** and conserve wildlife, she regularly donates money to organizations such as Doctors Without Borders and travels the world drawing attention to global issues.

SHAKIRA

[1] Born on February 2, 1977, in Barranquilla, Colombia, Shakira is a hugely successful pop singer and dancer. She wrote her first song at the age of 8. Her music is a blend of Latin, rock, and Arabic music styles. Her hit album, *Pies Descalzos*, meaning "bare feet," sold more than 3 million copies. By 2012, her U.S. album sales had reached nearly $10 million and her worldwide album sales had reached more than $70 million. She is the highest-selling Colombian artist of all time.

[2] In addition to her busy music career, Shakira is known for **philanthropic** work in her native Colombia. As a young girl, she often saw street children who slept in the park each night and she promised to do something to help them someday. After achieving her phenomenal musical success, she created the Fundación Pies Descalzos (Barefoot Foundation) to fight against social **injustice**. The aim of the foundation is to help **underprivileged** children escape a life of poverty. Since 2003, it has opened six schools in Colombia providing education, nutrition, and counseling to more than 4,000 children and their families. Although it is based in Colombia, the Barefoot Foundation is planning to expand to other countries and has started projects in South Africa and Haiti. Shakira is also a UNICEF Goodwill Ambassador and was named a member of President Obama's Advisory Commission on Educational Excellence for Hispanics in 2011.

C VOCABULARY: SOCIAL ISSUES Match the words (1–8) with the definitions (a–h).

1	humanitarian (*adj./n.*)	**a)**	a situation that is not fair or equal
2	refugee (*n.*)	**b)**	the state of not having enough money to pay for basic needs
3	ambassador (*n.*)	**c)**	someone who leaves their home country because it is not safe there
4	foundation (*n.*)	**d)**	helping people, especially by giving money to those who need it
5	philanthropic (*adj.*)	**e)**	not having as many advantages as other people
6	poverty (*n.*)	**f)**	an organization that provides money for a charity or things such as medical research
7	underprivileged (*adj.*)	**g)**	concerned with helping people who are suffering
8	injustice (*n.*)	**h)**	someone who represents an organization

D VOCABULARY: SOCIAL ISSUES Work in pairs and discuss the questions.

1 Which humanitarian causes do you feel are most important in the world today? Why?

2 What do you think is the role of a Goodwill Ambassador for an organization like the UN?

3 What do you think is the best way to help refugees? What about people who live in poverty?

4 What kind of social injustice is most serious in your country, in your opinion?

3 LISTENING: for main ideas page 71

A lecture usually consists of a series of main ideas, each followed by further details and examples. Often, key phrases tell you whether you are hearing the next main idea (*The next point I'd like to discuss is …*, etc.) or further details and examples (*such as …; for example …*).

A »)») **2.02** You are going to listen to a lecture. Look at the pictures and say what you think the speaker is going to talk about. Then listen to the introduction to the lecture and check your ideas.

B »)»)) **2.03** Listen to the rest of the lecture. As you listen, choose the option that best expresses each main idea. Work in pairs and compare your choices.

Purpose:
a) to give producers a fair price
b) to make sure that the producers make more money than the company selling the product

History:
a) Fair trade started with the selling of handmade objects in the 1960s, including things such as jewelry and fabrics.
b) There has been a change from an emphasis on handmade objects to an emphasis on agricultural products.

Labeling:
a) Labels allow fair-trade products to be identified more clearly in supermarkets.
b) Coffee is one of the products that often carries a fair-trade label on the packaging.

Criticism:
a) A number of economists think that coffee producers find it hard to make a living.
b) Several economists say that by paying higher prices, fair trade could make things worse.

C Listen to the lecture again and choose T (true) or F (false).

1	Changing fashions impacted on the kind of fair trade products produced.	T / F
2	Most fair trade these days involves agricultural products.	T / F
3	Fair-trade labels help consumers make their decision.	T / F
4	Anyone can decide to put a fair-trade label on a product.	T / F
5	Few people have benefited from fair trade.	T / F
6	Fair-trade products are usually cheaper than other products.	T / F

4 PRONUNCIATION: the contracted form of *would*

A »)»)) **2.04** Listen to the sentences. Notice that the contracted form of *would* ('d /d/ or /əd/) is used in the second sentence.

1 a) I would prefer them to give money to local people.
   b) I'd prefer them to give money to local people.
2 a) I would give money to this organization.
   b) I'd give money to this organization.
3 a) It would be better to provide medical equipment.
   b) It'd be better to provide medical equipment.

B Work in pairs. Practice saying one sentence from each pair in Exercise A. Your partner will identify the sentence.

5 SPEAKING: talking about social justice

A 🎧 **2.05** Listen to someone taking part in a debate and explaining why he agrees with the statement. Check the points he makes that support his argument.

"A fair society helps its poorer members."
1 ☐ Everyone should have enough to eat.
2 ☐ Each of us could be poor one day.
3 ☐ We may know some poor people personally.
4 ☐ We should give children a good chance in life.

B VOCABULARY: SOCIAL JUSTICE Replace each phrase in italics with the word or phrase from the box that the speaker in Exercise A actually used.

> benefits (*n.*)   can't afford (*phr.*)   have a responsibility (*phr.*)
> have the right (*phr.*)   live on (*phr. v.*)   unemployed (*adj.*)

1 Some people *manage to survive on* very little money every day.
   _____

2 They *don't have enough money* to buy food for their families.
   _____

3 The government should provide *money for the poor* so that no one goes hungry.
   _____

4 We should all *be allowed* to eat.
   _____

5 Anyone can lose their job and be *out of work*.
   _____

6 We all *have an obligation* to help the next generation.
   _____

C VOCABULARY: SOCIAL JUSTICE Complete each sentence with a word or phrase from Exercise B in the correct form.

1 We should all _____ to freedom and a good standard of living.
2 Many people who are _____ would prefer to work.
3 Unfortunately, life is expensive and we _____ to care for weaker members of society.
4 I'm shocked that some people _____ almost no money.
5 The _____ you get when you are out of work make life a little easier.
6 Do you agree we _____ to help other people if we can?

D 🗣 Work in pairs. Read the statement. Student A is for the statement. Student B is against the statement. Think of three reasons to support your opinion and make notes.

> "People who are unemployed should get financial support from the government."

_____
_____
_____
_____
_____
_____
_____
_____

E 👥 Independent Speaking Work in pairs. Explain your opinion to your partner. After you have both spoken, say whether your partner has convinced you to reconsider your opinion.

6 GRAMMAR: noun clauses as subjects

A 🎧 **2.06 LANGUAGE IN CONTEXT** Listen to the conversation. According to Lisa and Joe, why is it difficult for young people to get jobs?

Joe: Unemployment is a real problem for young people these days. What's really difficult for them is getting their first job, because employers always look for people with work experience.

Lisa: That's right. And if you don't have experience, you can't get a job in the first place! It's really unfair. What students need is good work experience while they're in school so they have a better chance of getting a job after they leave.

Joe: That's a good point. How students prepare for work is so important. Who gets the best job very often depends on already having the right skills and experience.

Lisa: Yes, I agree. And where you get your first job can influence your whole future career.

B **ANALYZE** Read the conversation in Exercise A again.

Form & Function Complete the table with examples from the text. Underline the verb in the noun clause and circle the verb in the main clause.

We can use a noun clause at the beginning of a sentence to highlight information that we think is important.

NOTICE!

Underline examples of *what*, *how*, *who*, and *where* in the conversation. What kind of clause does each word introduce?

Form	Example
noun clause about a subject: *What/Who* + base form + noun/adjective	**(1)** What _____ their first job … Who gets the best job very often (depends) on …
noun clause about an object: *What/How/Who/Where* + noun + base form	What students need (is) good work experience … **(2)** How _____ so important. **(3)** … where _____ influence your whole future career.

C **PRACTICE** Put the sentences in the correct order. Begin each one with a noun clause.

1 need / young people / are / what / more training opportunities

   _____

2 your job application / you write / is / very important / how

   _____

3 you / a big difference / makes / who / interviews

   _____

4 your self-confidence / you / where / work / affect / can

   _____

5 can create / a good impression / what / a positive attitude / is

   _____

WATCH OUT!

✓ What young people need is ….

✗ What do young people need is ….

D 🎙 **NOW YOU DO IT** Work in pairs. Explain what you would do to help reduce youth unemployment in your country or city.

What I would do first is …

What's really important is …

7 WRITING: sentence variety

⚙ You can often choose different grammatical structures to express an idea. Using a wider range of grammatical structures will make your writing more interesting.

A Read the extract. What problems does the writer suggest that international aid may cause?

Giving aid to countries that are facing economic problems seems like a good idea. ☐ It helps people in a time of crisis. ☐ It's important to continue to support very poor people in the world. However, there are also some dangers associated with giving aid. ☐ If an aid organization provides money and food, it can create dependence that is harmful for the local economy. ☐ Importing cheap food can also hurt local producers who cannot compete, and therefore lose their income. ☐ What world aid organizations need to do is provide training that will enable countries to develop their own economies. ☐ When a country has all its aid supplied in the form of money or food, it can easily become dependent. ☐ Providing medical care and education is a much better way of helping other countries. ☐ If all countries have access to good healthcare and education, they can develop the ability to become independent participants in the global market.

B Read the extract again. Find and underline examples of the following grammatical structures (1–7). Label each one with the number of the structure. Some sentences have more than one structure.

1 subject + verb + object sentence structure
2 noun clause as subject
3 gerund as subject
4 It's + adjective + infinitive
5 conditional
6 relative clause
7 causative (*have/get something done* or *have someone do / get someone to do something*)

C Rewrite each sentence starting with the words given. Use some of the grammatical structures from Exercise B.

1 It is not right to provide aid to countries that are at war.
Providing aid _____.

2 We should provide aid or people will suffer.
If we _____.

3 We should make people work for the aid they receive.
What we _____.

4 Giving suffering people a little money or food is fair.
It's fair _____.

5 The government should increase the size of aid payments.
We should get _____.

6 We provide aid to many countries. It has both advantages and disadvantages.
Aid, which we _____.

D Write two or three paragraphs explaining your opinion of international aid. Use different grammatical structures in your sentences.

You might want to write about
• how important you think international aid is and who you think should receive it.
• whether you think international aid should be increased or decreased.

lifeSkills

UNDERSTANDING RIGHTS AND RESPONSIBILITIES

- Understand what rights and responsibilities are.
- Decide what rights and responsibilities are valid in a given environment or situation.
- Be aware of rights and responsibilities in different contexts.

A Read the definitions of *right* and *responsibility*. As a class, discuss what is meant by "rights" and "responsibilities."

Eleanor Roosevelt with the Universal Declaration of Human Rights

right (*n.*): something that you are morally or legally allowed to do or have
Many new laws have been introduced to protect workers' rights.
Examples of workers' rights include fair pay, equal pay for equal work, and the right to work in a safe environment.
Common terms include: human rights, women's rights, workers' rights, children's rights, equal rights

responsibility (to/toward) (*n.*): a moral or legal duty to behave in a particular way
What is the individual's responsibility to others in modern society?
Examples of responsibilities include the responsibility to follow the law, to be tolerant, and to respect the rights of others in society.
Common terms include: individual responsibility, social responsibility, collective responsibility

B Work in pairs. Read and discuss the statements. Decide whether each one is a right or a responsibility. Some statements may be both. Which ones do you agree with?

Parents have the right/responsibility to:

		Right	Responsibility	Agree	Disagree
1	provide food and shelter for their child	☐	☐	☐	☐
2	be a good role model for their child	☐	☐	☐	☐
3	send their child to school	☐	☐	☐	☐
4	help choose their child's school / school subjects	☐	☐	☐	☐
5	teach their child at home	☐	☐	☐	☐
6	discipline their child	☐	☐	☐	☐
7	choose their child's husband or wife	☐	☐	☐	☐
8	provide their child financial support after the age of 18	☐	☐	☐	☐
9	_____				
10	_____				

Children have the right/responsibility to:

		Right	Responsibility	Agree	Disagree
1	study hard and get good grades in school	☐	☐	☐	☐
2	help choose their school / school subjects	☐	☐	☐	☐
3	work part-time after school or on weekends	☐	☐	☐	☐
4	get help and support from their parents when they are in trouble	☐	☐	☐	☐
5	help their parents with cooking and household chores	☐	☐	☐	☐
6	take care of younger siblings	☐	☐	☐	☐
7	take care of their parents when they are old or sick	☐	☐	☐	☐
8	get financial support from their parents after the age of 18	☐	☐	☐	☐
9	_____				
10	_____				

C Work in pairs. Add two more rights or responsibilities that parents have and two more rights and responsibilities that children have to Exercise B. Compare your ideas with another pair.

A: *I think parents have the right to …*
B: *I don't agree. Parents should never …*

D Work in pairs. Consider your society as a whole. Make lists of the rights and responsibilities you believe citizens of your country have. Think about the areas below.

Citizenship

Citizens in my country have a right to …	Citizens in my country have a responsibility to …

E Share your lists with the rest of the class. Did anyone come up with any rights or responsibilities that weren't on your lists?

F Work in groups. Discuss the questions.

1 Do you feel you now have a better understanding of rights and responsibilities in general?
2 What have you learned about your own rights and responsibilities?

REFLECT … How can awareness of rights and responsibilities be useful to you in **Study & Learning** and **Work & Career**?

RESEARCH …

Find a website that gives advice about citizens' rights and responsibilities in the U.S.A., the U.K., or another English-speaking country. Which of these rights and responsibilities do you think are international and apply in all countries, and which might be different elsewhere?

Language wrap-up

1 VOCABULARY

Complete the paragraph with the words and phrases from the box.
(12 points)

> afford Ambassadors foundations humanitarian injustice live on
> poverty refugees responsibility right underprivileged unemployed

Too many people in the world today are facing **(1)** _____ and hunger. There are
too many **(2)** _____, who have been forced to leave their homes by war or
natural disaster. Everyone has a **(3)** _____ to basic necessities such as food,
water, and shelter, but many people cannot **(4)** _____ them. There are too many
(5) _____ children who lack access to education and healthcare. How can we help
people who have lost their homes and are now **(6)** _____ without enough money
to **(7)** _____? Charities and aid organizations believe it is our **(8)** _____
to help fight against social **(9)** _____, and some celebrities use their fame to
support **(10)** _____ causes; some have started their own aid **(11)** _____
and others have been appointed as Goodwill **(12)** _____ for organizations like
UNICEF and the United Nations.

> **10–12 correct:** I can talk about social issues and social justice.
> **0–9 correct:** Look again at Sections 2 and 5 on pages 94, 95, and 97.   **SCORE:**   /12

2 GRAMMAR

A Choose the correct options to complete the sentences. (6 points)

1   We *would prefer / would rather* discuss the best way to raise money for charity.
2   I'd prefer charities *provide / to provide* more health education.
3   They'd rather *us not send / we didn't send* financial aid.
4   I'd rather *to start / start* a program to provide job training.
5   We'd prefer *to organize / organize* our own charity foundation.
6   I'd prefer *them / they* to support local organizations.

B Rewrite each sentence using a noun clause as a subject. (6 points)

1   The world needs more tolerance and understanding.
    What _____.
2   The topic of tonight's debate is the reason some countries are poorer than others.
    Why _____.
3   Most help is needed in schools and hospitals.
    Where _____.
4   The international community decides which countries receive the most aid.
    Who _____.
5   The worst time to think about training is just after you've lost your job.
    When _____.
6   It's really important to get help to people who need it most.
    What _____.

> **10–12 correct:** I can use *would rather* and *would prefer*. I can use noun clauses as subjects.
> **0–9 correct:** Look again at Sections 1 and 6 on pages 94 and 98.   **SCORE:**   /12

SPEAKING WORKSHOP

Proposing a solution

A 🔊 **2.07** Read the problem. Then listen to someone proposing some solutions. Complete the notes as you listen. What solutions are proposed?

The problem in my city is that rents are much too high. They just aren't affordable. For many people, rent takes up over half of their income. Landlords raise the rent every year and there's nothing we can do about it. If rents continue to rise, I'll have to leave the city and I'll lose my job. Soon, only rich people will be able to live here. It isn't fair. I think the city council should do something about it.

Karina Gomez, 32, mother of two children

KEEP COSTS LOW

Solution 1:

Solution 2:

B Listen again. Check the items below.

The speaker …
- [ ] restated the problem in her own words.
- [ ] suggested one solution.
- [ ] suggested two solutions.

- [ ] explained why one solution was better than another.
- [ ] added details to support each solution.
- [ ] made a concluding statement.

C Read the problem and make notes for your answer.

College fees set to rise …

The problem in my country is that college fees are too high. I can't afford to go to college. How can I get a good job if I don't have education and training? I don't think it's fair. Can't the government do something about it?

Solution 1:

Solution 2:

D 🗣 Present your ideas to the class and answer the question in Exercise C.

HOW ARE YOU DOING?
- ○ I restated the problem in my own words.
- ○ I suggested two possible solutions with supporting details.
- ○ I made a concluding statement.

UNIT 9 COMPETITIVE EDGE

IN THIS UNIT YOU

- ⚙ learn language to talk about competition, personality types, and science
- ⚙ read about the reasons for competitiveness
- ⚙ talk about different aspects of competition
- ⚙ listen to experts' opinions about the effects of competition on young people
- ⚙ write a description of a TV contest
- ⚙ learn about synthesizing information
- ▶ watch a video about a cat show competition

READING
understanding text organization
Do you often read factual texts? If so, for what reasons? What types of information do writers of factual texts tend to include?

SPEAKING
paraphrasing
In what situations do you need to paraphrase (say in different words) what another person has said or written?

LIFE SKILLS

STUDY & LEARNING

synthesizing information How is the skill of synthesizing information related to the skill of paraphrasing?

A 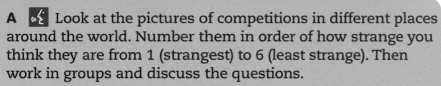 Look at the pictures of competitions in different places around the world. Number them in order of how strange you think they are from 1 (strangest) to 6 (least strange). Then work in groups and discuss the questions.

1 Did most people in the group have similar choices for the strangest and least strange competitions?
2 Do you know of any other unusual competitions? If so, do they take place in your country or other countries?

extreme ironing

Challenge: to iron a shirt while doing an extreme sport
Winner: most creative; best ironing skills

air-guitar world championships

Challenge: to pretend to play a guitar
Winner: best technical accuracy and artistic form

beard and mustache competitions

Challenge: to grow facial hair
Winner: most creative style

limbo skating

Challenge: to roller skate under low objects
Winner: the skater who clears the lowest object

cell-phone throwing world championships

Challenge: to throw a cell phone
Winner: farthest throw

wing suit flying

Challenge: to wear a flying suit and jump off a high point
Winner: the jumper who lands first

B 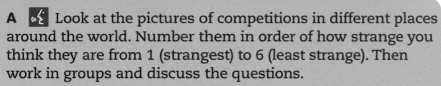 Work in groups. Come up with an idea for a new and unusual competition. Explain it to the class. Take a class vote on the best idea for a competition.

1 GRAMMAR: gerunds after prepositions

A LANGUAGE IN CONTEXT Read the text. Do you know people who fit each of the four personality types?

A, B, C, or D?

Do you get excited about having new challenges? Are you fond of competing in games or competitions? Do you complain about having to wait in lines? Are you easily bored with doing routine activities? Then you are probably a Type A personality.

Do you look forward to going to parties or other social events? Are you good at telling stories or jokes? Are you interested in having a career that involves working with lots of different people? Then you may be a Type B.

Do you care about having all the facts and insist on getting the details right? Do you like to be responsible for organizing information or events? Do you worry about making mistakes? You are probably a Type C.

Finally, do you feel happy about doing repetitive activities? Are you capable of following instructions and sticking to routines? Do you object to making changes in the way you do things? Those are traits of the Type D personality. Of course, the truth is that most people are a combination of two or more personality types, but we may have more traits of one type than of all the others.

B ANALYZE Read the text in Exercise A again.

Form Complete the table with verb and adjective phrases from the text.

verb + preposition (+ gerund)		adjective + preposition (+ gerund)	
complain about		excited about	
_____	_____	_____	_____
_____	_____	_____	_____
_____	_____	_____	_____
		_____	

NOTICE!
Underline the gerunds that follow prepositions. How do we form gerunds?

C PRACTICE Complete the sentences with the correct preposition and the gerund form of the verbs in parentheses.

1 Do you care _____ (use) correct grammar when you speak English, or are you more interested _____ just _____ (communicate)?
2 Do you object _____ (have) to wait in lines or on the phone?
3 Are you fond _____ (tell) stories and jokes or are you more interested _____ (listen) to other people talk?
4 Do you get excited _____ (compete) in games or sports?
5 Do you get bored _____ (do) repetitive activities, or do you feel happy _____ (do) routine things?
6 Do you look forward _____ (learn) to do new things, or do you worry _____ (make) mistakes if you have to do something new?
7 Do you enjoy being responsible _____ (organize) things or do you prefer to follow others' instructions?
8 Are you capable _____ (concentrate) on very detailed information for a long period of time?

WATCH OUT!
✓ I look forward to going out tomorrow.
✗ Sherrie is opposed to see violent movies.
✓ We want to go out tomorrow.
✗ I would like to seeing that movie.

D ▸ NOW YOU DO IT Work in pairs. Ask each other the questions in Exercise C and discuss which dominant personality type you are.

You said that you care about using correct grammar, you don't get excited about competing, and you don't get bored with doing repetitive activities. I think you're probably a Type C or D.

2 LISTENING: to experts' opinions

A 🗣 Work in pairs. Look at the title of the talk and brainstorm some of the things you think the speakers might mention.

Is competition healthy?

B »)) **2.08** Listen to the talk to check your ideas from Exercise A.

C 🗣 Listen again and take notes on the main arguments each speaker presents. Work in pairs and compare, then revise your notes if necessary.

D 🗣 Work in small groups. Say which speaker you agreed with more and why. You can refer to your notes.

E   VOCABULARY: SCIENTIFIC NOUNS AND VERBS Complete the table with nouns and the base form of verbs from the talk. Check your answers in a dictionary.

Verb	Noun	Verb	Noun
test	(1) _____	theorize	(5) _____
(2) _____	study	(6) _____	experiment
research	(3) _____	(7) _____	measurement
prove	(4) _____	(8) _____	conclusion

F   VOCABULARY: SCIENTIFIC NOUNS AND VERBS Complete the sentences with a word from Exercise E in the correct form. There may be more than one correct answer.

1   Psychologists use different methods to _____ theories to find out if they are true.
2   In the field of psychology, _____ are done on the behavior of both people and animals.
3   I don't think that theory has been _____ yet.
4   After reading this article, I have _____ that a limited amount of competition is good.
5   The desire to play sports is one _____ of competitiveness.
6   I want to do some internet _____ on the effects of competition on young adults.
7   I don't think scientists should _____ on animals.
8   His theory is interesting, but I want to see some _____ that it's true.

3 PRONUNCIATION: nouns and verbs with different pronunciation

A »)) **2.09** Listen to the words. Notice how the verb and noun are pronounced differently, with the stress on different syllables.

	Noun	Verb
1	record /ˈrekərd/	record /rɪˈkɔrd/
2	present /ˈprezənt/	present /prɪˈzent/
3	produce /ˈproʊdus/	produce /prəˈdus/
4	increase /ˈɪnkris/	increase /ɪnˈkris/

B 🗣 »)) **2.10** Work in pairs. Practice saying the sentences. Make sure you pronounce the verbs and nouns correctly. Then listen and check.

1   There is no record of any studies on this topic, so I'm going to research it for my thesis.
2   The paper presents two theories about why our brains produce certain chemicals.
3   This machine records data about when there is an increase in the levels of dopamine present in the brain.

4 SPEAKING: paraphrasing

To paraphrase something is to express information that you hear or read in your own words, usually in a simpler way. You can do this by changing words and/or sentence structure. Paraphrasing information shows that you have understood it.

A Read the list of paraphrasing techniques. Then read the text and the paraphrase below. Match the techniques (a–d) with the paraphrases (1–4).

a) Change words to different parts of speech, e.g., a noun to a verb. ☐
b) Use synonyms (words that have the same meaning as other words). ☐
c) Change the word order or the sentence structure and add or delete words as necessary. ☐
d) Use different connectors, or break a long sentence into two sentences. ☐

The results of one study suggested that what increased children's sense of self-worth and motivation the most was engaging in group activities, which led the researchers to conclude that more emphasis should be placed on cooperation-based activities.

(1) <u>One study indicated</u> that children experienced **(2)** <u>an increase</u> in **(3)** <u>self-esteem</u> and motivation when they did activities in **(4)** <u>groups. This</u> caused researchers to come to the conclusion that children should engage in more cooperative activities.

B 🔊 Work in pairs. Read the original text and the paraphrase. Find at least one example of each paraphrasing technique from Exercise A.

Original

If we use our brain for activities such as problem-solving or information recall, it will generate more neurons and axons related to those activities, which improves brain function and causes us to perform better. So the more we do something, the better we get at it, and very often the better we are at something, the more we want to do it. The implication of this may be that the more frequently we play competitive sports and games, the more we want to play them, which may make us more competitive.

Paraphrase

Using our brain for solving problems or recalling information causes it to create more neurons and axons connected with those activities. Our brain functions better, so we improve in these activities. When we are good at something, we often want to do it more often, so it's possible that competing a lot makes us want to compete even more.

C 🔊 2.11 🔊 Work in pairs. Listen to two people discussing a study on peer support among young adults. Paraphrase what each person says. Then compare your ideas with another pair.

D 🔊 Work in pairs. Choose a short text or a paragraph from a text that you have read previously in this book so far. Paraphrase your text for your partner. If you are not sure about any part of your partner's paraphrase, ask for clarification.

HOW TO SAY IT 🔊

Are you saying …?
So that means …
In other words, …

5 GRAMMAR: verb + gerund

A 🎧 **2.12 LANGUAGE IN CONTEXT** Listen to the conversation. Does Sandra dislike all reality shows?

Sandra: You know how my brother always laughs at me when I watch reality shows? Well, last night he was watching *Hunting Heroes*!

Rick: Seriously? That has to be the worst reality show in the world! Who would want to <u>watch a bunch of guys</u> hunting wild birds and animals?

Sandra: Yeah, I <u>have trouble</u> understanding why people <u>waste their time</u> watching shows like that.

Rick: <u>I've seen you</u> watching other reality shows though.

Sandra: Sure. I like some of the competition ones, like *The Voice* and *Project Runway*. It's interesting to <u>observe the competitors</u> going through the process of learning and growing in their field. You can just <u>feel their confidence</u> increasing every time they pass another round. I could <u>spend my life</u> watching those!

Rick: Not me. I can't <u>sit at home</u> watching TV. I <u>have more fun</u> doing outdoor activities.

B **ANALYZE** Read the conversation in Exercise A again.

Function Choose the correct option to complete the rule.
An object and a gerund often follow verbs of *action / perception*.

Form Complete the table with words and phrases from the conversation.

NOTICE!
Look at the underlined phrases in the conversation. What verb form follows them?

Form	
have + object + gerund	objects: *a good time / a hard time / difficulty /* **(1)** _____ / **(2)** _____
verb of perception + object + gerund	verbs: *notice / hear / listen to / imagine /* **(3)** _____ / **(4)** _____ / **(5)** _____ / **(6)** _____
spend/waste + expression of time + gerund	time: *a long time / most of your time / days / years /* **(7)** _____ / **(8)** _____
sit/stand/lie + expression of place + gerund	place: *there / at your desk /* **(9)** _____

C **PRACTICE** Complete the questions with appropriate verbs in the correct form. There may be more than one possible option.

1 Do you enjoy _____ around watching TV, or do you prefer to be more active?
2 In general, how much time do you _____ watching TV every day?
3 What do you _____ the most fun doing? What do you hate to _____ time doing?
4 Do you like _____ people compete on reality shows? If so, which ones?
5 How would you complete this statement? I have a hard time _____ why people watch …
6 On reality shows, you often _____ people behaving badly. Do you think shows like that are a bad influence on society? Why or why not?

WATCH OUT!
✗ He wastes too much time watch TV.
✓ He wastes too much time watching TV.

D 🗣 **NOW YOU DO IT** Work in groups. Discuss your answers to the questions in Exercise C.

⚙ Different text types have different features and are organized in different ways. A factual text, especially if it deals with a scientific topic, usually includes supporting information such as definitions or explanations, descriptions, and examples. Recognizing these features can help you understand the text.

A 🗣 **Work in pairs. Read the text and answer the questions.**

1 What is the main idea of the text?
2 What are the two theories in the text? Student A, explain the first theory. Student B, explain the second theory.

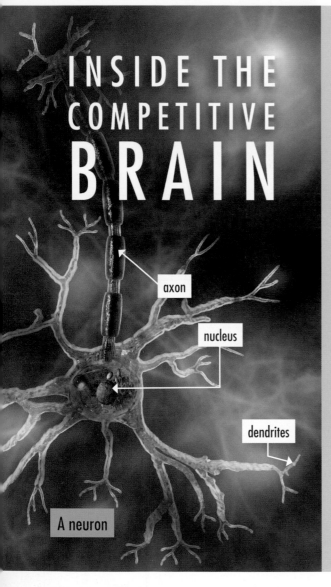

INSIDE THE COMPETITIVE BRAIN

axon

nucleus

dendrites

A neuron

[1] Can we really "just enjoy the fun of playing the game"? Recent scientific research indicates that the answer may depend on our brain structure and chemistry. There are various theories about how the joy of competing and the will to win may be controlled by nature.

[2] One theory is that our degree of competitiveness is connected to the levels of certain hormones and chemicals in our brain. The male hormone testosterone is actually present in both men and women, and winning causes a rise in testosterone levels, which gives a person a sense of power and success. The desire for this feeling may encourage us to be even more competitive. In contrast, losing appears to cause a drop in testosterone levels, which helps explain the agony of defeat. Winning also stimulates the production of the chemical dopamine, which is a neurotransmitter that produces a feeling of pleasure. The thrill of victory is caused by a combination of increased levels of testosterone and dopamine, and people who have naturally higher levels of these tend to enjoy competing more than those with naturally lower levels.

[3] An alternative theory is that of "plasticity." This means that the brain is constantly "rewiring," or changing its structure. The nerve cells in the brain are called neurons, and neurons have extensions called dendrites and axons.

Dendrites and axons are responsible for transmitting information to and from other cells in the body. Recent research has indicated that the brain can generate new neurons and axons with use, and this improves brain function. Therefore, if we use our brain for activities such as problem-solving or information recall, it will generate more neurons and axons related to those activities, which improves brain function and causes us to perform better. So the more we do something, the better we get at it, and very often the better we are at something, the more we want to do it. The implication of this may be that the more frequently we play competitive sports and games, the more we want to play them, which may make us more competitive.

[4] These two theories may help to explain why some people are more competitive than others, but can human behavior ever be attributed just to nature? For example, there may be people with high levels of the brain chemicals associated with competing and winning who don't actually enjoy competitive activities and prefer to channel their energy in other directions. We also all know people who aren't competitive at all who enjoy playing sports even though they seldom win, so the answer to whether we can "just enjoy the fun of playing the game" appears to be a very unscientific "it depends"!

B Look back at the text and underline the following things.

Paragraph 2

1 a definition of testosterone
2 an explanation of how testosterone is related to winning and losing
3 a description of dopamine
4 an explanation of the effects of testosterone and dopamine

Paragraph 3

5 an explanation of the theory of plasticity
6 a description of neurons
7 an explanation of what dendrites and axons do
8 examples of activities that increase brain function

C Repeat Question 2 in Exercise A. How did identifying the parts of the text in Exercise B help you understand the text and explain it better the second time?

D VOCABULARY: EXPRESSIONS OF EMOTION Follow the instructions for question 1. Then check the correct options for questions 2 and 3.

1   These three expressions all have a similar meaning, but they vary in intensity of feeling. Number them in order from the strongest emotion to the weakest.
the joy of ☐   the fun of ☐   the thrill of   ☐

2   Which two words are commonly used with "the agony of"?
defeat ☐   loss ☐   anger ☐   boredom ☐

3   Which two of these three phrases refer to wanting to do something?
a feeling of ☐   the will to ☐   the desire for/to ☐

E VOCABULARY: EXPRESSIONS OF EMOTION Work in groups. Discuss the questions.

1   Do you usually play a game or sport just for the fun of it, or do you have a strong will to win?

2   Does the thrill of victory give you a feeling of power and create a desire for more competition? When you lose, do you suffer from the agony of defeat?

3   Do you generally have a strong desire to compete and be the best? Give examples to support your answer.

7 WRITING: a description

A Read this description of a reality TV show. Would you like to watch it? Why or why not?

Little Lena

This show follows the life of a badly-behaved family from Alabama. The Larson family consists of dad Larry, mom Lynda, sons Larry, Jr. (15), Jason (13), Ryan (9), and daughter Lena (6). The Larsons were "discovered" when a TV producer observed Lynda and her spoiled daughter having a dramatic argument in a famous department store in New York. The audience listens to the family yelling at each other, watches them eating loads of horrible, unhealthy food, and follows them as they participate in strange competitions and other local events. Larry complains about having to help his wife in the house, and he tells his sons to ignore their mother. Lynda encourages Lena to be more and more competitive and rude to other children as they travel from one competition to another. The show is advertised as a comedy, but a lot of people don't find the family's behavior very funny.

B Work in small groups. Think of a TV reality show or game show that you know about and that you all agree is terrible. Make notes about what the show involves and why you think it's the worst show. With your group, write a description of the show similar to the model in Exercise A.

C Work in groups. Choose one member of your group to read your description to the rest of the class. Take a class vote on the worst TV show based on the descriptions you heard.

lifeSkills

SYNTHESIZING INFORMATION

- Gather information from different sources.
- Organize relevant information into categories.
- Combine the information to produce a new idea or a conclusion.

A Read the definition of *synthesizing information*. In what situations could synthesizing information be useful?

"Synthesizing information is the process of combining information and ideas from different sources to create or develop a new idea, focus, or perspective, or to reach a conclusion."

B 🗣 Work in groups. Read the instructions on the right and discuss the kinds of information that you need to find out and the types of sources you might use.

C 🗣 Work in groups. Assign one of the texts below and on page 113 to each group member and follow these steps.

- Read your text in detail and underline the main idea, supporting details, and any examples.
- In your notebook, briefly summarize the information that you've underlined in your text.
- Share the information you found out with your group. Decide which information is relevant to your task in Exercise B and put the relevant information into appropriate categories: *description*, *claims*, *evidence*, *conclusions*.
- Analyze the information and discuss your conclusions.

Ginkgo biloba—what is it, and does it work?

In teams, prepare a report on what ginkgo biloba is and whether there is any proof that it works. Include information on the following things:

- a description of ginkgo biloba: what it is and what it is used for
- claims made about it by manufacturers of supplements
- statistical or anecdotal evidence to support or refute these claims
- your team's conclusions/ opinions based on your findings

A

Ginkgo biloba:

a species of medicinal tree found in China. The leaves contain compounds called flavonoids and terpenoids, which are antioxidants that can help protect the cells of the body. People who want to increase their competitive edge in sports or in their profession often take ginkgo biloba because it is thought to support memory and other brain functions. The substances in ginkgo biloba increase the flow of oxygen to the cells, which can help with blood circulation and produce feelings of energy, physical vitality, and mental sharpness.

a *Ginkgo biloba* tree

B

Ⓖ Ginkgo biloba Capsules

Do you want to perform at the top of your ability? It's a competitive world out there, and whether you are hoping for a promotion at your company or competing in a sport, you want to be at your best. Studies have shown that the ancient Chinese tree *Ginkgo biloba* has properties that increase the flow of oxygen to all of the cells in the body, including the brain. Benefits of taking gingko biloba supplements may include improvements in memory and other cognitive functions, increased energy, and a general feeling of well-being. You will observe your cognitive abilities improving in just a few weeks with ginkgo biloba!

200 capsules 30 ml

$15.00 + shipping and handling

Healthy & Happy SUPPLEMENTS

C

Botany 101, spring semester   Nutritional supplements

Review of independent studies to test the effectiveness of ginkgo biloba in increasing cognitive function

Summary	Some data suggest that ginkgo biloba may be effective in increasing mental function and energy levels.
Research	All studies evaluated the effectiveness of taking 30 ml capsules of ginkgo biloba once a day for six months. One third of the participants were older people with memory problems while the others were younger adults who wanted to increase their brain function and energy in general.
Results	Three clinical studies in the U.S.A., the U.K., and Brazil were evaluated. Results were mixed. In one study, 75% of the participants experienced an improvement in memory, and at least a slight increase in energy. In the other two studies, the results were inconclusive; about 20% of the participants experienced some improvement, but the majority showed little to no improvement. In all three studies, researchers observed participants experiencing side effects such as nausea and headaches.
Conclusions	Most of the claims that ginkgo biloba increases brain function are made by manufacturers of supplements, and further studies are needed to prove whether or not ginkgo biloba is actually useful for improving cognitive functions and energy levels. There is some evidence that it is effective; however, there appear to be some negative side effects associated with the compound.

D

sallyck: I have a high-stress job, and I wanted to increase my energy and mental function. I heard that ginkgo biloba was great for both of those things. I took a supplement for 30 days, and my advice? Don't waste your money! The only real effects I had were headaches and nausea, and I didn't feel myself improving in either memory or energy levels. Forget it!

timo34: My grandfather was worried about not being able to remember things, so he started taking ginkgo biloba supplements. After about a month, our family noticed his memory improving, and it also seemed that he had a little more energy. I decided to try ginkgo biloba to see what it would do for me, and I'm glad I did! I have to remember a lot of details in my job, and I think ginkgo biloba has definitely made my memory better.

D **Work in groups and prepare your report. Then present your report to the rest of the class.**

E **Work in groups. Discuss the questions.**

1 How can organizing information into categories, in this case descriptions, claims, evidence, and conclusions, help you synthesize information for a report?

2 Why is it a good idea to use a variety of different sources when doing an analytical report like this one?

REFLECT ... How can the skill of synthesizing information be useful to you in **Self & Society** and **Work & Career**?

RESEARCH ...
Choose another health- or performance-related product that is currently popular. Look up different sources of information on the product. Prepare a synthesis of the information with a short conclusion based on what you have read. Give a short report to the class.

HOW TO SAY IT

In my opinion, this is/isn't relevant, because ...
This information can help us prove/conclude ...
Although this information suggests ..., there is no/some proof here that ...

Language wrap-up

A Complete the sentences with the phrases from the box. (6 points)

> agony of   desire for   feeling of   joy of   thrill of   will to

1 Sitting in the garden gives me a _____ peace.
2 Most athletes have a strong _____ success.
3 Some people enjoy the _____ danger in extreme sports.
4 I don't compete; I run just for the _____ being outdoors.
5 You won't be a champion if you don't have a strong _____ win.
6 It's always sad to see athletes experiencing the _____ defeat.

B Complete the paragraph with the correct verb or noun forms of the words from the box. More than one answer may be possible. (6 points)

> conclude   experiment   measure/measurement   research   test   theory/theorize

We did an **(1)** _____ in science class to **(2)** _____ competitiveness in rats. First, we read some **(3)** _____ on the subject, and we decided that our **(4)** _____ was that male rats were more competitive than female rats. We designed a **(5)** _____ in which we put hungry male and female rats together and put a small amount of food at one end of their cage. We found that the four most competitive rats were two females and two males, so we **(6)** _____ that competiveness, at least in rats, is not based on gender.

> **10–12 correct:** I can use scientific nouns and verbs and expressions of emotion.
> **0–9 correct:** Look again at Sections 2 and 6 on pages 107, 110, and 111.   **SCORE:**   /12

Choose the correct options to complete the paragraph. (12 points)

> I guess I'm a Type A personality because I love all kinds of competition. For example, I'm not interested **(1)** *in / about* exercising by myself; I want to compete! I **(2)** *am / have* trouble understanding it when I hear people **(3)** *to say / saying* that they just exercise for the fun of it. I'm good **(4)** *at / about* running, and I can **(5)** *feel / catch* my energy **(6)** *increases / increasing* during a race. I'm capable **(7)** *to run / of running* much faster when I feel the thrill of competition. I'm pretty competitive at work, too. My colleagues usually spend an hour or more **(8)** *to have / having* lunch, but I get bored **(9)** *with / about* sitting **(10)** *around / on* talking when I could be getting ahead with my work. I like being responsible **(11)** *for / of* managing important projects, and I'm looking forward **(12)** *to / about* being in top management some day!

> **10–12 correct:** I can use verb constructions with gerunds.
> **0–9 correct:** Look again at Sections 1 and 5 on pages 106 and 109.   **SCORE:**   /12

A Read the assignment and the letter. What points does the writer make to support her case?

> You are a business owner. Write a letter to your city government recommending that they submit a proposal for your city to host a large national or international event. It can be a sports event such as the Olympics, a music festival, or any other type of large event that you are interested in having in your city.

¹ Subject: Bid for Olympics 2028

² To the Members of the City Council:

³ As a hotel owner and citizen of Miami, I am interested in ways to promote our city and to stimulate its economy. For that reason, I am writing to propose that the City Council submit a bid to host the 2028 Summer Olympic Games.

⁴ My understanding is that the Olympic Committee bases its selection on the following criteria:

• the availability of at least 45,000 hotel rooms
• space for building an Olympic Village with housing for 16,500 people
• a large international airport
• a good public transportation system
• a large number of non-Olympic tourist attractions, restaurants, etc.

⁵ I believe that Miami qualifies in all areas but one. There are over 300,000 hotel rooms in and near the city, and Miami has one of the largest international airports in the country. There is plenty of open space near the city for building the Olympic Village and new sports facilities. The only weak point for our city is public transportation. As you know, our bus service is limited, and we do not have a light rail or other alternative system of public transportation. However, the Olympics would provide a good reason to improve our transportation system.

⁶ I'm sure you will agree that hosting the Olympics would be an excellent opportunity for the city, and I hope that you will consider submitting a bid. The Miami Hotel Association would be interested in meeting with you to discuss how we could help in this effort.

⁷ Thank you for considering this proposal. I look forward to hearing from you.

⁸ Paula Stevens
President, Miami Hotel Association
pbstevens@MHA.net (777) 555–8731

B Write the number that corresponds to each part of the letter.

a) summary paragraph with an offer ___
b) opening paragraph giving reason for writing ___
c) subject of email ___
d) list of criteria for selection ___
e) contact information ___
f) closing ___
g) arguments for proposal ___
h) greeting ___

C Read the assignment in Exercise A again. Then make notes to plan a similar letter.

D Write your letter. Remember to include all the necessary information. Write about 200 words.

HOW ARE YOU DOING?
○ I have included a correct greeting and closing.
○ I have stated my reason for writing in my opening paragraph.
○ I have included several points to support my proposal.

UNIT 10 RISKY BUSINESS

LISTENING
rapid speech
Why is it more difficult to understand what someone is saying when they speak quickly in English?

WRITING
requesting action
In what circumstances might you write a letter requesting action? Would you use a formal or informal style? Why?

LIFE SKILLS

SELF & SOCIETY

managing stress Which of these statements describes how you feel about stress at work/school/college?

⦿ Stress affects me badly. I get anxious and can't concentrate.
⦿ I don't mind a little stress, but too much pressure gets me down.
⦿ Stress is just another name for excitement! I love working under pressure!

A 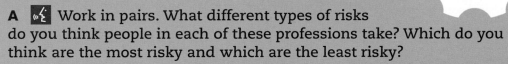 Work in pairs. What different types of risks do you think people in each of these professions take? Which do you think are the most risky and which are the least risky?

a firefighter

an actor

a politician

a stock trader

a small business owner

B 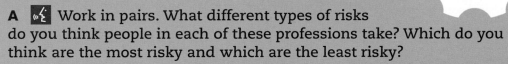 Work in pairs. Discuss the questions.

1 How much of a risk-taker are you? What risks, if any, do you regularly take?
2 Complete this questionnaire and add up your points. Is the result what you expected? Why or why not? Compare your result with your partner.

Domain		Would you ...	Yes	Maybe	No	Score
Physical: health and safety	a)	take part in a sport like caving or horseback riding?				
	b)	go bungee jumping?				
	c)	ride a bicycle in traffic without a helmet?				
	d)	eat food from a sidewalk stand?				
Lifestyle: social status and relationships	a)	argue for something everyone else in your group is against?				
	b)	move to another country?				
	c)	run for a public office?				
	d)	wear something uncool or out of style?				
Livelihood: career and finance	a)	quit your job before finding a new one?				
	b)	start your own business?				
	c)	work freelance?				
	d)	invest money in the stock market?				

Scoring: Yes = 2, Maybe = 1, No = 0

Score by Domain: 0–2 Not a risk-taker   3–5 Moderate risk-taker   6–8 High risk-taker

Total score: 0–7 Not a risk-taker   8–16 Moderate risk-taker   17–24 High risk-taker

A 🔊 Before you read the article, decide whether you agree or disagree with the statements. Work in pairs and compare your answers.

		Agree	Disagree
1	People worry about physical safety too much these days.	☐	☐
2	People who succeed are people prepared to fail.	☐	☐
3	People should do their best to avoid risks.	☐	☐

B Read the article. Decide whether the writer would agree or disagree with each of the statements in Exercise A. Do you agree with the points the writer makes? Why or why not?

WHAT ARE YOU **SCARED** OF?
We should all take more risks in our lives, argues Tina Brandon

[1] I think it must have been some time in the 1990s when we all started to **play it safe**. My father talks of his own youth as a time of outdoor adventure, of **risky** activities such as playing on rope swings in the woods and camping out with friends. Sure, they picked up minor injuries along the way, and at worst a few broken bones, but they enjoyed their **freedom** and they learned to accept risk as a normal part of life. My own generation is different. Rather than playing outside in the woods, we spent our time playing inside on our computers. Instead of **taking chances** with friends, we were protected from all harm by adults.

[2] And I think we're suffering now because of it. Think about the successful people you know. What do they all have in common? Whether they are musicians, actors, politicians, or people who have succeeded in business or sports, you can be pretty sure that they have all taken risks at key moments in their lives. Perhaps they haven't been **exposed to** physical danger but they've exposed themselves to an even greater risk: the risk of **failure**.

[3] I believe that too many of us have become so afraid of failure that we don't **dare to** take any chances. Instead of looking for opportunities, we look for **security** and safety. But we need to learn to take more risks if we want to get the rewards. It's only through risking failure that we learn what works and what doesn't.

[4] All of us can challenge ourselves by introducing more risk into our lives. Take up a new sport and risk being bad at it in the beginning. Go to your boss with that idea you've been thinking about but were too scared to share before. Take a risk! You never know what might happen.

C VOCABULARY: SAFETY AND RISK Find the words and phrases in bold (1–8) in the article and match them with the definitions (a–h) to complete the sentences.

1	If you **play it safe**, you	a)	involves the possibility of danger, harm, etc.
2	Something that is **risky**	b)	are not protected from it.
3	**Freedom** is	c)	a feeling of safety.
4	If you **take a chance**, you	d)	do it without fear, even though it may be dangerous.
5	If you are **exposed to** something, you	e)	avoid taking any risks.
6	**Failure** is	f)	do something in spite of the risk.
7	If you **dare to** do something, you	g)	the right to do what you want.
8	**Security** is	h)	a lack of success in doing something.

D 🔊 **VOCABULARY: SAFETY AND RISK** Work in pairs and answer the questions.

1 When was the last time you dared to do something new or took a chance? Were you afraid of failure?
2 Do children today have less freedom than in the past? Are they exposed to less danger?
3 How important is a feeling of security to you? Do you like to play it safe or do you like to take part in risky activities?

2 GRAMMAR: expressing ability

A LANGUAGE IN CONTEXT Read the article and comments. To what extent do you agree with each comment?

ENTREPRENEURS AND RISK

What does it take to succeed in setting up and developing a business? Of course, you're good at running your business on a day-to-day level, and no doubt you are able to deal well with clients. But are you capable of evaluating the level of risk? Are entrepreneurs risk-takers, or do they actually avoid risk? I'm interested in your comments.

Steve Field   *August 12, 10:00 a.m.*

Entrepreneurs manage to grow businesses because they ignore the risk of failure. They have a strong belief in themselves and can stick to their vision despite obstacles. When I started out, I could see clearly where I wanted to get to, and that was a big advantage, whatever the risk!

Amy Drinkwater   *August 12, 10:29 a.m.*

It's easy to think entrepreneurs are high risk-takers, but actually the opposite is true! Anyone who ignores risk is incapable of making the right long-term decisions. Without a proper risk assessment, you are unable to tell what kind of return you're likely to get on your investment. The best entrepreneurs collect all the information they can to reduce the risk as much as possible.

> **NOTICE!**
> Underline all the expressions in the text that refer to the ability or inability to do something. How many different expressions can you find?

B ANALYZE Read the text in Exercise A again.

Form Complete the table with the phrases from the box.

> be able   be capable of   be good at   be incapable of   be unable
> can/can't   could/couldn't   (not) manage   (not) succeed in

verb + infinitive	verb + base form	verb + gerund

> **WATCH OUT!**
> ✗ Not everyone will succeed in run their own business.
> ✓ Not everyone will succeed in running their own business.

C PRACTICE Rewrite each sentence with the word in parentheses.

1 Some people are not able to deal with risk. (*incapable*)

_____

2 How did you manage to make the business profitable? (*succeed*)

_____

3 Jeff can't evaluate the acceptable level of risk. (*unable*)

_____

4 In the end, we couldn't accept that level of risk. (*weren't*)

_____

5 Successful entrepreneurs are capable of controlling risk. (*manage*)

_____

D NOW YOU DO IT Work in pairs and answer the questions about how good an entrepreneur you think you would be.

1 What are you good at that would be a useful skill for an entrepreneur?
2 Would you be capable of judging business risks well? Why or why not?
3 What personal qualities do you have that would help you succeed in developing a business?

3 WRITING: requesting action

If you are writing a letter to request action, it should be short and should include only the most important points. The action(s) you want should be stated clearly, possibly in bullet points. The letter should be formal and polite.

A Read the letter and answer the questions.

1 Who has written the letter? What organization does she represent?
2 What problem is the letter trying to solve?
3 What is the purpose of the first paragraph?
4 What is the purpose of the final paragraph?

To the Parks and Recreation Department,

We are writing to call your attention to a potential safety issue in Bowen Park. The park is very popular because of its caves, and most of the caves are shallow and safe for exploration. However, the cave known as Deep Mouth has long tunnels and deep pools of water that put inexperienced explorers at risk. We feel that since those who enter Deep Mouth run the risk of getting lost or injured, the cave should be closed to the public.

We are aware that there is a sign at the entrance of Deep Mouth cave, but unfortunately, many people, particularly teenagers, ignore it and in doing so, risk their lives. Because of this, we request the following action:

- Block the entrance to Deep Mouth cave.
- Carry out a complete risk assessment on Deep Mouth and other caves in the park.
- Require park rangers to stop any high-risk behavior they observe.

We have great confidence in your ability to deal with potential safety hazards in our parks, and we would appreciate your prompt action to reduce the risks to the general public.

Sincerely,

Janet West

Chairperson

Citizens for Safety

B VOCABULARY: EXPRESSIONS WITH *RISK* Find and underline words and phrases in the text that include or are derived from the word *risk*. Then complete the sentences with the words or phrases you underlined. Use the definitions in parentheses to help.

1 If the authorities carried out a _____, the place would be a lot safer. (*analysis of the dangers*)
2 Who is most _____, and why? (*in danger*)
3 Do you think people are actually _____, or is the situation less dangerous than that? (*doing things that may result in death*)
4 What could the authorities do to _____? (*make the situation less dangerous*)
5 If the authorities try to change the situation, do you think they _____ of causing a worse problem? (*face a possible danger*)
6 The only way to prevent _____ behavior is to educate people. (*dangerous*)

C VOCABULARY: EXPRESSIONS WITH *RISK* Work in pairs. Think of a high-risk situation in your local area and ask and answer the questions in Exercise B. Here are some ideas.

- a road where the traffic puts people at risk
- a river or other body of water that isn't safely fenced off
- a playground that poses a risk to children

D Write a letter requesting action about the situation from the proper authority. Use your ideas from Exercise C and phrases from Exercise B.

4 GRAMMAR: past modals of deduction

A 🎧 **2.13** **LANGUAGE IN CONTEXT** Listen to the conversation. Who are they talking about and why do you think he did what he did?

Lili: I've just been reading about Felix Baumgartner, you know, the guy who did the highest skydive ever, from 24 miles up. He reached over 800 miles per hour. That's faster than the speed of sound! You **may have** seen the video of it.

Neil: Yeah, I know who you mean. He **must have** been terrified. I mean, he **can't have** been sure he'd survive diving from that height.

Lili: Exactly! He **couldn't have** known what to expect. In fact, halfway through the dive he started spinning. He **must not have** expected that to happen.

Neil: So what did he do?

Lili: I'm not sure. He **might have** put out his arms and legs, maybe. Or he **could have** used his body weight in some way. Anyway, he got the dive back under control and landed safely.

Neil: His family **must have** been relieved.

Lili: I bet he was, too!

NOTICE!
What form of the verb follows each phrase in bold?

B **ANALYZE** Read the conversation in Exercise A again.

Form Complete the table with the correct modals in bold from the text.

Past modals of deduction: modal + (*not*) *have* + past participle

Strong probability	Moderate probability/improbability		Strong improbability
(1) _____	(2) _____	(4) _____	(5) _____
	may not have		(6) _____
	(3) _____		(7) _____
	might not have		

Function Choose the correct options to complete the explanation.

We use past modals of deduction to **(1)** _____ about the past. This may be based on evidence or on our **(2)** _____. The choice of modal verb depends on whether we think our deduction is moderately probable or **(3)** _____.

1   **a)** draw conclusions   **b)** express regret   **c)** express criticism
2   **a)** hopes   **b)** assumptions   **c)** wishes
3   **a)** undesirable   **b)** very probable   **c)** illogical

WATCH OUT!
✗ She must know what she was doing.
✓ She must have known what she was doing.

C **PRACTICE** Rewrite the sentences with past modals of deduction.

1   Baumgartner almost certainly felt nervous as he waited to jump.

_____

2   I'm sure it wasn't the first time he'd made a very high skydive.

_____

3   It's possible that he made a number of practice jumps first.

_____

4   I'm sure he didn't plan it alone and I expect he had a team of people behind him.

_____

5   It's possible that he didn't know he would break the sound barrier.

_____

6   It's possible that his family didn't want him to make the jump.

_____

D 🗣 **NOW YOU DO IT** Work in pairs. Look at the picture. Use past modals of deduction to talk about what you think happened just before the picture was taken.

5 PRONUNCIATION: reduction of *have*

A »🎧 **2.14** Listen and practice the phrases. Notice that *have* is unstressed and that it joins with the word before it.

Affirmative:
must have gone /mʌstəv gɔn/
might have taken /maitəv 'teikən/
may have been /meijəv bin/
could have given /kʊdəv 'giv(ə)n/

Negative:
must not have gone /mʌst natəv gɔn/
might not have taken /mait natəv 'teikən/
may not have been /mei natəv bin/
couldn't have given /'kʊd(ə)ntəv 'giv(ə)n/

B »🎧 **2.15** Listen and practice the sentences.

1 Baumgartner must have known the risks before he jumped.
2 He may not have known how fast he'd fall.
3 He couldn't have known exactly where he'd land.
4 He must have been very brave to do it.

6 LISTENING: rapid speech

⚙ The difficulty in understanding rapid speech is that people tend to run words together. If you learn some common phrases that run together, your ability to understand rapid speech will improve.

A 🔊 Work in groups. Look at the picture and read the paragraph. Discuss whether you think David Blaine was in real danger.

Magician and endurance artist David Blaine risked electrocution during an amazing stunt, which he named "Electrified: One Million Volts Always On." Blaine managed to spend 72 hours on a 22-foot high pillar, surrounded by huge coils that generated a million volts of electricity. That million volts was aimed at Blaine, who didn't eat or sleep for the duration of the stunt. He wore a metal suit that conducted the electricity away from his body, but even so, doctors found that the stunt had caused him to have an irregular heartbeat.

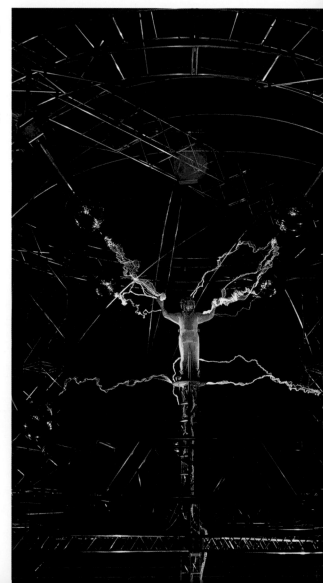

B »🎧 **2.16** Listen to two people talking about David Blaine's stunt. What is Evan's opinion of the stunt? What is Jenna's opinion?

C Listen to the conversation again. Check the phrase in each pair that you hear.

1 a) You could have seen it! ☐
  b) You've got to see it! ☐
2 a) Why, do you think? ☐
  b) What do you think? ☐
3 a) It could have been real. ☐
  b) It couldn't have been real. ☐
4 a) He must have practiced a lot of times. ☐
  b) He missed practice a lot of times. ☐
5 a) I don't know. ☐
  b) I want to know. ☐
6 a) I've got to find some pictures of it. ☐
  b) I'm going to find some pictures of it. ☐
7 a) I don't want to see the picture. ☐
  b) I want to see the picture. ☐
8 a) I've got to go. ☐
  b) I'm going to go. ☐

7 SPEAKING: speculating about events

A  **2.17** Look at the picture and listen to the news report. What speculations do the reporters make about the event?

B Work in groups. Discuss why you think the man did this and what you think happened in the end.

HOW TO SAY IT

I think he must have / could have wanted to …
I guess he managed to / was able to …
He must not have been able to …
I imagine what might have happened was that …

C Read the news story. Were your guesses about what happened correct?

News Features

Larry Walters had always wanted to fly and was willing to risk his life to do it. One day, he bought a lawn chair and 45 weather balloons. He tied the balloons to the chair, filled them with helium, and then strapped himself into the chair. He brought some sandwiches, a drink, and a pellet gun with him. The idea was to float up about 30 feet, enjoy the view, and then shoot a few of the balloons with the pellet gun so that he could return to the ground. But when he cut the cord holding the chair to the ground, the balloons pulled the chair up at a very high speed, quickly reaching an altitude of 16,000 feet! Larry was too scared to shoot any of the balloons with his gun, so he stayed sitting there for 14 hours. Passing airline pilots reported seeing a man in a lawn chair. They may never get over the shock of seeing a man in a chair at 16,000 feet! Finally, Larry overcame his fear and shot a few of the balloons. He descended safely, but was arrested after landing.

When a reporter asked him why he'd done it, Larry replied, "A man can't just sit around." The police were unsure how to deal with Mr. Walters because they didn't know what to charge him with. Police officers have to put up with people doing a lot of risky stunts, but this was definitely one of the craziest!

D Work in pairs. Decide which of the two headlines you will each talk about. Speculate about the news story behind your headline and make notes about what you think may have happened.

DRIVER CHASES RUNAWAY BUS ON BUSY HIGHWAY

BOY WHO SWALLOWED METEORITE LIVES!

E Independent Speaking Work in pairs. Tell your partner what you think happened. When you have both finished talking, check the answers with your teacher.

lifeSkills

MANAGING STRESS

- Recognize the symptoms of and risk factors for stress.
- Consider different ways of relaxing.
- Develop your stress-management strategy.

A Read the article about stress. Do you ever experience stress in your life? What do you think of the advice offered in the article?

COPING WITH STRESS

Some stress is good. It prepares you for action and gives you the adrenaline boost you need for a busy modern lifestyle. However, too much stress can be bad. Have you ever suffered from any of these symptoms?

- low mood
- an inability to relax
- a short temper for no reason
- difficulty concentrating

- unexplained aches and pains
- headaches
- sleeping problems

If so, you could be suffering from stress. Stress can be caused by a number of different factors, including exams, relationship problems, pressure at work, and money problems. It's important to figure out what causes you stress and to develop a strategy for dealing with stress when it happens, such as finding positive ways to relax or communicating with those around you. And for each cause of stress, you need to ask yourself these key questions to develop a strategy that works for you:

- Can I avoid the thing that causes me stress? (*avoid strategy*)
  e.g., *If some aspects of your job cause you stress, can you say "no" to those tasks?*
- Can I change the thing that causes me stress? (*alter strategy*)
  e.g., *If something is causing you stress, be assertive and ask for the change you need.*
- Can I change my reaction to the thing that causes me stress? (*adapt strategy*)
  e.g., *You might be putting yourself under pressure to be perfect. Maybe you need to adjust your standards.*
- Can I learn to live with the thing that causes me stress? (*accept strategy*)
  e.g., *Sometimes we just need to accept that we can't control every aspect of our lives.*

Find the right strategy for each cause of stress and you'll succeed in taking back control of your life and reducing the amount of stress in it.

B What makes you stressed? Look at each of the situations and rate them according to how stressful you find them (1 = not stressful at all, 5 = very stressful).

You have to …	1	2	3	4	5
1 speak in front of a group of people you don't know.	○	○	○	○	○
2 speak to one person you don't know at a party.	○	○	○	○	○
3 take a test at college or at work.	○	○	○	○	○
4 take a long trip on your own.	○	○	○	○	○
5 manage with little money for a while.	○	○	○	○	○
6 find a new place to live.	○	○	○	○	○
7 take care of children or relatives for a day.	○	○	○	○	○
8 complain about something, such as service in a restaurant.	○	○	○	○	○

C Work in pairs and compare your answers. Discuss what causes each of you stress. Are you both stressed by the same things?

D Look at the following ways of relaxing. Under each one, write *I already do this*, *I'd like to try this*, or *I'm not interested in this*. Make a note of any other ways of relaxing that you do regularly.

1 _____

2 _____

3 _____

4 _____

5 _____

6 _____

7 Other: _____

E Choose one cause of stress in your life. Make notes on how you might use different strategies to cope with the stress. Use the example to help you. Then work in pairs and compare your ideas. Which strategy or strategies do you think would be most effective?

Cause of stress: taking exams at college

AVOID strategy

I could change to a course that uses continuous assessment instead of exams.

ALTER strategy

I wonder if I could ask my tutor about taking oral exams, which I find less stressful, rather than written exams.

ADAPT strategy

I could study more and make sure I'm fully prepared for each exam so that I don't worry about it.

ACCEPT strategy

If I tried to see exams as a chance to show what I know, maybe that would help.

REFLECT ... How can the skill of managing stress be useful to you in **Work & Career** and **Study & Learning**?

RESEARCH ...

One technique some people use for managing stress is meditation. Find out what meditation is and how it works. In your next lesson, tell the class what you have learned.

F **Work in groups. Discuss the questions.**

1 What have you learned about managing stress?
2 Do you think you will be able to manage stress better in the future?

Language wrap-up

1 VOCABULARY

Complete the paragraph with words and phrases from the box in the correct form. There may be more than one correct answer. (12 points)

| at risk   dare   exposed   failure   freedom   high-risk   play it safe |
| risk your life   risky   run the risk   security   take a chance |

Walt Disney once said, "I dream, I test my dreams against my beliefs, I **(1)** _____ to take risks, and I execute my vision to make those dreams come true." He recognized that there was no advantage in **(2)** _____. By risking **(3)** _____, he made success possible. He **(4)** _____ on unlikely heroes, such as Mickey Mouse, and it paid off. Each of us has to decide whether to **(5)** _____ of failing or to seek **(6)** _____, even if it means accepting less. For those in business, it can sometimes feel as if you're **(7)** _____, so it's important to remember that it's not exactly a game of life and death—although it's true that your career and livelihood are often **(8)** _____. When you are **(9)** _____ to risk, it can in fact give you a great sense of **(10)** _____, since it can feel like you've got nothing more to lose. It may be this, which means many entrepreneurs engage in **(11)** _____ behavior away from work, such as hot-air ballooning or motor sports. Perhaps these **(12)** _____ activities give them the same excitement they get from their working lives.

10–12 correct: I can use words and phrases to talk about safety and risk.
0–9 correct: Look again at Sections 1 and 3 on pages 118 and 120.   **SCORE:**   /12

2 GRAMMAR

Choose the correct options to complete the newspaper story. Some answers depend on grammatical form and others on meaning. (12 points)

Investigators have been **(1)** *unable / incapable* to determine the cause of the crash of an Inter-City commuter plane last Thursday. The small plane, en route from Boston to New York, did not **(2)** *succeed / manage* to reach the runway, and it crashed into some nearby trees. All 20 people aboard the aircraft were killed. Firefighters **(3)** *succeeded in / were able to* controlling the resulting fires, and no homes were damaged. Fortunately, all of the homeowners **(4)** *could / were able to* get out of their houses with no injuries. Lead investigator Carol Owens said that she wouldn't be able **(5)** *make / to make* a full statement until more facts were known. She did say that the crash **(6)** *may / could* not have been caused by weather because Thursday was clear and calm. She said that it **(7)** *may / must* have been caused by a mechanical failure, but that more information is needed. However, airline officials have stated that they feel strongly that the crash **(8)** *must / couldn't* have been caused by mechanical failure. "Our mechanics are extremely good at **(9)** *keep / keeping* our planes in top condition. We **(10)** *are able / can* say with great confidence that this tragedy was not the result of poor maintenance," said IC spokesman Jim Carr. "It **(11)** *must / might* have been pilot error, but there's no clear evidence of that, or possibly a pilot medical emergency. Whatever the cause was, it **(12)** *may / couldn't* have been easy to control the plane and the pilot did well to avoid loss of life on the ground."

10–12 correct: I can use expressions of ability and past modals of deduction.
0–9 correct: Look again at Sections 2 and 4 on pages 119 and 121.   **SCORE:**   /12

A 🔊 **2.18** 👂 Listen to someone answering the question. Make a note of the main points the speaker makes. Work in pairs and compare your notes.

> Some people find high risk activities, such as mountain climbing or extreme sports relaxing. Others find quieter activities relaxing. Which type of activity do you find most relaxing? Include details and examples in your explanation.

B Listen again for phrases the speaker uses to express her preferences.

1 I _____ do something quiet than …
2 I find quieter activities _____ extreme sports because …
3 The second reason I _____ quieter activities is …
4 Finally, quieter activities appeal _____ because …
5 I _____ to do activities that don't cause me more stress.

C You are going to answer the question in the box in Exercise D. Before you do that, make notes to answer the questions.

1 What examples of high-risk professions can you think of?
_____

2 What examples of professions with less risk can you think of?
_____

3 Which type of profession would you prefer?
_____

4 What is the first reason for your choice?
_____

5 What is the second reason for your choice?
_____

6 What is the third reason for your choice?
_____

D 👥 Answer the question. Talk to your group or to the whole class.

> Some people would like to do a high-risk job, such as being a police officer, and would find it exciting. Others would find it stressful and would prefer a less risky profession. Which type of profession would suit you most? Include details and examples in your explanation.

HOW ARE YOU DOING?

○ I expressed my choice clearly.
○ I used good examples and provided detail in my explanation.
○ I gave three clear reasons for my choice.

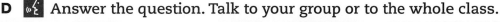

UNIT 11 THROUGH THE LENS

IN THIS UNIT YOU

- learn language to talk about pictures and make comparisons
- read about selfies
- talk about the similarities and differences between two pictures
- listen to a podcast about photography
- write a memo about pictures of staff members
- learn about giving and receiving feedback
- ▶ watch a video about how photography can help change people's perception of a country

READING
understanding text organization

Different sentences have different functions. What functions can you think of, e.g., *providing an example?*

SPEAKING
making comparisons

What words, phrases, or grammar do you know that we use for comparing one thing to another, e.g., *comparative adjectives?*

LIFE SKILLS

WORK & CAREER

giving and receiving feedback
Who do you receive feedback from in your everyday life? Do you find it a positive experience? Why or why not?

A Work in pairs. Look at these images of people taking pictures. Check the situations you have taken pictures in. Say what kind of pictures you like to take and why.

B Work in pairs. Say how much you agree or disagree with the statements. Explain why.

"I can't stand having my picture taken."
"I prefer pictures of people to pictures of beautiful scenery."

1 GRAMMAR: verb + gerund/infinitive with a change in meaning

A LANGUAGE IN CONTEXT Read what this person says about an old family picture. Summarize the speaker's response to the picture in your own words.

Oh, I remember being in this picture! That was so long ago! My dad made us try to look natural, but we couldn't do it. Oh, look at that hair! I regret having that style now. What was I thinking? And those clothes! So old-fashioned! Everyone stopped wearing those years ago! What an embarrassing picture! Still, I'll never forget laughing and having fun with my family when we took it. We're all grown up now and living busy lives, but it's good to stop to think about those days sometimes. Remember to treasure every moment with your family because time goes by so fast!

NOTICE!
Underline all the gerunds (*–ing*) and infinitives (*to* + verb) in the text. Which verbs do they follow?

B ANALYZE Read the text in Exercise A again.

Form Complete the table with examples from the text.

verb	+ gerund	+ infinitive
forget	(forget that you have done sth.; have no memory of sth.) (1) _____	(forget that you need to do sth.) *Don't forget to show him the picture.*
regret	(regret that you have done sth.) (2) _____	(apologize for bad news) *We regret to inform you that your pictures have been deleted.*
remember	(remember that you have done sth.; have a memory of sth.) (3) _____	(remember that you need to do sth.) (4) _____
stop	(stop an action/habit) (5) _____	(stop in order to do sth. else) (6) _____
try	(do sth. to see what result it will have) *Try cleaning the lens.*	(in the past = attempt sth. without success; in the present/future = attempt sth. you may/may not be able to do) (7) _____

Function Write *gerund* or *infinitive*.

1 not remember something you have to do: *forget* + _____
  not have a memory of something: *forget* + _____
2 feel bad about something you have to tell someone: *regret* + _____
  wish you hadn't done something in the past: *regret* + _____
3 have a memory of something: *remember* + _____
  not forget something you have to do: *remember* + _____
4 stop an action or habit: *stop* + _____
  stop so that you can then do something else: *stop* + _____
5 attempt something you may or may not be able to do: *try* + _____
  do something to see what result it will have: *try* + _____

WATCH OUT!
✗ I really regret to wear that outfit!
✓ I really regret wearing that outfit!

C PRACTICE Write each verb in the correct form.

1 Have you ever taken a picture you regretted _____ (*take*)? What happened?
2 Do you remember ever _____ (*have*) a family picture taken? Who was there? How did you feel?
3 Do you agree with the writer that we should stop _____ (*think*) about our family history sometimes? Do you ever look at family pictures and do that?
4 Do you ever try _____ (*avoid*) having your picture taken? When? Why?

D 🎤 **NOW YOU DO IT** Work in pairs. Ask and answer the questions in Exercise C. Use as many of these verbs as you can: *forget, regret, remember, stop, try.*

2 LISTENING: to a podcast

A 🎙️ You are going to listen to a podcast. Work in pairs. Look at the pictures and say what you think the podcast might be about.

B 🎧 **2.19** Listen to the podcast. As you listen, write a word or short phrase you hear in each blank.

1 Jackson went to an exhibition of work by _____.

2 Penny says we often assume pictures only appear on _____ these days.

3 Jackson was most _____ by Judy Anderson's picture of a local homeless man.

4 Nothing takes _____ from the man and his expression.

5 The picture is also a comment on the area's recent _____.

C VOCABULARY: DESCRIBING PICTURES Listen to the podcast again. As you listen, label the pictures with the words from the box. One of the words can be used more than once.

| background   focus   foreground   landscape   portrait   side   subject |

1 a _____

2 in the _____

3 out of _____ (*opposite*: in focus)

4 the _____ of the picture

5 a _____

6 on the left-hand _____

7 on the right-hand _____

8 in the _____

D 🎙️ **VOCABULARY: DESCRIBING PICTURES** Work in pairs. Choose one of the pictures in Exercise C and describe it to your partner. Say what you like or don't like about it. Then swap and listen to your partner describe the other picture.

3 SPEAKING: making comparisons

We may be in a situation where we need to make a choice between two or more things. By comparing and contrasting, we can judge the things against each other and make a better decision.

A Work in pairs. Look at the pictures. Make notes on what the pictures have in common and what the differences are between them.

Things the pictures have in common
both are pictures of groups of people

_____
_____
_____
_____

Things that are different between the pictures
the first shows a family, the second shows a group of friends

_____
_____
_____
_____

B 2.20 Listen to two people comparing the two pictures in order to choose one to illustrate an article. Check the points they make against the notes you made in Exercise A. Make a note of any points they mention that you didn't.

C VOCABULARY: MAKING COMPARISONS Listen again and complete the sentences with a word or phrase from the box. Two words can be used in one of the blanks.

| alike   in contrast   in that   point of difference   similarity   unlike   whereas   while |

1 Both pictures are _____ because they're both pictures of groups of people.
2 The first is a family portrait and looks like it's been taken by a professional, _____ the second shows someone taking a selfie with their friends.
3 Another _____ is that the people are posing and smiling in both pictures.
4 However, maybe the first situation is a little formal for my article, _____ the second situation is much more informal.
5 Another _____ is the reason they're having their picture taken.
6 _____, the second group wants a picture they can send to friends or put online to show people what a good time they're having.
7 Both pictures are similar _____ the people want to record this moment in their lives, but the second one is more modern.
8 It'll appeal to younger people, _____ the first one.

D VOCABULARY: MAKING COMPARISONS Work in pairs. Take turns choosing one of these sets of pictures and comparing them.

A LANGUAGE IN CONTEXT Read the opinions. Who do you most agree with?

THE GREAT DEBATE

Home   Archive   About us   Links

Here at The Great Debate, we invite two people to comment on a current issue and then invite you to join the debate! This week, the topic is "edited pictures" and joining us are fashion photographer Shannon Atkins and mental-health campaigner Connor Rourke. Add your comments below.

Shannon Atkins

The vast majority of images we see every day are edited in some way **because of** the demands placed on photographers by the clients. They want their product to be presented in the best way, whether it's a new clothing line, a new perfume, or a new car, so people want to go out and buy it. **Moreover**, consumers themselves want edited pictures. Who wants to see celebrities with pimples and a few extra pounds? I edit the unattractive aspects out of my fashion images **due to** the expectations of both clients and consumers, and I'm not ashamed of that. **Besides that**, I think my job is to give people images to aspire to, to show them a perfect ideal to aim for. Most people don't want reality. They want dreams.

Connor Rourke

I'm very concerned about the number of pictures we see these days that have been edited. We are surrounded by images that have been altered to make the subject seem more attractive. **As a result of** this heavy editing, these images present an unrealistic idea of beauty. **Furthermore**, they imply that we ordinary people with our ordinary lives and ordinary bodies are inadequate. **As a consequence**, young people, in particular, feel like failures because they will never match the ideal. This can lead to very low self-esteem. **In addition to** these problems, these images can also make us unhappy with our partners, the people around us, and the lives we lead.

NOTICE!
Which of the words in bold have similar meanings?

B ANALYZE Read the opinions in Exercise A again.

Form Complete the table with the words and phrases in bold from the text.

connectors of addition	connectors of cause and effect
and, also, _____, _____, _____, _____	because, _____, _____, _____, _____, _____, therefore

Function Choose the correct options to complete the rules.

1 Connectors of *addition / cause and effect* are used to add further points or to provide more information in support of a point.
2 Connectors of *addition / cause and effect* are used to show how one thing makes another happen, or how one thought follows logically from another.

WATCH OUT!

✗ She looked perfect in the photo but it was all because heavy editing.

✓ She looked perfect in the photo but it was all because of heavy editing.

C PRACTICE Rewrite each pair of sentences as one sentence with the words and phrases given. You may need to add other words as well.

Many people cannot live up to the ideal they see in images. They get depressed.

1 (because of, fact) _____
2 (result, not being able) _____

Models are made to appear more beautiful. They are often also made to appear thinner.

3 (and, besides) _____
4 (and, furthermore) _____

D 🎧 NOW YOU DO IT Work in pairs. Discuss the questions. Use connectors of addition and of cause and effect to explain your opinion.

1 Are images around us edited too much? Give reasons for your opinion.
2 What do you think the expression "the camera never lies" means? Do you agree? Why or why not?

In a well-organized text, different sentences have different functions. Some sentences introduce a new topic, some give additional information or supporting details, and some argue for or against an idea. Recognizing the function of sentences improves your understanding of the text.

A Read the article. Do you agree with the writer's views on selfies? Explain why or why not.

The selfie ◉

selfie, early 20th century

selfie, early 21st century

¹ The selfie has become the defining document of the modern age. In the world of social networking, no event, whether life changing or mundane, can truly be said to have happened unless the participants have taken a photograph of themselves doing it.

² Selfies are visual diary entries, offered to the world as evidence that you were in a certain place at a certain time. ª They are also, in some ways, a perfect reflection of the digital age, being usually pointless and ephemeral. ᵇ No one treasures someone else's selfie.

³ The selfie is the modern postcard. It says: "I am here"; it possibly also says: "Wish you were here"; it frequently says: "Don't you wish you were here? Because then your life would be as glamorous/popular as mine."

⁴ The selfie feels new, but people have been taking photographs of themselves since the invention of the camera. ᶜ The first documented case of a teenager taking a selfie was in 1914, when Russia's Grand Duchess Anastasia Nikolaevna, then aged 13, took her own photograph using a Kodak Brownie and sent it to a friend with a letter that read: "I took this picture of myself looking at the mirror. It was very hard as my hands were trembling." The instant self-portrait, instantly self-published, is one of the fastest-growing internet phenomena. ᵈ According to a survey, two-thirds of Australian women aged 18–35 take selfies, which are usually then posted on Facebook. According to another, nearly a third of all photographs taken by people age between 18 and 24 are selfies.

⁵ So what does it say about us, this need to picture ourselves to others, however briefly, however little the rest of the world cares? Inevitably, some sociologists are worried (as sociologists usually are). Some link the selfie-craze to an obsession with looks and the objectification of the body.

⁶ This is, of course, ridiculous. ᵉ Human beings have been picturing themselves, trying to hone their self-images, and showing off to their friends for centuries. The citizens of Pompeii had their portraits painted on their walls, the Roman equivalent of Facebook, to impress the neighbors. The Victorian selfie was the studio portrait, a ritual requirement of middle-class life. The growth of photography brought a boom in self-photography, but the relationship between sitter and picture was always interrupted by a mirror: today's technology enables photographic self-portraits in which the camera is invisible.

⁷ Today we picture ourselves faster, more frequently, and with greater self-irony, but the selfie says what the self-portrait has always said: this is me, in my world, with the background and friends that define me.

B Read the article again. Match each underlined sentence (a–e) with the correct function (1–5).

This sentence …

1 summarizes what comes before it. _____
2 presents a further explanation of an important idea. _____
3 provides evidence against a point of view mentioned. _____
4 provides evidence in support of a claim. _____
5 gives a specific example of something mentioned. _____

C Choose the correct options to complete the sentences.

1 The writer says that people take selfies …
a) because diaries and postcards are old-fashioned.
b) because other people want to see what they are doing.
c) as a way of proving that they really did something.

2 According to the writer, the selfie …
a) is more popular than ever before.
b) is mainly popular in Australia.
c) is only popular among young people.

3 The writer thinks that sociologists …
a) are right to be worried about selfies.
b) are obsessed with appearances.
c) worry too much about this kind of thing.

D 🔊 Work in pairs and answer the questions.

1 Do you ever take selfies? If so, why and in which types of situations?
2 Why are selfies more popular now than ever before?
3 Are there situations where it's not appropriate to take selfies? Where would you not take a selfie?

6 PRONUNCIATION: stress timing

A 🔊 **2.21** Listen to the quotations about photography. Notice how the underlined stressed syllables fall in a regular rhythm and how the syllables between are said very quickly.

"You <u>don't</u> make a <u>photo</u>graph just with a <u>camera</u>. You <u>bring</u> to the act of photo<u>graphy</u> all the <u>pictures</u> you have <u>seen</u>, the <u>books</u> you have <u>read,</u> the <u>music</u> you have <u>heard</u>, the <u>people</u> you have <u>loved</u>."
Ansel Adams, American photographer (1902–1984)

"You can <u>look</u> at a <u>picture</u> for a <u>week</u> and never <u>think</u> of it a<u>gain</u>. You can <u>also</u> look at a <u>picture</u> for a <u>second</u> and <u>think</u> of it <u>all</u> your <u>life</u>."
Joan Miró, Catalan Spanish artist (1893–1983)

B 🔊 **2.22** 🔊 Work in pairs. Practice saying the quotations using a regular rhythm like the examples above. Listen and check your answers.

"What I <u>like</u> about <u>photo</u>graphs is that they <u>capture</u> a <u>moment</u> that's gone for<u>ever</u>, im<u>poss</u>ible to repro<u>duce</u>."
Karl Lagerfeld, German fashion designer, artist and photographer (1933–)

"The <u>camera</u> is an <u>in</u>strument that <u>teaches</u> people how to see with<u>out</u> a camera."
Dorothea Lange, American photographer (1895–1965)

7 WRITING: a memo

A 🔊 **2.23** Your manager needs new images from staff members for the company website. Listen to the phone message and make a note of what the manager tells you.

B Write a memo in the form of an email to staff members based on the notes you have made. Start by completing the details.

● ● ●   Memo

To: All staff members
From: _____
Subject: _____

A memo is a short letter or email that is sent to people in an organization. It is often used to pass on information or report on meetings. A memo should be direct and clear and use a neutral tone.

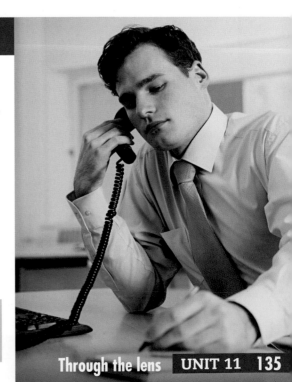

Through the lens | **UNIT 11** | **135**

lifeSkills

GIVING AND RECEIVING FEEDBACK

Giving feedback
- Start by making at least a couple of positive comments.
- Give the other person a chance to respond.
- Use friendly language and positive body language.

Receiving feedback
- Listen with an open mind.
- Ask questions to fully understand the feedback.
- Stay calm and consider the validity of any criticism.

A 🎧 **2.24** Listen to the feedback session. Do you think Mrs. Vaughan gives feedback well? Does Paul receive the feedback well? Explain what they do well or badly.

B 🗣 Work in groups. You work as a member of a team in a public relations company. Read the email from your manager and discuss the questions.

1 What two elements need to be included in the campaign?
2 What steps does your manager want you to take?

From: JPatel@mastermail.mac.wd

Subject: Local tourism campaign

Hello, everybody,

As you probably know, the number of tourists visiting our local area has been falling in recent years. It's not clear whether this is due to increasing prices or other factors. However, the local government is eager to reverse this trend, so they've approached us for ideas.

We need to design a whole campaign, and it needs to be visual. We need to really use the beauty of the local area in images for ads, both in the traditional media and online, and we need to come up with some good slogans for the campaign. Think of as many ways of promoting the area as you can, and I'm sure we'll come up with something powerful between us.

Work with your own team first to come up with good ideas. Then I want you to present your ideas to another team and listen to their constructive feedback. That will guide you in improving your ideas.

I'd like to see what you've come up with in a few days. I'll contact you to arrange a meeting.

Regards,
J. Patel
Project Manager

NEW FRIENDS
NEW ADVENTURES
NEW ZEALAND

C Work in groups and discuss the ideas. Say what you like or dislike about them and decide which ones you might be able to use in your campaign. Make a note of any other ideas.

- organize a competition for pictures taken of the area by local people and use the best ones
- hire a professional photographer to take pictures of local sights
- create social media pages with lots of images of different kinds
- survey local people to see what they think
- make a short professional movie about the area to go online
- use local people to make a short movie
- create a poster campaign with an interesting slogan

D Using ideas from your discussion, and other ideas of your own, plan your local tourism campaign. Make notes below. Give as much detail as you can.

Key features of the campaign

E Work with another group. Group A, describe your campaign to Group B. Explain how you think it will boost local tourism. Group B, listen and make notes. Then give Group B feedback on their ideas. Follow the steps below. Finally swap roles.

1 Comment on what you liked about the other group's ideas.
2 Comment on any problems you can see with the other group's ideas. Allow the other group to respond.
3 Try to suggest ways to improve the ideas.

F Work in groups and improve your ideas. Take into account the feedback you received. Then present your ideas to the whole class.

G Work in groups. Discuss the questions.

1 What did you learn about giving and receiving feedback?
2 How well do you usually respond to feedback? Do you think what you've learned will change your reaction in the future? Why or why not?

HOW TO SAY IT

We thought … was a really good idea. In addition, we liked …

Can you tell us why you decided to …?

Have you thought about …? Also, …

Do you think … might be better?

I see your point, and I could change things so that …

Yes, I understand, but the reason I did that was …

REFLECT … How can the skill of giving and receiving feedback be useful to you in **Self & Society** and **Study & Learning**?

RESEARCH …

Find out about performance reviews. What are they and how do people feel about them? What kind of questions do you need to be prepared for?

Language wrap-up

1 VOCABULARY

Choose the correct options to complete the sentences. (12 points)

1 I can't tell what's in the background because it's *out of / off* focus.
2 One *similar / similarity* between the pictures is that they were both taken in exotic locations.
3 I'm a big fan of *portrait / landscape* pictures of mountains, lakes, and beautiful sunsets.
4 This picture carries a lot of emotion, *alike / unlike* this one, which is very cold.
5 One *mark / point* of difference between the pictures is the time of day they were taken.
6 I just bought a wonderful *portrait / landscape* of an old man, and you can really see what he's thinking.
7 The *subject / object* of the picture is a young girl playing with her pet dog.
8 The two pictures are similar *from / in* that they both show problems within families.
9 *In / By* contrast to the first picture, the second picture shows people enjoying their free time.
10 On the left-hand *part / side* of the picture there's a sign, but I can't read what it says.
11 I'm planning to study photography, *whereas / otherwise* my brother is going to study law.
12 In the *background / foreground*, close to the camera, there's a young child.

> **10–12 correct:** I can describe pictures and make comparisons.
> **0–9 correct:** Look again at Sections 2 and 3 on pages 131 and 132.　　**SCORE:**　　**/12**

2 GRAMMAR

A Complete each sentence with the verb in parentheses in the correct form. (6 points)

1 I'll never forget _____ (*take*) my grandfather's picture for the last time.
2 I tried _____ (*get*) my old camera to work, but I couldn't figure out how.
3 As we walked along the bridge, James stopped _____ (*take*) a picture.
4 Don't forget _____ (*send*) a picture with your passport application.
5 I'll always regret _____ (*get*) rid of our old family picture albums.
6 I wish people would stop _____ (*take*) selfies all the time!

B Complete the paragraph with the phrases from the box. There may be more than one answer. (6 points)

> as a consequence　　as a result　　because of　　besides that　　due to　　in addition to

Henri Cartier-Bresson's pictures demonstrate that he truly was the father of street photography. **(1)** _____ of his work, street photography with a 35 mm camera became the standard of photojournalism. This is **(2)** _____ the fact that he showed that great art could be produced by capturing "the decisive moment." This is when the photographer is looking at a scene and, **(3)** _____ the way the elements come together perfectly, they feel they must take a picture. **(4)** _____, the phrase "the decisive moment" has entered the vocabulary of all photographers. **(5)** _____ popularizing this phrase, he also showed that it is possible to find great beauty in ordinary life. **(6)** _____, he brought out the beauty of the city he loved—Paris.

> **10–12 correct:** I can use verbs + gerund/infinitive with a change in meaning. I can use connectors of addition and cause and effect.
> **0–9 correct:** Look again at Sections 1 and 4 on pages 130 and 133.　　**SCORE:**　　**/12**

WRITING WORKSHOP

A Read the report. What problems does the writer identify? What recommendations does she make?

To: Mr. Delaney   **Subject:** The company website
From: Maria Agosti

Introduction
As requested, I have carried out a review of the company website. In particular, I was asked to consider the images on the website. My findings and recommendations appear below.

Overall design
The website was redesigned five years ago. As a consequence, it is badly in need of an update. Visitors to the website are able to read about our products and can order them online. However, right now they are not able to share what they find with their friends on social networks. In contrast, our competitors have much more up-to-date sites in that they are well connected to social networks.

Company image
The current images on the website are very formal and professional. They mostly consist of pictures of staff members at work or in a professional studio. This gives the website a formal feel, and as a result of this, it isn't very attractive to our young customers, who would react better to a more modern company image.

Suggestions for improvement
In terms of overall design, we need to modernize the website. One key part of that is having better links to social media. In addition to that, it's essential that we update the staff pictures. I suggest we ask all staff to provide informal selfies, which would make the company image far more fun and modern.

B Read the report again and answer the questions.

1 How does the writer clearly show what this is and who it is for?
2 How does the writer clearly show which particular topic she is discussing?
3 Why is it important in this kind of report to show clearly who it is for and what topics are being covered?
4 How formal is the report? Why?

C You are going to write a similar report. Before you write the report, read the instructions and make notes to answer the questions.

> You work in your local tourism office. Your manager has asked you to write a report about tourism in your area and how it might be improved. Identify any areas that need improvement and make suggestions.

1 Complete the opening of your report:
   To: _____
   From: _____
   Subject: _____
2 What two problem areas could you talk about? What problems are you going to identify?
   _____
   _____
3 What suggestions are you going to make to address those problems?
   _____
   _____

HOW ARE YOU DOING?

○ I have used an appropriate format for a report.

○ I have used an appropriate tone.

○ I have identified areas for improvement and made suggestions.

D Use your notes to write a report of about 200 words in response to the instructions in Exercise C.

UNIT 12 BRIGHT LIGHTS, BIG CITY

IN THIS UNIT YOU

- learn language to talk about cities and city life
- listen to people discuss tourist sites
- write a letter of complaint about a city tour
- read an extract from a guidebook about Fez, Morocco
- talk about cities of the future
- learn about plagiarism
- ▶ watch a video about life in Belfast, Northern Ireland

LISTENING
rapid speech

How easy is it to understand native English speakers? What kinds of things cause difficulties for you? Do you have any techniques that help you?

WRITING
a letter of complaint

When you write a letter or email of complaint about a product or service, what information do you think you should include?

LIFE SKILLS

STUDY & LEARNING

recognizing and avoiding plagiarism
What is plagiarism and why is it important to understand what it is?

A Read the list and check the criteria you think are important in defining a "great" city. If there are other things that you think are essential to a great city, add them to the list.

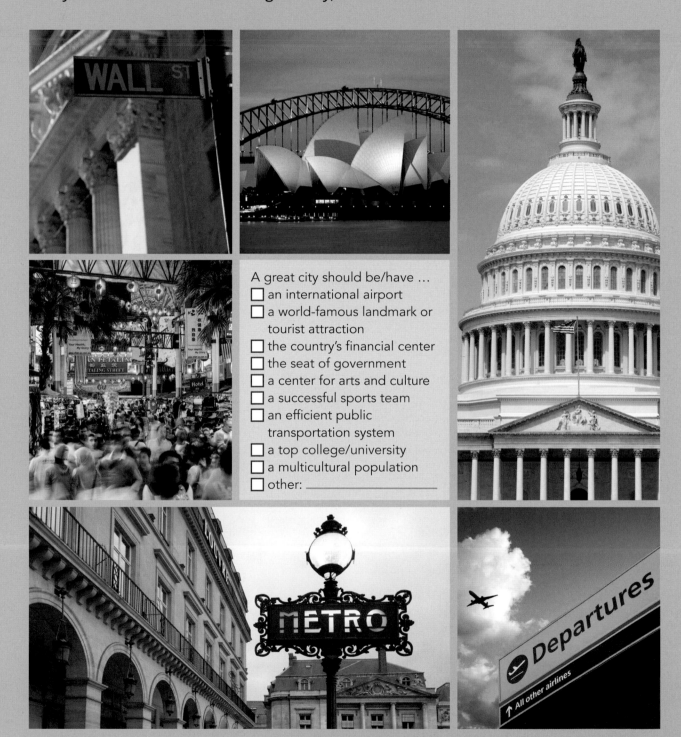

A great city should be/have …
- [ ] an international airport
- [ ] a world-famous landmark or tourist attraction
- [ ] the country's financial center
- [ ] the seat of government
- [ ] a center for arts and culture
- [ ] a successful sports team
- [ ] an efficient public transportation system
- [ ] a top college/university
- [ ] a multicultural population
- [ ] other: _____

B Work in groups. Think about the most important city in your country. Is it the capital city? According to the criteria you chose in Exercise A, would you define it as a great city? Why or why not?

OK, our most important city is the capital. It has an international airport, but the transportation system isn't that great because it doesn't have a subway …

1 GRAMMAR: connectors of contrast

A LANGUAGE IN CONTEXT Look at the picture. Can you guess which country and city the writer is visiting? Read the extract from a travel blog post to check your answer.

It was a long trip, but I'm feeling OK <u>despite</u> the long flight! The weather is beautiful even though spring is just beginning. Today, I walked around the city and took pictures of the jacaranda trees with their beautiful purple flowers. Although Pretoria is full of jacarandas, the trees are not native to South Africa. Just two jacarandas were imported from Rio de Janeiro in 1888; however, later many more trees were planted along Pretoria's streets. They are gorgeous; nevertheless, they are a non-native species and some ecologists want to get rid of them. In spite of the fact that the trees are an invasive species, I find myself hoping that they are allowed to stay to add their beauty to this attractive city.

NOTICE!
Look at the underlined word. What two ideas are being contrasted in this sentence?

B ANALYZE Read the extract in Exercise A again.

Function Answer the question in your own words.

What do we use words like *but*, *nevertheless*, and *despite* for? _____

Form Complete the table with connectors from the text. Then answer the questions below.

Position	Example
beginning of second clause, after a comma	*It was a long trip,* **(1)** _____ *I'm feeling OK …*
beginning of second clause, after a period or semicolon; comma after the connector	*… Rio de Janeiro in 1888;* **(2)** _____, *later many more trees were planted …* *They are gorgeous;* **(3)** _____, *they are a non-native species …*
beginning of first clause, clause is followed by a comma / beginning of second clause, no comma	**(4)** _____ *Pretoria is full of jacarandas, the trees are not native …* *The weather is beautiful* **(5)** _____ *spring is just beginning.*
beginning of first or second clause, followed by a gerund phrase, noun phrase, or *the fact that*	*In spite of / Despite having to work, I'm having a great time.* *… I'm feeling OK* **(6)** _____ *the long flight.* **(7)** _____ *the trees are an invasive species, I find …*

8 Which connectors can go at the beginning of the first or the second clause or phrase?
9 Which connectors have to go at the beginning of the second clause or phrase?

C PRACTICE Choose the correct options to complete the sentences.

1 *In spite of / However* the tourist crowds, Rio de Janeiro is an amazing city.
2 San Francisco is one of the world's top cities *even though / despite* it can be very windy!
3 *But / Although* Diane lives in Sydney, she's never been to the Opera House.
4 Travel abroad is expensive. *Nevertheless, / Despite,* you can find some bargains online.
5 Personally, I couldn't live in a city, *however / but* I know it must be exciting.
6 My favorite city has to be Delhi, *in spite of / in spite of the fact that* it can be really chaotic!
7 *Despite / Nevertheless* hating the cold, I loved Stockholm.
8 *But / Even though* Alberto speaks Catalan, he's never visited Barcelona.

WATCH OUT!
✗ In spite we got really lost, we had an amazing day.
✓ In spite of the fact that we got really lost, we had an amazing day.
✓ In spite of getting really lost, we had an amazing day.

D 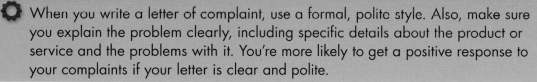 **NOW YOU DO IT** Work in pairs. Tell your partner about a popular city or landmark that you've visited, but don't say the name of the place. Your partner will try to guess the place. Use connectors from the table in Exercise B to express contrasting ideas.

I visited … in …, but …　　　　　　*It was …; however, …*
In spite of the fact that …, …　　　*Although it's a popular place/landmark, …*

2 WRITING: a letter of complaint

When you write a letter of complaint, use a formal, polite style. Also, make sure you explain the problem clearly, including specific details about the product or service and the problems with it. You're more likely to get a positive response to your complaints if your letter is clear and polite.

A Read the letter of complaint about a city tour. Underline four complaints. Then underline the writer's request.

Dear Sir/Madam:

I am writing concerning a city tour that I took with your company on July 12 this year. My wife and I booked the tour because we thought the price was reasonable and because it included some of the landmarks of Bangkok that we wanted to see. However, we were very disappointed with it for a number of reasons.

First of all, it lasted only three hours despite being advertised as a five-hour tour, and we didn't visit Wat Pho or the Grand Palace even though these were included on the itinerary. Furthermore, they gave us only 30 minutes at The Golden Mount, but the itinerary said we would have an hour there. Finally, although the tour guide said he spoke good English, he wasn't easy to understand.

For these reasons, I request a refund for the cost of the tour. I enclose the tickets and a copy of my receipt for $88 as proof of payment.

I look forward to hearing from you.

Sincerely,

James Thompson

B Read the letter again. What is the writer's purpose in each of the three main paragraphs? What specific details does he include in each paragraph?

C **VOCABULARY: FORMAL LETTERS** Write the words or phrases the writer uses to do the following.

1 open his letter _____
2 say why he is writing _____
3 say that he didn't like the tour _____

4 list his main complaints _____
   _____ _____
5 ask the person to reply _____
6 close his letter _____

D 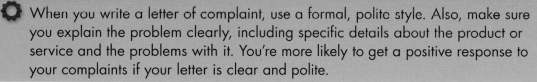 **VOCABULARY: FORMAL LETTERS** Work in pairs. Make a list of things that could go wrong on a tour of your city. Then write a formal letter of complaint to a tour company saying what you were unhappy about and what you want the tour company to do.

E 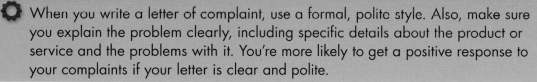 Now work with another pair. Read their letter and make suggestions for possible ways to improve the following things:

Content	Language		
organization of paragraphs	grammar	vocabulary	use of formal language
details	spelling	punctuation	use of connectors

3 READING: a guidebook

A Work in pairs. Have you ever been to Fez, Morocco? If not, say what you imagine it to be like. Then read the guidebook to see if your ideas were correct. If you have been there, read the guidebook and say whether it describes Fez as you know it.

Fez, founded around 790 A.D., is located in the geographical **heart** of Morocco and is also considered by many to be the cultural heart of the country. The main attraction in this ancient **settlement** is the medieval medina, the old **village** at the center of the city. It has been inhabited since the 10th century and still bustles with crowds of people involved in everything from the spice **trade** to selling street food. The medina of Fez is an important archeological **site** and is the most complete medieval town still in existence. In fact, it is a UNESCO World **Heritage** site. The Fez medina forms a working model of daily life from when civilization was still young.

A guided tour is the easiest way to tackle Fez, but the brave can take on the narrow **alleys**, risking getting lost and having to haggle with a local to be guided back out. The noise of buying and selling is often interrupted by the cries of mule drivers pushing heavy carts that warn shoppers to get out of the way. The most stunning **views** over the ancient walled city are from the ruined Merenid tombs on a hilltop. From here, it is possible to see some of the magnificent palaces, green-roofed holy places, and the Karaouine Mosque. Fez is secretive and shadowy, but captivating and colorful at the same time. It is an important part of world heritage as well as of the national heritage of Morocco.

B VOCABULARY: DESCRIBING PLACES Write the nouns in bold from Exercise A that mean the same as the following.

1 the things you can see from a particular place: _____
2 the art, buildings, or traditions that are important to a country and its history: _____
3 the central part of something: _____
4 a place where something interesting happened; an important building or other construction: _____
5 the activity of buying and selling things: _____
6 a very small town: _____
7 a place where people have come to live: _____
8 small passages between buildings: _____

C VOCABULARY: DESCRIBING PLACES Complete the noun collocations (1–8) with words from Exercise B. Look back at the text in Exercise A to check. In some cases, there is more than one option.

1 old–historic–tiny _____
2 coastal–mountain–ancient _____
3 narrow–dark–old _____
4 religious–mystical–archeological _____
5 waterfront–rooftop–stunning _____
6 religious–cultural–national–world _____
7 spice–gold–cloth _____
8 cultural–commercial–geographical _____

D Work in groups. Take turns describing a city you know for your group to guess. Use words and phrases from Exercise C where possible.

A: *This is an ancient city on an island near here.*
B: *Is it …?*
A: *No. It's a coastal city, and it has an important archeological site.*

It's not necessary to understand every single word in a conversation, or even every sentence, so don't panic when you hear a word or several words that you don't recognize. Focus on what you do understand.

A Look at the pictures. Where do you think each one was taken?

B ✎ **2.25** Listen and match the extracts from a guided tour with the pictures. Listen for key details and ignore anything that is too fast to understand.

Extract 1: ___

Extract 2: ___

Extract 3: ___

Extract 4: ___

C ✎ **2.26** Listen to the guided tour again, this time with comments from participants. Ignore anything you don't understand. Then choose T (true) or F (false).

1	The man and the woman agree that the houses look very similar to houses in England.	T / F
2	The woman thinks the downtown area may be dangerous.	T / F
3	The guide says they have to be careful, even during the day.	T / F
4	The guide wants the tourists to eat Chinese food.	T / F
5	All of the residents in the Mission District are from Mexico.	T / F
6	The guide says the city isn't very international.	T / F

D ✎ Work in pairs. Listen to the conversation again. Then discuss what you understood and what you didn't understand. Did you understand the main topics and ideas?

5 GRAMMAR: ways of talking about the future

A LANGUAGE IN CONTEXT Read about a city of the future. Would you like to live in a city like this? Why or why not?

CITY OF THE FUTURE
—MASDAR CITY, ABU DHABI

Thousands of people in Abu Dhabi in the U.A.E. (United Arab Emirates) are moving to a new city soon. The government has started building a carbon-neutral city, and on completion in 2025, it will have approximately 50,000 residents. The city is going to function entirely on solar, wind, and hydrogen power. There won't be any gasoline-powered cars in Masdar; people will travel on electric trains. Some people might also have small electric cars that run on tracks. Several countries are starting to build eco-cities or communities, and some will be finishing them in the last years of this decade, but Masdar City may be the first completely carbon-neutral city.

B ANALYZE Read the text in Exercise A again.

Function Complete the rules with the words from the box. Then complete the examples with words from the text.

> future progressive   going to   ~~may, might, or will~~   present progressive

Function	Example
Use **(1)** <u>may, might, or will</u> to make predictions about the future.	… it **(5)** _____ approximately 50,000 residents. Masdar City **(6)** _____ the first completely carbon-neutral city.
Use **(2)** _____ to make predictions about the future and to talk about intentions.	The city **(7)** _____ function entirely on solar, wind, and hydrogen power.
Use **(3)** _____ to talk about fixed arrangements and plans.	Thousands of people in the U.A.E. **(8)** _____ to a new city soon.
Use **(4)** _____ to talk about events in progress at a particular time in the future.	… some **(9)** _____ them in the last years of this decade.

> The future progressive is formed: *will/won't/may/might + be + –ing form*
> It can be used with (*by*) *this time tomorrow / next week,* etc., and *when.*
> *By this time next year, we may be living in Masdar City.*
> *I will be waiting for you when you arrive in Abu Dhabi.*

NOTICE!

Look back at the text and underline all of the verb forms that are used to refer to the future. Which form can be used for either the present or the future?

WATCH OUT!

✓ This time tomorrow, I'll be flying to Rome.
✗ This time tomorrow, I'll fly to Rome.

C PRACTICE Choose the correct options to complete the sentences.

1 By July, *I'm working / I will be working* in the new office downtown.
2 *I'm going / I'll go* on vacation on Friday. Can you drive me to the airport, please?
3 I think Tom *will visit / is visiting* Dan when he's in New York.
4 This time next month, we *are getting ready / will be getting ready* to move to Perth.
5 I *might be working / might work* when you call, so wait for me to answer.
6 Heather *will fly / is flying* to Berlin on Monday.
7 The new city *will look / will be looking* very impressive.
8 By this time tomorrow, *I'll drive / I'll be driving* down to Buenos Aires.

D  **NOW YOU DO IT** Work in pairs. Think of predictions, plans, and intentions for your life at the points in the future listed below. Use different future forms to tell a partner about them.

- this time tomorrow
- next week
- by next summer
- in about two years
- ten years from now
- when you're 50

A: *This time tomorrow, I'll be traveling to the beach for a vacation.*
B: *Next week, I'm visiting my aunt in Santa Fe.*

6 PRONUNCIATION: connected speech

A ⏵ **2.27** Listen to the phrases and compound words. Notice how the final consonant sound of the first word is connected to the same first consonant sound of the next word with no vowel sound in between.

next time	/'nekstaɪm/	love Venice	/lʌv'venɪs/
good day	/gʊd'deɪ/	Club Bayview	/klʌb'beɪvju/
electric car	/ə,lektrɪk'kɑr/	same manager	/seɪm'mænɪdʒər/
will live	/wɪl'lɪv/		

B ⏵ **2.28** Listen to the sentences, paying special attention to the underlined phrases. Then practice saying the sentences using connected speech.

1 The weekend is the <u>best time</u> to travel.
2 We <u>will live</u> in a city where <u>electric cars</u> run on tracks.
3 They <u>love Venice</u> and had a <u>great trip</u> there last year.
4 They might also <u>visit Turin</u> <u>and Dolo</u> <u>next time</u>.
5 <u>Club Bayview</u> has had the <u>same manager</u> for a long time.

7 SPEAKING: talking about cities of the future

A You are going to talk about what you think cities of the future will be like. First, use the guide opposite to make some notes about your ideas.

B ⏵ **2.29** Listen to three people talking about what they imagine cities of the future will be like. Match each speaker with the correct statement. Were any of the notes you made in Exercise A similar to what the speakers said?

Speaker 1	**a)**	thinks that rural areas will disappear.
Speaker 2	**b)**	thinks cities are going to become more environmentally responsible.
Speaker 3	**c)**	thinks that people will mostly live below ground in the future.

C  Work in pairs. Say which of the ideas (a–c) mentioned in Exercise B you most agree with and which ideas, if any, you disagree with.

D 🗣 **Independent Speaking** Work in pairs. Think about your ideas from Exercise C and the notes you made in Exercise A. Add any additional points you want to include. Then describe your vision to your partner.

> - *Very different from today's cities?* yes / no
> - *More / less environmentally responsible than cities now?* yes / no
> - *If so, how?* _____
> - *Type and location of buildings and homes:* _____
> _____
> - *Transportation:* _____
> - *Population distribution:*
>   *more urban / more rural / the same*
> - *Other ideas:* _____
> _____
> _____
> _____

lifeSkills

RECOGNIZING AND AVOIDING PLAGIARISM

- Understand what plagiarism is.
- Learn to recognize plagiarism in your own work or others' work.
- Learn and use strategies for avoiding plagiarism.

A 🔊 **Read the definition of *plagiarism*. Work in small groups and discuss the questions.**

1 For what purposes or in what situations do people have to write texts?
2 Where might the information for different types of texts come from?
3 Is it always wrong to use material from someone else's work? Why or why not?
4 What are the possible consequences of plagiarizing someone's work?

> **plagiarism** /ˈpleɪdʒəˌrɪzəm/ **(n.)** taking someone else's work, ideas, or words and using them as if they were your own. Plagiarism also includes borrowing facts, statistics, pictures, or even song lyrics without giving credit to the source they came from. Because we use the internet as a source of information (which means we have access to so many different people's ideas), it's easy to find that you've plagiarized someone without actually meaning to. Recognizing what constitutes plagiarism is a necessary starting point in learning to avoid it.

B 🔊 **How much do you know about what constitutes plagiarism? Work in pairs and take the online quiz.**

Is it plagiarism if you …

		YES	NO
1	copy and paste a paragraph of text from a website into your work?	YES	NO
2	take someone else's text, but change a few of the words and sentences around?	YES	NO
3	copy a diagram or other data from a source and provide a reference for the source?	YES	NO
4	use another author's ideas as your own ideas?	YES	NO
5	include a fact in your work which is general knowledge?	YES	NO

SUBMIT >

C Match each strategy for avoiding plagiarism (1–4) with the correct definition (a–d).

1 paraphrasing
2 quoting
3 referencing/citing
4 summarizing different sources

a) mentioning the sources of the information that you have included in your written work
b) using several different texts on a topic and synthesizing the information from all of them
c) rewriting what someone has written or said using your own words
d) using quotation marks (" ") around words that you have taken directly from another source and listing the source

COPYRIGHT

D Work in pairs. Read the extract from a book called *Urban Culture* by J.E. Short. Then decide which one of the texts (1–4) plagiarizes the original and why.

United States urbanization, which began in the late 1800s, created many new cities. Cities like Boston and Philadelphia sprang up, and they attracted industry, which in turn attracted people. The population in these new cities grew rapidly. Many poverty-stricken farmers, immigrants, and African Americans from the South came to these major cities in search of jobs and a better life.

¹ In the late 1800s, the urbanization of the United States started with the expansion of cities such as Boston. As industries developed, more people, particularly those from nearby farming settlements, began to arrive in these new cities in search of work. According to J.E. Short, many of these new arrivals were "poverty-stricken farmers, immigrants, and African Americans from the South."

² United States urbanization, which started in the late 1800s, created a number of new cities. Cities like Boston and Philadelphia grew, and this attracted people to them. The population in these new cities increased rapidly. African Americans from the South, as well as farmers and immigrants, came to these major new cities to look for work and new lives.

³ As J.E. Short argues in *Urban Culture* (2009), cities such as Boston and Philadelphia grew out of the need for poor workers from rural areas to find regular paid work. Their arrival helped industries expand at a speed which had never been seen before.

⁴ By the end of the 19th century, rural areas of the United States could no longer support large numbers of immigrant and African-American workers. In search of work, they ended up in places such as Philadelphia—a new urban area, which, like Boston, was steadily growing. Here the work was plentiful and reasonably well-paid.

HOW TO SAY IT

Even though this writer has used some of the same words, …

I think / don't think this writer has plagiarized because …

The writer has/hasn't used … although …

Despite …, this writer has …

E Work in pairs. Discuss how the writers of the other three texts have avoided plagiarism. Say which of the strategies in Exercise C they used.

F Work in groups. Discuss the questions.

1 Have you ever been in a situation when you may have accidentally plagiarized, e.g., by copying and pasting from the internet?

2 What would you do differently now to avoid plagiarism in a similar situation?

REFLECT … How can the skill of recognizing and avoiding plagiarism be useful to you in **Self & Society** and **Work & Career**?

RESEARCH …

Choose a city you want to know more about and do research on it. Use the information you find to write a short report about the city. Use the techniques in this section to ensure you do not plagiarize any content.

Language wrap-up

1 VOCABULARY

Complete the text with the words and phrases from the box.
Then choose the correct options to complete it. (10 points)

> Dear Madam   Despite the large numbers of people   I am writing concerning
> I look forward to hearing from you   Sincerely

To: Young, Sarah
From: Harper, Zena
Subject: Celebrations

(1) _____,

(2) _____ the local celebrations that took place recently. I thought the event was great and even though the weather wasn't very good, I was glad so many people came.

First of all, may I congratulate the organizing committee on their decision to hold the celebrations in the **(3)** *heart / alleys* of the city—it really gave visitors the chance to see our cultural **(4)** *settlement / heritage* at its best. We had a stunning **(5)** *site / view* of the firework display from the main square. **(6)** _____, it was easy to get in and out of the city.

I'm attaching some pictures of the evening that you might like to include on your website. Some of them were taken at the archeological **(7)** *alley / site* and others were taken from our **(8)** *village / settlement* ten miles from the city at the start of the evening. Please let me know if you have any problems downloading them.

(9) _____.

(10) _____,

Zena Harper

8–10 correct: I can use formal written language in letters and describe interesting places.
0–7 correct: Look again at Sections 2 and 3 on pages 143 and 144.   **SCORE:**   /10

2 GRAMMAR

Write the appropriate future forms of the verbs in parentheses and choose the correct options to complete the diary entry. (10 points)

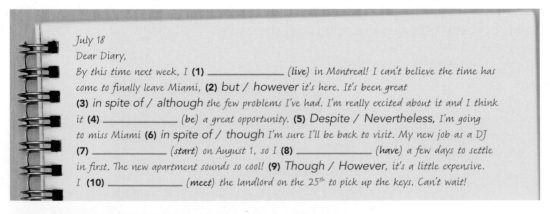

July 18
Dear Diary,
By this time next week, I **(1)** _____ *(live) in Montreal! I can't believe the time has come to finally leave Miami,* **(2)** but / however *it's here. It's been great*
(3) in spite of / although *the few problems I've had. I'm really excited about it and I think it* **(4)** _____ *(be) a great opportunity.* **(5)** Despite / Nevertheless, *I'm going to miss Miami* **(6)** in spite of / though *I'm sure I'll be back to visit. My new job as a DJ*
(7) _____ *(start) on August 1, so I* **(8)** _____ *(have) a few days to settle in first. The new apartment sounds so cool!* **(9)** Though / However, *it's a little expensive. I* **(10)** _____ *(meet) the landlord on the 25th to pick up the keys. Can't wait!*

8–10 correct: I can use connectors of contrast and talk about the future.
0–7 correct: Look again at Sections 1 and 5 on pages 142 and 146.   **SCORE:**   /10

A 🎧 **2.30** Listen to someone talking about what she thinks her city will be like in the next century. Answer the questions.

1 Does the speaker think Dallas will be completely different in the 22nd century from how it is now?
2 What aspects of 22nd century Dallas does she talk about?
3 In what area does she think there will be the most changes? The fewest changes?

B Listen again. Make a note of the words and phrases the speaker uses for the following purposes.

To express contrast	To express a reason or result	To express an opinion
however	*because*	*I think*
_____	_____	_____
_____	_____	_____
_____		

C You are going to talk about what you think your city will be like in the 22nd century. Use the format below to make some notes.

Introduction to the areas you are going to talk about
Point 1:
• things you think will change and how
• things you think won't change much and why
Point 2:
• things you think will change and how
• things you think won't change much and why
Point 3:
• things you think will change and how
• things you think won't change much and why

D 👥 Work in groups. Talk about your city in the 22nd century. You can refer to your notes, but you should not read.

HOW ARE YOU DOING?

○ I talked about at least three aspects about a city of the future.
○ I used correct phrases to express contrasting ideas, results, or opinions.
○ I used correct future verb forms.

Communicative wrap-up
Units 1–2

1 GLOBAL WINNERS AND LOSERS

A Work in small groups. Look at these people and discuss to what extent you think each of them gains or loses through globalization.

a businesswoman

a local farmer

a factory worker

a consumer

B With your group, imagine you're having a discussion with the people in Exercise A. Role-play, expressing your opinion and explaining why you agree or disagree with the statement below.

Increasing globalization is the best future for mankind.

2 CHANGES

A Work in pairs. Discuss how your country is changing in each of these categories. What effects are these changes having on society? What do you think of these changes?

- economy
- shopping
- work
- media
- education

B Tell the class about one change in each category and ask the class if they agree with your opinion.

Online shopping is becoming more and more popular. We think it's a good thing because you can save money by shopping online. What do you think?

3 THE WISH GAME

🗣️ **Work in groups of four. Follow these instructions to play the game.**

- With your group, cut one piece of paper into 16 squares. Each person should take four squares and write a different word on each, one for each of the following topics: *personal life, community, school/work, the world.*

- Shuffle the squares and put them in a pile in the middle.

- Decide who will start. When it's your turn, take a square and say what category it is. You have 30 seconds to make a wish about the category, e.g.:
  Neighborhood, that's the "community" category. I wish people in my building wouldn't leave their trash outside their door.

- You get one point for a correct sentence. If you make a mistake in grammar, or if you take longer than 30 seconds, you do not get a point.

- Continue until you run out of squares. The person with the most points wins.

4 NEW IDENTITIES

A 🗣️ **Work in pairs. Read what these people say. Then say which opinion you agree with more, and explain why.**

"I think learning English has really changed me. I feel like a different person when I speak English, so I feel like I can explore different ideas. The better my English becomes, the more I feel it becomes part of my identity."

"I can see that learning English is very useful, but it hasn't really changed me. The more I learn, the better the career I can aim for, but I'll always be basically the same person. It just means that I can express my ideas to more people."

B 🗣️ **With your partner, complete these sentences. Compare your ideas with another pair.**

The stronger your sense of national identity, …
The more time you spend with people from other countries, …
The more multicultural our society becomes, …

SCORE YOURSELF!
Score 1–5 for the items below. Score 5 for things that are easy and 1 for things that are difficult.

I can talk about the effects of globalization.	5	4	3	2	1
I can talk about changes in society.	5	4	3	2	1
I can express how I would like situations to be different.	5	4	3	2	1
I can express my opinions on personal and national identity.	5	4	3	2	1

If you gave yourself 1 or 2 for any of the statements, look at Units 1 and 2 again.

Communicative wrap-up

1 INFORMATION POOL

A 🗣️ Work in pairs. Choose a celebrity and make a list in your notebook of what you know about the person. Make a second list of what you want to know.

> We Know ...
> what she does. (actress)
> if she has kids. (yes)
>
> We want to Know ...
> how she became famous.
> what she's like.

B 🗣️ Work individually. Walk around the class and ask your classmates questions to try to complete the information that you don't know.

Do you know how Sandra Bullock's career started?

C 🗣️ Work with your partner from Exercise A again and report the information you found out.

A: *Carrie said that Sandra Bullock had won an Oscar for best actress in 2010. She also said that she had been nominated for best actress in 2014 for the movie Gravity.*

B: *Yeah, Ali told me about the Oscar, too. And he said that she had also won a Razzie for worst actress back in 2010 for the movie All About Steve! I don't think that has ever happened again though!*

2 BUMPER STICKERS

A 🗣️ Work in pairs. Decide what you think each bumper sticker means and whether the message is positive or negative.

Monday is an awful way to spend 1/7 of your life ✖

IF YOU DON'T THINK EVERY DAY IS A GOOD DAY, TRY MISSING ONE

SAY NO TO NEGATIVITY

 EAT RIGHT, 👟 EXERCISE, 🪦 DIE ANYWAY

B 🗣️ With your partner, create a bumper sticker with a saying about life's ups and downs. Your message can be optimistic or pessimistic, funny or serious. Then present your idea to the class and discuss the meaning of each bumper sticker. Vote on the best idea.

YOU CAN'T HAVE A RAINBOW WITHOUT RAIN

3 WHAT IF ...?

A 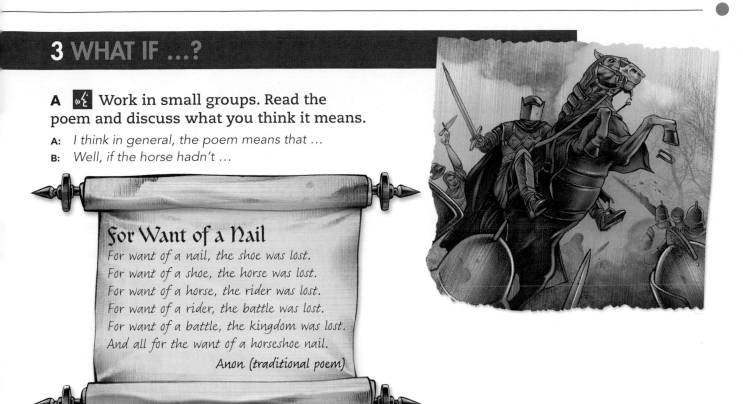 Work in small groups. Read the poem and discuss what you think it means.

A: *I think in general, the poem means that ...*
B: *Well, if the horse hadn't ...*

For Want of a Nail

For want of a nail, the shoe was lost.
For want of a shoe, the horse was lost.
For want of a horse, the rider was lost.
For want of a rider, the battle was lost.
For want of a battle, the kingdom was lost.
And all for the want of a horseshoe nail.

Anon (traditional poem)

B With your group, think of an event in history or in a famous person's life that had important consequences. Discuss these questions.

1 What was the event?
2 What were the consequences?
3 What qualities did the person possess or lack that influenced the outcome?
4 How would things have been different if this hadn't happened?

4 RUMORS

A Work in pairs. Think of an interesting event in the life of a famous person. Discuss what happened and what you think the outcome will be.

A: *You know that politician who is accused of election fraud? I don't think he's guilty.*
B: *You mean the mayor? Of course he's guilty! If his opponent had asked for a recount, Mayor Sanders wouldn't have won!*
A: *Well, they're saying that on the news, but I think the media just wants to cause a scandal to create excitement. Sanders won't be found guilty.*

B With your partner, work with another pair. Tell them who and what you talked about. Comment on what you hear.

A: *Marty said he thought Mayor Sanders had paid people to vote for him and that if they had recounted the votes, he would be in jail by now.*
B: *No, I didn't! I said that he wouldn't have been elected!*

SCORE YOURSELF!					
Score 1–5 for the items below. Score 5 for things that are easy and 1 for things that are difficult.					
I can gather and report information about celebrities.	5	4	3	2	1
I can speculate about positive and negative messages.	5	4	3	2	1
I can read a poem and analyze its meaning.	5	4	3	2	1
I can discuss events and consequences in people's past and present lives.	5	4	3	2	1
If you gave yourself 1 or 2 for any of the statements, look at Units 3 and 4 again.					

Communicative wrap-up
Units 5–6

1 MAKING THE SALE

A 🎙️ Work in small groups. You work for an advertising agency, and a company has approached you to promote a new brand of eco-friendly bottled water. Decide on a name for the product and complete the marketing strategy.

Marketing Strategy

Project description

The company wants to take into account environmental issues when marketing the product and has requested that it have an "eco-friendly" look and marketing strategies. Think of which water-related environmental issues you would like to deal with in your marketing strategy.

Product	Bottled water
Name	
Retail price	
Target market (age, etc.)	
Key adjectives to describe the product (healthy, modern, etc.)	
Main advertising media (TV, internet ads, etc.)	
Brief outline of advertisement ideas	

B 🎙️ With your group, prepare to present your ideas to the rest of the class. Practice your presentation to make sure you know what each person is going to say. Each member of your group should participate equally.

Our product is called …, and it's being marketed to …
In order to interest our market, we have to describe our water as …
We think consumers are tired of …, so we have to persuade them to …

C 🎙️ Give your presentation to the rest of the class. When all the groups have finished, vote on the best marketing strategy.

2 TEAM SPIRIT

A 🎧 **2.31** 🗣️ Work in pairs. Listen to a conversation about a college ritual. Then see how many details you can remember about it.

B 🗣️ With your partner, work with another pair. Discuss which of the following statements you agree with more, and explain why.

"Rituals like the one that's being described in the conversation don't really get people to identify more with their college. They just encourage people to place importance on the wrong things, like whether the football team wins or loses. These things are unimportant, and they're just a way to avoid taking your education seriously!"

"Things like mascots and school colors are symbolic of deeper, more important things like loyalty, group identity, and respect for an organization. They exist to help students form a strong bond and sense of identity with their college. Also, college is hard, and students need activities that are fun and help them make friends."

3 THE DREAM OFFICE

A 🗣️ Work in small groups. Look at this traditional office and discuss what it might be like to work there. Make a short list of three or four advantages and disadvantages of working like this.

Advantages:
Managers can easily see
what everyone is doing.

Disadvantages:
Employees might feel
observed while they work.

B 🗣️ You are going to design a nontraditional working environment. Read these comments from employees to help prompt ideas. Make notes on what your dream office looks like and what the office rules and regulations might be.

"I get easily distracted at work. I think it's because I get bored working alone."
"We're so used to working in a particular way that it stops us from being creative. Things need to change all the time."
"Our office seems to be designed around the work, not around the people. It's not somewhere I look forward to going on Monday morning."

C 🗣️ With your group, work with another group. Explain your ideas to them and comment on their ideas. Use the questions below as a guideline.

What would the advantages of each suggestion be?
Are there any potential disadvantages?
How would managers/employees feel about working in such a nontraditional environment?

SCORE YOURSELF!					
Score 1–5 for the items below. Score 5 for things that are easy and 1 for things that are difficult.					
I can discuss alternative ideas and explain reasons behind choices.	5	4	3	2	1
I can talk about traditions.	5	4	3	2	1
I can make suggestions for working in nontraditional ways.	5	4	3	2	1
If you gave yourself 1 or 2 for any of the statements, look at Units 5 and 6 again.					

Communicative wrap-up

1 DESIGN CRITIQUE

A Work in groups. Read the forum entry and discuss what you like and dislike about each T-shirt design.

collegenet

| HOME | ARTICLES | FORUMS | GAMES | ADVICE | WRITING | QUIZZES |

SUBJECT: Check out my design!

POSTED: Mon, June 3, 12:42 a.m.

Hey, guys. OK, what I'm trying to do is come up with a good idea for a submission in the T-shirt designing contest. The T-shirt has to be about the college camping trip. Which one of these designs do you think I should continue to develop? Please rate the following things: the general image the design projects; the color scheme; the typeface; the artwork.

Thanks for the input!

B With your group, make a list of good and bad points for each design, and decide which one you think the designer should develop further. Then make notes on what the person needs to do to improve the design and why.

We'd rather you didn't use those colors because …
We'd prefer to have a different picture because …

C Report your decision to the class. Explain which design you chose and why. Tell the class some of your ideas for improvements.

2 CAMPAIGNING FOR JUSTICE

A 🗣 Work in groups. Look at the poster and discuss these questions.

1 What is the topic of the poster?
2 In your opinion, is the text effective?
3 How do the graphics illustrate the message?

B 🗣 With your group, design a social justice poster that would be relevant to your country or community. Complete the design guide below. You do not have to be an artist to come up with a good design!

SOCIAL ISSUE:	
AUDIENCE (CHILDREN, TEENS, ADULTS, ETC.):	
TEXT:	
GRAPHICS (DRAWINGS, PICTURES, ETC.):	
IDEAS FOR ARRANGEMENT ON POSTER:	

C 🗣 With your group, present your poster idea to the class. Vote on the best idea and explain your reasons.

We think this group's poster is the best because …

ANIMALS HAVE RIGHTS, TOO!

Did you know that many animals are mistreated, abused, and kept in terrible conditions? Animal activists believe all living creatures have the right to good health, food, and shelter, and it is our responsibility to care for them.

Whether you are a vegetarian or eat meat, you should support animals being treated in the best possible way while they are alive. Help us fight animal cruelty and injustice! Come to our meeting in the campus Reading Room at 8:30 p.m. on Thursday.

3 CHANGING THINGS FOR THE BETTER

A 🗣 Work in pairs. Think of a person who you think has had a positive impact on a specific country or region, or on the world. Complete the notes.

B 🗣 With your partner, work with another pair. Tell them about the person you talked about. Decide which of the two people your group thought of has had a more positive impact.

Name:
Title/Job:
What they did or are doing to help a cause:
What they had done / had been doing before taking on this cause:
What the situation had been like before they got involved:

SCORE YOURSELF!
Score 1–5 for the items below. Score 5 for things that are easy and 1 for things that are difficult.

I can use *rather* and *prefer* to give opinions and make suggestions about design.	5	4	3	2	1
I can compare and contrast and explain my preferences.	5	4	3	2	1
I can talk about social issues and justice.	5	4	3	2	1

If you gave yourself 1 or 2 for any of the statements, look at Units 7 and 8 again.

Communicative wrap-up

1 HOW COMPETITIVE ARE YOU?

A Take this quiz to find out what types of jobs and leisure activities are best suited to your personality!

1 Do you get excited about learning to do new things? **Yes / No**

2 Are you good at convincing people to agree with you? **Yes / No**

3 Do you have trouble following instructions? **Yes / No**

4 Do you hate wasting time when you could be getting things done? **Yes / No**

5 Do you like watching sports? **Yes / No**

6 Have you ever taken a big risk? **Yes / No**

7 When you work with a group, do you prefer to be the leader? **Yes / No**

8 Do you think playing it safe in business or sports is boring? **Yes / No**

9 Do you often take chances, either in your work or in your personal life? **Yes / No**

Mostly *yes* answers:
You are very competitive. You will not be happy doing a job or hobby that doesn't challenge you or give you opportunities to be a winner. You should play sports or games that allow you to express your competitive nature. You want to win in whatever you do!

Mostly *no* answers:
You are not very competitive and you are happy doing jobs or other activities that allow you to work in a cooperative way with other people. You feel anxious and unhappy when you have to compete, so the key to your happiness is team activities, whether at work or at play.

B Work in groups. Discuss these questions.
1 Did most people in the group have mostly *yes* or *no* answers?
2 Do you agree with the results of the quiz? Why or why not?
3 What types of jobs and leisure activities might be best suited to competitive people and non-competitive people?

2 AN UNEXPLAINED SITUATION

A Read this description. Think about what might have happened.

A single shoe is found in the middle of the desert. However, as far as anyone knows, no one has crossed the desert for at least three months, and there are no footprints in the sand leading to or from the shoe. What happened, and how did the shoe get there? Where is the other shoe?

B Work in pairs. Discuss what you think might have happened. Make notes of your best ideas.

C With your partner, work with another pair. Compare your ideas. Who has the most convincing explanation?

D Listen to the best ideas from all the groups. Then check the answer with your teacher. Did anyone guess correctly?

3 ASSESSING RISK

A 🗣 Work in small groups. For each of the following activities, talk about what you think the main risks are.

performing in front of a crowd ⬜

canoeing ⬜

riding a rollercoaster ⬜

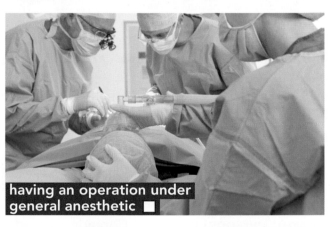
having an operation under general anesthetic ⬜

scuba diving ⬜

starting your own business ⬜

B 🗣 With your group, rank the activities in Exercise A from 1 (the riskiest) to 6 (the least risky).

C 🗣 Compare your ranking with another group's and explain your choices.

SCORE YOURSELF!					
Score 1–5 for the items below. Score 5 for things that are easy and 1 for things that are difficult.					
I can talk about competition and competitive behavior.	5	4	3	2	1
I can speculate about a past event and difficulties in the past.	5	4	3	2	1
I can talk about and assess levels of risk.	5	4	3	2	1
If you gave yourself 1 or 2 for any of the statements, look at Units 9 and 10 again.					

Communicative wrap-up
Units 11–12

1 PICTURES OF THE PAST

A Work in pairs. Decide together which decade each picture comes from and why.

B With your partner, imagine you work for a publisher who is planning to bring out a book called *The History of Photography*. You have been asked to choose an image for the cover of the book. Discuss what each image in Exercise A says about the history of photography. Then decide which image you would choose and why.

2 PERSONAL PARADISE

A Look at these pictures of places to live and decide which one would be your personal paradise. Consider the advantages and disadvantages and choose the one that has the most advantages for your lifestyle.

B Work in pairs. Tell each other which place you chose and why. Mention any disadvantages of the place your partner chose. Do these disadvantages change your opinion?

3 A CITY OF DREAMS

A 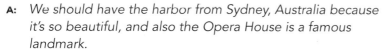 Work in pairs. You are going to design your ideal city using characteristics of other cities around the world. Make a list of cities you have visited or heard about and the positive characteristics of each one. Then choose the characteristics you want to include in your dream city.

- culture
- environment
- entertainment
- transportation
- nightlife
- famous landmarks
- people
- food

A: *We should have the harbor from Sydney, Australia because it's so beautiful, and also the Opera House is a famous landmark.*

B: *Good idea. And how about the nightlife of New Orleans? There are so many great clubs and music venues there.*

B With your partner, work with another pair. Present your ideas and explain which parts you want to take from which cities and what your ideal city will be like.

Our city will have Sydney's beautiful harbor and Opera House. In addition, it's going to have … The nightlife will be great because it will have lots of music venues like New Orleans.

4 JUST A MINUTE

Work in groups. Read the rules and play the game "Just a minute."

- Choose a timekeeper. This person will tell the class or team when the minute starts and ends.
- One player chooses a topic from the list below and tries to talk for one minute about that topic without hesitating, repeating anything, or changing the topic.
- If the person does any of these, another player can interrupt and say, "Just a minute! You hesitated/repeated yourself/changed the topic."
- If the player who interrupted is correct, he or she then continues to talk on the same topic for the remaining time.
- Other players are free to challenge this player in the same way. The person who is speaking at the end of the minute gets a point.
- A different player then chooses a different topic and the game starts again.
  Topics:
  - the "selfie"
  - city life
  - family pictures
  - plagiarism

SCORE YOURSELF!
Score 1–5 for the items below. Score 5 for things that are easy and 1 for things that are difficult.

I can discuss historical pictures.	5	4	3	2	1
I can compare and contrast places to live.	5	4	3	2	1
I can discuss and justify ideas.	5	4	3	2	1

If you gave yourself 1 or 2 for any of the statements, look at Units 11 and 12 again.

Grammar reference

REVIEW OF PAST TENSES

Form	Function	Examples
simple past –ed, irregular forms (was, had, etc.)	used to describe a completed event, action, or state in the past. It is usually the main tense used to talk about the past.	I grew up in Minnesota. They spoke to us in a different language.
simple past with did for emphasis did + base form	used to describe a completed event, action, or state in the past and is used for emphasis, often for contrast	**A:** You didn't find it difficult to settle in when you came to the U.S.A., right? **B:** Not really, but I did feel a sense of culture shock at first.
past progressive was/were + –ing form	used to describe actions or states in progress at a particular time in the past. It is often used to describe background action (e.g., the weather.)	Two years ago, I was living in Canada and researching the customs of indigenous communities.
past perfect had + past participle	used to describe a completed event, action, or state that took place before another past event, action, or state. It is used to talk about things that happened before the main action.	We practiced the traditional activities that our parents had taught us.

1 Choose the correct options to complete the sentences.

1 Emily *took / was taking* a bath when her cell phone *rang / was ringing*.
2 She *learned / had learned* the local dialect even though no one *spoke / had spoken* it for 50 years.
3 I don't play many sports now, but I *had played / did play* a lot of basketball when I *had been / was* at school.

2 Complete the sentences with the correct past tense form of the verbs in parentheses.

1 We _____ (not get into) the concert because the tickets _____ (sold out).
2 I _____ (see) Jane earlier. She _____ (read) in the library.
3 When he got home, Jack _____ (open) the letter he _____ (receive) that morning.

WOULD, USED TO, BE + ALWAYS + –ING

Form	Function	Examples
would (always/never) + base form	used to talk about habits or customs in the past	Sara would never remember to buy milk on her way home.
(always/never) used to + base form	used to talk about habits or customs in the past, or to express something that was true in the past, but is no longer true	The wind always used to blow really hard in Montreal. When I was younger, I used to have short hair.
be + always + –ing form (present or past progressive)	used to talk about habits or customs in the present and past	They are always laughing and joking. He was always singing.

1 Find the mistake in each sentence and write the correct sentence.

1 I used struggle with my sense of identity when I first arrived. _____
2 Jessica would never to arrive on time for meetings. _____
3 They are always try to meet new people. _____

2 Complete the sentences with the verbs in parentheses and the forms in the table.

1 Where is he? The meeting began ten minutes ago. He _____ (run) late.
2 The school director usually had lots of activities planned. The students _____ (get) bored.
3 Amy had her hair cut. She looks really different; she _____ (have) long hair.

VERBS WITH STATIVE AND DYNAMIC USES

Function Some verbs are rarely used in progressive forms. They are called stative verbs because they usually refer to states or conditions which continue over a period of time, for example *know*, *prefer*, or *agree*. However, some stative verbs commonly have both stative and dynamic uses, with different meanings.

verb	Stative use (simple verb form)	Dynamic use (progressive verb form)
be	(permanent state, general truth) *Lupita is married.*	(acting, behaving) *Michael is being really weird.*
have	(possession, characteristics) *I have five minutes before class starts.*	(causing, experiencing) *I'm having problems with my car.*
see	(notice, observe, understand) *Do you see what I mean?*	(meet or date) *They've been seeing each other for a while.*
think	(have an opinion) *I think it's a good idea.*	(the process of thought) *I was thinking about it all day.*

1 Choose the correct options to complete the sentences.

1 *Do you see / Are you seeing* that sign on the wall? It says "No smoking."
2 Maria *is / is being* really thoughtful at the moment.
3 We *think / are thinking* about where to go on vacation.

2 Complete the sentences with *have*, *see*, or *be* in the correct stative or dynamic form.

1 Paul and I _____ really happy in our new home.
2 I _____ much money right now. Could we stay home this evening instead of eating out?
3 "Susanna, _____ anyone now, or are you single?"

REPEATED AND DOUBLE COMPARATIVES

Form	Function	Examples
comparative + *and* + comparative *more and more* + multisyllable adjective *less and less* + multisyllable adjective	**Repeated comparatives** are used to describe something that is changing.	*As a result of social media, it has become easier and easier to maintain friendships around the world.* *Global corporations are becoming more and more powerful.* *These days, it is less and less common for people to spend their whole lives in the same job.*
the + *more* (+ noun) + verb phrase… *the* + comparative + verb phrase… *the* + comparative + *the* + noun + verb phrase…	**Double comparatives** are used to describe how two things are changing at the same time, or how one thing changes as a result of a change in something else.	*The more you study, the more you learn.* *The more food you buy from local farmers, the easier it is to support the local economy.* *The more expensive the item, the fewer people will buy it.*

1 Put the words into the correct order to make sentences.

1 are / multinationals / less / in / up / more / developed / countries / and / setting / more / .

_____

2 more / face-to-face / have / rely / the / we / less / social media, / on / interaction / we / the / .

_____

3 the / more / world / globalized / the / more / foreign / cities / resemble / each / other / becomes, / the / .

_____

2 Write sentences with a repeated comparative (RC) or double comparative (DC) using the prompts and any other words you need.

1 average temperatures / in the U.S.A. / become / warm / each year (*RC*)

_____

2 difficult / class / you need to study (*DC*)

_____

3 good / healthcare / long / life expectancy / in a country (*DC*)

_____

UNIT 3

REPORTED SPEECH—MODAL VERBS AND PAST PERFECT

Form

No tense change	past perfect → past perfect	"I hadn't added him as a friend on Facebook." _He said that he hadn't added him as a friend on Facebook._
modal change	may → might will → would can → could must → had to	"I may have to work part-time in the future." _She admitted that she might have to work part-time in the future._ "Candidates must do a presentation in the job interview." _They stated that candidates had to do a presentation in the job interview._
no modal change	might → might would → would could → could should → should	"Could you help me download a new app?" _She asked him if he could help her download a new app._ "Celebrities should use their fame to help others." _He claimed that celebrities should use their fame to help others._

1 Choose the correct options to complete the sentences.

1 "I must come up with some new ideas."
I explained that I *must / had to* come up with some new ideas.
2 "They will assume we can do the task."
She said that they *will / would* assume we *could / can* do the task.
3 "Would you like some coffee?"
I asked him if he *would / will* like some coffee.

2 Complete the reported speech sentences.

1 "I would never miss the final of *The X Factor*."
She told me _____.
2 "If I had known, I would have gone."
Bill said _____.
3 "We should read this best-selling book."
They admitted _____.

REPORTED SPEECH—OPTIONAL BACK-SHIFTING

Function	Examples
a general truth = optional "The oceans are warming too quickly."	_The article said that the oceans **are** warming too quickly._ _The article said that the oceans **were** warming too quickly._
something that is still true at the moment of reporting = optional "The Chicago Bears are this year's winners."	_He announced that the Chicago Bears **are** this year's winners._ _He announced that the Chicago Bears **were** this year's winners._
future possibilities or plans = optional "The 2020 Olympics will be held in Tokyo."	_The IOC declared the 2020 Olympics **will** be held in Tokyo._ _The IOC declared the 2020 Olympics **would** be held in Tokyo._
something that is no longer true = necessary "We're having a New Year's party."	_(On January 3): She told me they **were having** a New Year's party._

1 Choose the correct options in the sentences. In some cases, both options may be correct.

1 "Ellen and Craig are getting married today."
  She said that Ellen and Craig *are / were* getting married that day.
2 "More and more people are buying organic food."
  The manager reported that more and more people *are / were* buying organic food.
3 "Daft Punk will be in the spotlight at next week's Grammy awards."
  The journalist commented that Daft Punk *would / will* be in the spotlight at next week's Grammy awards.

2 Report the sentences using back-shifting where appropriate.

1 "Globalization is a threat to many indigenous communities."
  He stated _____.
2 "I don't eat meat anymore."
  She declared _____.
3 "Unemployment figures are going to decrease next year."
  The government claimed _____.

UNIT 4

NOUN CLAUSES AS OBJECTS

Form	Example
what = the thing(s) that	*Psychologists are interested in **what makes people happy**.*
how = the way that	*Do you know **how we can cheer Julia up**?*
when = the time that	*Maria still remembers **when you surprised her with a bunch of flowers at work**.*
where = the place that	*I'm not sure **where I can find more information**.*
why = the reason that	*He explained **why he didn't answer your text**.*

1 Underline the noun clauses in the sentences. Then match them with the purpose.

1 Do you know why no one was interested in the talk today?
2 I think people often feel pessimistic about how the world is changing.
3 I think he'll be happier when he starts his new job.

a) the way that
b) the time that
c) the reason that

2 Complete the sentences with the missing question word.

1 I was fascinated by _____ we learned in the class.
2 Are you trying to decide _____ to go for your anniversary?
3 Thanksgiving is _____ many people choose to visit their families.

REVIEW OF CONDITIONAL FORMS

Form	Function	Example
third conditional *If + past perfect, would(n't) have + past participle*	used to talk about unreal situations in the past.	*If he hadn't taken a year off before going to college, he wouldn't have discovered his true passion.*
second conditional *If + simple past, would(n't) + base form*	used to talk about things the speaker feels are unreal or unlikely in the present or future.	*If you were friendlier, you'd be more popular.*
first conditional *If + simple present, will (won't) + base form*	used to talk about things that the speaker thinks are likely or possible in the future.	*If she goes to the class, her English will definitely improve.*
zero conditional *If + simple present, simple present*	used to talk about things that are generally true.	*If I have time, I go to the gym three times a week.*

1 Find the mistake in each sentence and write the correct sentence.

1 If we finished early, we usually go for coffee. _____
2 If the company doesn't make a loss this year, salaries would increase. _____
3 He said he would come if he would finish work on time. _____

2 Write conditional sentences with the prompts provided in parentheses.

1 I / more outgoing / I / get / job in sales (unreal situation)

_____

2 people / often / less happy / they / focus on / material goods (general truth)

_____

3 team members / get along / project / complete / on time (likely)

_____

UNIT 5

THE PASSIVE

Function We use the passive when the action is more important than the person doing the action, or when we don't know who is doing the action.

Tense	Form	Example
simple present passive	*is/are* + past participle	*Modern buildings are designed to withstand heavy rains.*
simple past passive	*was/were* + past participle	*Many homes were destroyed by the floods last year.*
present progressive passive	*is/are being* + past participle	*Traffic is being diverted due to roadworks.*
present perfect passive	*has/have been* past participle	*Tourists have been informed of severe delays on major routes.*
past perfect passive	*had been* + past participle	*We had already been told about the next press conference.*

1 Complete the sentences with the correct passive form of the verb in parentheses.

1 In the last few days, dates for the summer music festival _____ (*confirm*).
2 Possible causes of climate change _____ (*discuss*) right now.
3 Most of the region's infrastructure _____ (*rebuild*) before heavy rains a few weeks ago.

2 Rewrite each sentence in the correct passive form.

1 Researchers are carrying out studies into laughter therapy. _____
2 Recently, more and more companies have outsourced jobs. _____
3 They have announced the comeback tour. _____

EXPRESSIONS OF PURPOSE

Form	Function	Examples	Formality
to + base form *in order (not) to /* *so as (not) to* + base form	used to express why someone does or uses something	*I showed my students a meditation technique* **to** *help them relax.* **In order to** *register, please bring your ID with you.* *Please turn off your cell phone* **so as not to** *disturb other visitors.*	neutral more formal very formal
for + gerund (*–ing*)	used to express the use or purpose of a thing	*We'll rent a car* **for** *sightseeing.*	neutral
so (that) + noun + clause	used to express why someone does or uses something	*We bought rain barrels* **so (that)** *we could collect rainwater.*	neutral

1 Cross out the two incorrect answers.

1 My friend didn't get the job, so I took him to see a movie *for / to / so that* cheer him up.
2 I turned the volume down at midnight *to / so as not to / for* wake up the neighbors.
3 Use these scissors *for / so as to / so that* opening the wrapping.

2 Complete the sentences with an expression of purpose. More than one answer may be possible.

1 Write down a reminder _____ forget your appointment.
2 _____ work well on a team, you need to be a good communicator.
3 We can use the internet _____ booking a last-minute flight.

UNIT 6

BE USED TO / GET USED TO

Form	Function	Examples
be + used to + noun / gerund	used to talk about things we are / are not already familiar with	I'm used to a live audience. He wasn't used to performing to so many people.
get + used to + noun / gerund	used to talk about the process of becoming familiar with something	He's getting used to his new job. She had to get used to wearing a suit.

1 Jack has gone back to college after working as an accountant. Match the sentences to their meanings.

1 He's getting used to writing essays.
2 He's used to working long hours.
3 He's not used to long lectures.

a) He's not familiar with this.
b) He's in the process of becoming familiar with this.
c) He's familiar with this.

2 Complete the sentences with the correct form of *be/get used* to and the verb in parentheses.

1 I was a teacher for years, but I retired last week. I _____ (not, have) so much free time!
2 I had to get up at 6:30 a.m. every morning. So it's taking me a while to _____ (wake up) late.
3 At first it felt strange to spend so much time at home because I _____ (work) long hours in school.

VERB + OBJECT + INFINITIVE

Form	Verbs	Example
verb + noun + infinitive	advise, allow, ask, encourage, expect, force, get, invite, need, order, permit, persuade, tell, want, warn, would like	They persuaded me to open a Twitter account.
negative verb + noun + infinitive		The company doesn't encourage staff to work from home.
verb + noun + *not* + infinitive		He asked me not to invite his ex-girlfriend to the party.

1 Cross out the mistake in each sentence.

1 The emergency workers told people do not to stay in their homes if they began to flood.
2 Teachers don't expect that you to speak perfect English.
3 Airlines warned to passengers not to carry liquids over 200 ml in their hand luggage.

2 Complete the second sentence with the verb in parentheses so it has a similar meaning to the first.

1 Meteorologists convinced people that it's better to avoid unnecessary trips this weekend.
Meteorologists _____ (persuade) take unnecessary trips this weekend.

2 Colleges tell freshmen they don't have to take part in initiation ceremonies.
Colleges _____ (not expect) take part in initiation ceremonies.

3 In some companies, employees are permitted four personal days each year when they don't have to work.
Some companies _____ (allow) take four personal days off work each year.

UNIT 7

POSSESSIVE APOSTROPHE

Form		possessive 's	possessive '
singular nouns		Chicago's best park, Luis's house	Luis' house
plural nouns		The children's school	The students' schedule
compound nouns	Separate ownership	Carla's and Max's noses	
	Joint ownership	Carla and Max's house	
double (two consecutive nouns)		My friend's parents' house	
with gerund		The store's opening	The boys' shouting

1 Find and correct the possessive mistake in each sentence.

1 I suppose if Caleb's and Joanna's mom had called, she would have left a message.

2 Do you have Max brother's phone number?

3 The mens' soccer league organizes games every Sunday.

2 Write 's in the correct place(s) in the sentences.

1 The dog barking is getting louder and louder.

2 Would you mind looking at Julia and Adrian contracts?

3 I wonder if Chris and Ben sister is coming to the party.

PAST PERFECT VS. PAST PERFECT PROGRESSIVE

Tense	Form	Function	Example
past perfect	had + past participle	used to describe a completed event, action, or state that took place before an event, action, state, or time in the past	Beyoncé had released several albums when she began recording with Jay Z.
past perfect progressive	had + been + gerund	used to emphasize the duration of an event, action, or state that continued up to another event, action, state, or time in the past	By the time her friend arrived, she had been waiting for 45 minutes.

1 Choose the correct options to complete the sentences.

1 I had been having / had a really weird dream when the alarm clock woke me.

2 Susie finally bought her ticket to Japan! She had been talking / talked about buying it for months.

3 I got to the theater late, but the movie hadn't started / been starting yet.

2 Find and correct the mistake in each sentence.

1 Every time he checked his inbox, he was disappointed to see that she still hadn't been replying.

_____

2 Unfortunately, the band had played for 30 minutes when we arrived, but we heard a few songs.

_____

3 I had never really been thinking about living in another country until I saw the ad for this job in Spain.

_____

WOULD RATHER AND WOULD PREFER

Form	Function	Examples
would rather (not) + base form	used to express the subject's preference about their own actions	*I'd rather have coffee.* *She'd rather not have coffee now.*
would prefer (not) + infinitive		*We'd prefer to have coffee.* *I'd prefer not to have coffee now.*
would rather + subject + (negative) base form in past tense	used to express a preference about the actions of the subject and someone else, or someone else alone	*The manager would rather customers paid by card.* *The manager would rather they didn't pay in cash.*
would prefer + object + (not) + infinitive		*The manager would prefer customers to pay by card.* *The manager would prefer them not to pay in cash.*

1 Find and correct the mistake in each sentence.

1 Farmers would prefer consumers buy products that promote fair trade.
2 We'd rather you come with us.
3 I would rather to get there by lunchtime.

2 Complete the second sentence so it has a similar meaning to the first.

1 I'd like to come up with my own ideas for a website instead of contracting a designer.
   I would prefer _____.
2 I'd be happier if you didn't post pictures of me on social media sites.
   I'd prefer _____.
3 We would like richer countries to cancel poorer countries' debt instead of giving them financial aid.
   We would rather _____.

NOUN CLAUSES AS SUBJECTS

Form	Example
Form 1: Question word is the subject: **What/Who** + base form + noun/adjective	**What <u>is clear</u>** is that young people are finding it harder to get a job these days.
Form 2: Question word is the object: **What/How/Who/Where** + noun + base form	**Where a child <u>grows up</u>** will influence his/her development.

1 Choose the correct options to complete the sentences.

1 *What / Where* you choose to stay in the city will depend on your budget.
2 *What / Who* you meet in college will influence how hard you study.
3 *How / Where* you get there is up to you—you can go by car, by train, or by bus.

2 Put the words into the correct order to make sentences containing noun clauses.

1 made / lunch / was / how / you / quickly / amazing / .

_____

2 decided / the / government / what / unfair / was / .

_____

3 win / predict / to / is / hard / who / will / .

_____

GERUNDS AFTER PREPOSITIONS

Form	Examples	
verb + preposition (+ gerund)	care about, complain about, fond of, insist on, look forward to, object to, worry about	We're looking forward to seeing you this weekend.
adjective + preposition (+ gerund)	bored with, capable of, excited about, good at, happy about, interested in, responsible for	Anna's interested in learning more about the country.

1 Complete with the correct preposition.

1 Is he good _____ playing soccer?
2 She always complains _____ doing the housework.
3 We're really excited _____ moving to our new house.

2 Complete the sentences with the words from the box and the correct preposition.

1 The world is _____ producing enough food for everyone.
2 She is _____ designing her own home next year.
3 I always _____ giving presentations; I'm terrible at public speaking!

> capable
> looking forward
> worry

VERB + GERUND

Form		Example
have + object + gerund	objects: a good time / a hard time / difficulty / trouble / fun	Sam was having a hard time adjusting to the long hours of his new job.
verb of perception + object + gerund	verbs: find / notice / hear / feel / listen to / imagine / watch / see / observe	They found him watching TV downstairs.
spend/waste + expression of time + gerund	time: days / years / my time / a long time / most of your time / your life	I spent years studying for my postgraduate degree.
sit/stand/lie + expression of place + gerund	place: there / at your desk / on the sofa / around	The crowd just sat there listening to the music all afternoon.

1 Put the words into the correct order to make sentences.

1 for / imagine / day / hours / can't / training / I / five / every / . _____
2 homework / you / difficulty / having / the / understanding / are / ? _____
3 work / long / commuters / waste / hours / traveling / to / distances / . _____

2 Rewrite the sentences with the verbs in parentheses and a gerund.

1 I heard a sound. My brother arrived home. (hear) _____
2 James repaired a boat over many years. (spend) _____
3 The girls stood on the beach and watched the sunset. (stand) _____

EXPRESSING ABILITY

Form	Examples	
verb + infinitive	be able, be unable, manage	I won't be able to help you redecorate tomorrow.
verb + base form	could/couldn't, can/can't	She couldn't call you back because she was driving.
verb + gerund	be good at, succeed in, be capable of	I'm pretty good at singing.

1 Complete the sentences with an expression of ability.

1 Not many people _____ to work full-time and study.
2 They said they _____ come because they're taking care of Ella's dog.
3 I always have to help them. They _____ doing it themselves.

2 Rewrite each sentence with the words in parentheses so the meaning is similar.

1 A few years ago, I successfully ran a half marathon (*manage*).

_____

2 Do you think you will be able to raise $1,000 for charity? (*succeed in*)

_____

3 Sam can design websites. I saw some of her work and it was fantastic. (*good at*)

_____

PAST MODALS OF DEDUCTION

Form modal + *(not) have* + past participle	
Strong probability	John **must** have heard some good news this morning. He can't stop smiling.
Moderate probability/improbability	I can't find my glasses. I **might/could/may** have left them at home.
Strong probability	Sarah **must not** have come to work. I haven't seen her all day.
	Julia **can't / couldn't** have eaten her lunch. Her sandwich is still on her desk.

1 Complete with the correct modal verb: *might/may/could*, *must*, or *can't/couldn't*.

1 Susan got the teaching job. She _____ have impressed the interviewer.
2 They _____ have discussed the new project. The team didn't know anything about it.
3 One possible explanation is that he _____ have forgotten about the meeting.

2 Complete with a past modal verb in the correct form and the verb in parentheses.

1 Sally _____ (*get along*) with Steve's parents last week because they're going on vacation!
2 My brother _____ (*go*) out last night because he doesn't have any money.
3 Where's Owen? I'll check my phone; he _____ (*send*) a text.

UNIT 11

VERB + GERUND/INFINITIVE WITH A CHANGE IN MEANING

verb	gerund example	infinitive example
forget	(have no memory of sth.) I'd completely forgotten seeing that movie.	(forget that you need to do sth.) I forgot to reserve tickets for the movie theater.
regret	(regret that you have done sth.) I regret spending so much money.	(apologize for bad news) We regret to inform you that your account has been suspended.
remember	(have a memory of sth.) I definitely remember texting Jane earlier because I had to look for her number.	(remember that you need to do sth.) I remembered to text Jane because Mark reminded me.
stop	(stop an action/habit) I stopped eating gluten a few months ago.	(stop in order to do sth. else) I stopped to eat lunch because I was hungry.
try	(do sth. to see what result it will have) Try going to the gym more if you want to lose weight.	(in the past = attempt sth. without success; in the present/future = attempt sth. you may/may not be able to do) I tried to go to the gym but it was closed.

1 Choose the correct options to complete the sentences.

1 I regret *to eat* / *eating* so much at lunch. I feel really tired now.
2 I tried *to fix* / *fixing* the washing machine, but I think I made it worse.
3 Don't you remember *to book* / *booking* an appointment with the dentist? It's in your organizer.

2 Write the sentences with the prompts and the correct form of the words in bold.

1 I've try / **call** / work several times but nobody answers.

_____

2 I remembered / **mail** / that letter for you. It should get there by tomorrow.

_____

3 Do you think you could stop / **eat** / chocolate for a week?

_____

CONNECTORS OF ADDITION / CONNECTORS OF CAUSE AND EFFECT

Form	Function	Examples	
connectors of addition	used to add further points or provide more information in support of a point	*and, also, besides that, furthermore, moreover, in addition*	*I like reading and listening to music.* *This forest is an area of natural beauty. Besides that, it is home to many wild animals.* *The new supermarket will be bad for local businesses. Furthermore, it will also be bad for the environment.*
connectors of cause and effect	used to show how one thing makes another happen, or how one thought follows logically from another	*so, therefore, because of, as a result (of), as a consequence, due to*	*She loves playing tennis. Therefore, she plays as often as possible.* *The ice cream melted because of the heat.* *As a result of not studying, I failed my exams.*

1 Choose the correct options to complete the sentences.

1 We need to improve local transportation. *In addition,* / *Therefore,* we need to create new work opportunities in the area.
2 A lot of processed food products today contain high amounts of fat. *As a consequence,* / *Furthermore,* this is usually saturated fat.
3 There have been many forest fires in Western Australia *as a result of* / *in addition* extreme temperatures.

2 Connect the two sentences with a connector from the box. You may need to omit some words.

| because of | Furthermore | Therefore |

1 It's important to enjoy what you do. Earning a large salary should not be the most important factor when choosing a career. _____
2 It is claimed that anorexia is increasing. A possible reason is the presence of very thin models in magazines. _____
3 Some studies find that children are more productive when they cooperate with others. Collaborative work increases self-esteem. _____

UNIT 12

CONNECTORS OF CONTRAST

Position	Connector	Examples
beginning of second clause, after a comma	but	*New York isn't the capital city, but it is the cultural capital of the U.S.A.*
beginning of first clause, comma after the connector	however nevertheless	*I'm not really enjoying the story of the book I'm reading. However, I do like the author.*

beginning of first clause, clause is followed by a comma	although	Although the talk only lasted 15 minutes, it was very informative.
beginning of second clause, no comma	even though	The talk during the excursion was very informative even though it only lasted 15 minutes.
beginning of first or second clause, followed by a gerund phrase, noun phrase, or *the fact that*	despite	*Despite his qualifications, he can't get a job.*
	in spite of	*Despite being qualified, he can't get a job.*
		In spite of the fact that he's qualified, he can't get a job.

1 Complete the sentences with the words from the box.

Even though   Nevertheless   Despite

1 _____ there was a transportation strike in her city, Mia got to work on time.
2 My brother says he doesn't really enjoy going to the movies. _____, he goes all the time.
3 _____ complaining about his job all the time, Adrian never looks for a new one.

2 Complete the sentences with a connector of contrast. Use the correct punctuation.

1 _____ her business idea didn't take off at first, now it's very successful.
2 We warned him not to go hiking in the bad weather. _____, he ignored our advice.
3 He only speaks a few words of Spanish _____ having lived in Peru for five years.

WAYS OF TALKING ABOUT THE FUTURE

Form	Function	Example
Simple future *will, won't may (not), might (not)* + base form	used to make predictions about the future	*People won't travel on diesel trains in the cities of the future.*
going to be + going to + base form	used to make predictions about the future and to talk about intentions	*The World Cup hosts are going to build three new stadiums.*
Present progressive be + –ing form	used to talk about fixed arrangements and plans	*I'm starting my new job on Monday. Can you give me a ride?*
Future progressive *will, won't, may (not), might (not)* + be + –ing form	used to talk about events in progress at a particular time in the future It can be used with *by this time tomorrow / next week* and *when*.	*By this time next week, we will be living in our new house.*

1 Choose the correct options to complete the sentences.

1 I won't be able to come on Saturday; *I'm having / I will have* friends over for dinner.
2 I don't think people *will use / are using* cars in cities in ten years.
3 This time next year, consumers *will be designing / will design* their own clothes and shoes.

2 Rewrite the sentences with prompts and the correct future form.

1 **Lili:** What are you doing this weekend?
  Neil: I / stay / hotel / L.A.

2 By this time tomorrow, we / sit / on / a sunny beach.

_____

3 In the future, I think most schools / use / digital notebooks.

_____

Macmillan Education
4 Crinan Street
London N1 9XW
A division of Macmillan Publishers Limited

Companies and representatives throughout the world

ISBN 978-0-230-45763-8

Text, design and illustration © Macmillan Publishers Limited 2015
Written by Mickey Rogers, Joanne Taylore-Knowles, Steve Taylore-Knowles with
Ingrid Wisniewska

The authors have asserted their rights to be identified as the authors of this work
in accordance with the Copyright, Designs and Patents Act 1988.

This edition published 2015
First edition published 2010

Designed by emc design limited
Illustrated by Alek Sotirovski (Beehive Illustration) p155; Oscar Spigolon p158
Cover design by Tony Richardson, Wooden Ark Ltd.
Cover photograph courtesy of Getty Images/Zero Creatives.

Picture research by Susannah Jayes

The authors would like to thank the schools, teachers and students whose
input has been invaluable in preparing this new edition. They would also like to
thank the editorial and design teams at Macmillan for doing such a great job of
organizing the material and bringing it to life.

The publishers would like to thank the following educators who reviewed
materials and provided us with invaluable insight and feedback for the
development of *masterMind* 2nd edition:

Isidro Almedarez, Deniz Atesok, Monica Delgadillo, Elaine Hodgson, Mark
Lloyd, Rufus Vaughan-Spruce, Kristof van Houdt, Rob Duncan, James Conboy,
Jonathan Danby, Fiona Craig, Martin Guilfoyle, Rodrigo Rosa

The authors and publishers would like to thank the following for permission to
reproduce the following material:

Extract from 'Science gets the last laugh on ethnic jokes' by Kathleen Wren
originally published on NBCnews.com. Material adapted from the Al Arabiya
New Website. Material adapted from: 'Reveille First Lady of Texas A&M' by
Rusty Burson and Vanessa Burson, published by Texas A & M University
Press. Used with permission. Material adapted from 'Why 'selfie' is the word of the year'
by Ben Macintyre. Originally published on the Times online website on 20th
November 2013. Reprinted with permission. Material adapted from the Cardiff
University website. www.cardiff.ac.uk Figures adapted from 'Press Release:
Bottled Water Sustains Strength' by the Beverage Marketing Corporation. www.
beveragemarketing.com/ Material adapted from 'Would you pay $55 for bottled
water?' by John Fuller originally published on How Stuff Works. http://www.
howstuffworks.com/

The authors and publishers would like to thank the following for permission to
reproduce their photographs:

Alamy/Charlotte Allen p148, Alamy/Allstar Picture Library pp38(tml), 84(tm),
Alamy/Marc Anderson p141(bl), Alamy/Asia File p21(2), Alamy/Mario Babiera
p64(bl), Alamy/Patrick Batchelder p140, Alamy/Blend Images pp31(tr), 48, 75,
Alamy/Blue Jean Images p132(tl), Alamy/Serge Bogomyako p161(cl), Alamy/BSIP
SA p47, Alamy/james cheadle p69(4), Alamy/ClassicStock p14, Alamy/Neil
Cooper p62, Alamy/Couria Media p161(tr), Alamy/James Davis Photography
p163(tcr), Alamy/Design Pics Inc. p92(bcr), Alamy/Dex Image p153(tl), Alamy/
Reinhard Dirscherl p161(bcl), Alamy/Lev Dolgachov p162(tr), Alamy/Dundee
Photographics p32(cr), Alamy/epa european pressphoto agency b.v. p105(cl),
Alamy/FALKENSTEINPHOTO p81(bl), Alamy/foodfolio p26(cr), Alamy/Andrew Fox
p63(3), Alamy/fStop Images GmbH p104(cr), Alamy/I. Glory p147, Alamy/Robert
Harding World Imagery p145(B), Alamy/Horizons WWP p69(6), Alamy/
imageBROKER p51, Alamy/Image Source Plus p79(A), Alamy/D Johnson p79(B),
Alamy/Juice Images p161(cr), Alamy/Robert Kneschke p9(1), Alamy/B Lawrence
p141(tc), Alamy/MBI pp60(cl), 132(bl,br), Alamy/Kari Martilla p160, Alamy/
Mediablitzimages p111, Alamy/Aiva Mikko p81(tr), Alamy/Moodboard p45(2),
Alamy/Bob Pardue – Lifestyle p98, Alamy/PHOVOIR p161(bcr), Alamy/Pixellover
RM 9 p24, Alamy/Vova Pomortzeff p69(5), Alamy/Purestock p53, Alamy/Ian
Shaws p65(b), Alamy/Adrian Sherratt p57(5), Alamy/Ian Shipley ARC p73, Alamy/
Paul Solloway pp12, 13, Alamy/Mele Stemmermann p125(6), Alamy/Devon
Stephens p96(cl), Alamy/SuperStock p145(D), Alamy/Jochen Tack p21(3), Alamy/
Matjaz Tancic p69(3), Alamy/Tetra Images p117(cm), Alamy/Mark Thomas
p33(bcr), Alamy/Gregg Vignal p117(tr), Alamy/wales_heritage_photos p69(2),
Alamy/Wavebreak Media ltd p80(cl), Alamy/Zooner GmbH p112(cml); **Anouska
Hempel Design** pp87; **Arte Luise Kunsthotel** p91; **Corbis** pp46(br), 129(tr),
Corbis/PIYAL ADHIKARY p93(bl), Corbis/Adrianko p89, Corbis/Aflo p104, Corbis/
age footstock Spain S.L./Iain Masterton p162(cr), Corbis/All Canada Photos/Paul
Zizka p127(tr), Corbis/arabianEye/Patrick Eckersley p55, Corbis/GAETAN BALLY
p105(br), Corbis/Phil Banko p56, Corbis/Blend Images/JGI/Tom Grill p125(1),
Corbis/Blend Images/Mike Kemp p45(6), Corbis/Blend Images/John Lund/Marc
Romanelli p109, Corbis/Blend images/Jacqueline Veissid p10, Corbis/Sam
Diephuis p119, Corbis/Galeries/Brian Shumway p101(cl), Corbis/GraphicaArtis
p149, Corbis/Karl-Heinz Haenel p20, Corbis/Ingolf Hatz p156, Corbis/Lindsay
Hebberd p68(br), Corbis/Hero Images pp9(4), 29, 125(5), 132(tr), Corbis/Hill Street
Studios p117(tl), Corbis/Image Source pp97, 125(3), 135, Corbis/Maskot p40(cr),
Corbis/Lori Adamski-Peek p9(3), Corbis/Jose L. Pelaez p93(tr), Corbis/Marcus
Prior p99, Corbis/Martin Puddy p141(cl), Corbis/Radius Images pp36, 107,
Corbis/Reuters/CARLO ALLEGRI p68, Corbis/Reuters/HOWARD BURDITT
p95(cr), Corbis/Reuters/RICARDO MORAES p115,Corbis/H. Armstrong Roberts
p162(tl), Corbis/Tomas Rodriguez p134(cr), Corbis/Sajjad/Xinhua Press p58,
Corbis/Hugh Sitton p93(br), Corbis/Somos Images/Steve Hix p86, Corbis/Sylvain
Sonnet p116, Corbis/Les Stone/Sygma p63(1), Corbis/Studio Eye p81(br),Corbis/
Keren Su p91(cr), Corbis/Ada Summer p133, Corbis/Topic Photo Agency p77,
Corbis/Betsie van der Meer p117(cr), Corbis/Matthew Visinsky p72, Corbis/
Visuals Unlimited, Inc./Carol & Mike Werner p110, Corbis/Jessie Walker p162(bcl),
Corbis/wangiei/Xinhua Press p21(1), Corbis/WEST/Westend61 p61, Corbis/Arman
Zhenikeyev p125(4); **Ecoscene**/Chinch Gryniewicz p57(4); ©**Fairtrade** Foundation
p96(tr); **Getty Images**/AFP pp9(5), 85(br), Getty Images/alohaspirit p33(tcr), Getty
Images/Petri Artturi Asikinaen p8(cr), Getty Images/asiseei p131(tr), Getty Images/
Allan Baxter p92, Getty Images/Don Bayley p33(cr),Getty Images/ADEK BERRY
p38(tl), Getty Images/Chris Bott p17(bcr), Getty Images/Mark Bowden p76, Getty
Images/Paul Bradbury p39, Getty Images/Cavan Images p131(bl), Getty Images/
Chabruken p117(cl), Getty Images/Siong Heng Chang p161(tl), Getty Images/
Comstock p16, Getty Images/Cultura RM/Christin Rose p132(bm), Getty Images/
Mark Cuthbert p35(tcl), Getty Images/damircudic p88(b), Getty Images/Michael
DeLeon p153(tl), Getty Images/Richard Drury p64(br), Getty Images/EMMANUEL
DUNAND p122, Getty Images/Echo p125(2), Getty Images/Amanda Edwards
p35(tcm), Getty Images/John Elk p120, Getty Images/Evening Standard p34,
Getty Images/davidf p94, Getty Images/John Fedele p44(cr), Getty Images/
Fertnig p20(cr), Getty Images/Mitchell Funk p145(A), Getty Images/Christopher
Futcher p9(2), Getty Images/Geber86 p45(5), Getty Images/Justin Geoffrey p130,
Getty Images/GordonsLife p11, Getty Images/Steve Granitz p154, Getty Images/
Daniel Grill p152(cm), Getty Images/Jamie Grill p129(bl), Getty Images/Bartosz
Hadyniak p65(tr), Getty Images/laflor p124, Getty Images/Image Source p19,
Getty Images/ImagesBazaar p88(tr), Getty Images/Erik Isakson p31(b), Getty
Images/Ivan Ivanov p112(tr), Getty Images/Johner Images p45(4), Getty Images/
Chris Jongkind p8, Getty Images/Jupiterimages p33(cl), Getty Images/Nancy
Kaszerman p84(tr), Getty Images/Christopher Kimmel p140(cr), Getty Images/
Wilfred Krecichwost p136(cr), Getty Images/Clarissa Leahy p49, Getty Images/
Kristina Lindberg p60(tl), Getty Images/SAUL LOEB p70, Getty Images/ Anna
Lubovedskaya p41, Getty Images/Hector Mandel p116(cm), Getty Images/Nino
Mascardi p63(2), Getty Images/Marianna Massey p35(tcr), Getty Images/Jamie
McCarthy p84(tl), Getty Images/Pam McLean p129(tl), Getty Images/P.Medicus
p136(b), Getty Images/Chris Mellor p143, Getty Images/Ethan Miller p85(tr), Getty
Images/Maria Taglienti-Molinari p162(tm), Getty Images/Dave Nagel p46(tr), Getty
Images/NASA p37, Getty Images/Danny Nebraska p52(tr), Getty Images/Tom
Nevesely p118, Getty Images/Kali Nine LLC p127(bl), Getty Images/Panoramic
Images p26(cl), Getty Images/Douglas Pearson p144, Getty Images/Jose Luis
Pelaez p108, Getty Images/polygraphus p22, Getty Images/Claude Robidoux
p131(br), Getty Images/Amanda Rohde p51(br), Getty Images/Lee Rogers
p162(cl), Getty Images/Eleanor Scriven p128, Getty Images/Zen Sekizawa p45(1),
Getty Images/kristian sekulic p132(cr), Getty Images/Margo Silver p17(cl), Getty
Images/Wayne Simpson p129(cl), Getty Images/Ariel Skelley p45(3), Getty
Images/Andy Smith p128(cr), Getty Images/SONNET Sylain p32, Getty Images/
Matthew Spolin p145(C), Getty Images/Justin Sullivan pp40(b), 81(cl), Getty
Images/kali9 p152(cl), Getty Images/Karwai Tang p35(cr), Getty Images/Tempura
p136(tr), Getty Images/Tang Ming Tung p129(cr), Getty Images/Betsie Van der
Meer p17(cr), Getty Images/Bill Varie p157(cr), Getty Images/Klaus Vedfelt
p129(br), Getty Images/Visuals Unlimited, Inc./Carol & Mike Werner p.110, Getty
Images/Dougal Waters p56(cr), Getty Images/Westend61 p28, Getty Images/
Willowpix p17(bcl), Getty Images/Xinhua Press/wangle p21(1), Getty Images/
yulapopkova p33(tl), Getty Images/Zero Creatives p52(b), Getty Images/
zhouyousifang p80; **IMAGE SOURCE** pp60(tcl), 141(tll); **Photoshot** p69(1),
Photoshot/africanpictures.net p57(1), Photoshot/Anka Agency p142, Photoshot/
Imago p121(br), Photoshot/TIPS p23, Photoshot/UPPA p105(bl), Photoshot/
Xinhua p105(cr); **Press Association Images**/Sean Dempsey/PA Archive p83,
Press Association Images/RANDY MUDRICK/AP p123; **Rex Features** pp35(cr),
104(tl), Rex Features/Everett Collection p100, Rex Features/Imaginechina p82,
Rex Features/LAURENTVU/TAAMALLAH/SIPA p43, Rex Features/JAY NEMETH/
SPORTSANDNEWS/SIPA p112(tr), Rex Features/Ray Tang p95(tl), Rex Features/
Tom Watkins p104(tr); **Reuters Picture Library**/Jumanah El-Heloueh p146;
Thinskstock/alice-photo p141(br), Thinkstock/KatarzynaBialasiewicz p101(cr),
Thinkstock/Michael DeLeon p152(tl), Thinkstock/Franco Deriu p81(tl), Thinkstock/
Antonio_Diaz p25(tm), Thinkstock/Digital Vision p103, Thinkstock/Fuse p74,
Thinkstock/Jupiterimages p44, Thinkstock/mastaka p15, Thinkstock/miflippo
p57(3), Thinkstock/mofles p152(tm), Thinkstock/Monticello p112(br), Thinkstock/
Nirian p57(2), Thinkstock/Mohamed Osama p59, Thinkstock/phaendin p71,
Thinkstock/Darren Patterson p162(bcr), Thinkstock/Top Photo Group RF p163(tr),
Thinkstock/tupungato p141(tr), Thinkstock/ViewApart p157(tr), Thinkstock/Mike
Watson Images p33(tr).

This material may contain links for third-party websites. We have no control over,
and are not responsible for, the contents of such third-party websites. Please use
care when accessing them.

Printed and bound in Thailand

2018 2017 2016 2015
10 9 8 7 6 5 4 3 2 1